As We
Were Saying

As We Were Saying

SEWANEE WRITERS ON WRITING

EDITED BY
WYATT PRUNTY MEGAN ROBERTS
AND ADAM LATHAM

LOUISIANA STATE UNIVERSITY PRESS
BATON ROUGE

Published by Louisiana State University Press
www.lsupress.org

LSU Press Paperback Original

DESIGNER: Mandy McDonald Scallan
TYPEFACE: Whitman

Charles Martin's "Is There a Plot in This Poem?" first appeared in the *Southwest Review*, Vol. 99, No. 2 (2014).

Jill McCorkle's "Haunted" first appeared in the *Writer's Chronicle*, February 2017.

Mary Jo Salter's "S Is for Something: Mark Strand and Artistic Identity," first appeared in the *Sewanee Review*, Winter 2017.

Library of Congress Cataloging-in-Publication Data

Names: Prunty, Wyatt, editor. | Roberts, Megan, editor. | Latham, Adam, editor.
Title: As we were saying : Sewanee writers on writing / edited by Wyatt Prunty, Megan Roberts, and Adam Latham.
Description: Baton Rouge : Louisiana State University Press, [2021] | Includes bibliographical references and index.
Identifiers: LCCN 2020054232 (print) | LCCN 2020054233 (ebook) | ISBN 978-0-8071-7506-4 (paperback) | ISBN 978-0-8071-7576-7 (pdf) | ISBN 978-0-8071-7577-4 (epub)
Subjects: LCSH: Authorship.
Classification: LCC PN145 .A786 2021 (print) | LCC PN145 (ebook) | DDC 808/.02—dc23
LC record available at https://lccn.loc.gov/2020054232
LC ebook record available at https://lccn.loc.gov/2020054233

for Randall Kenan

CONTENTS

1 Introduction, *by Wyatt Prunty*

11 ALICE McDERMOTT / FICTION / Story

25 ADRIANNE HARUN / FICTION / Narrative Architecture and the Inhabitation of Story

45 RANDALL KENAN / FICTION / The Character of Our Character: Reality, Actuality, and Technique in Fiction and Nonfiction

56 CHARLES MARTIN / POETRY / "Is There a Plot in This Poem?"

71 NAOMI IIZUKA / PLAYWRITING / What Makes a Play a Play?

84 WILLIAM LOGAN / POETRY / Seven Types of Ambivalence: On Donald Justice

98 MARY JO SALTER / POETRY / S Is for Something: Mark Strand and Artistic Identity

114 MARGOT LIVESEY / FICTION / The Train Stops Here: The Optimism of Revision

127 STEVE YARBROUGH / FICTION / The Starting Line

139 DAN O'BRIEN / PLAYWRITING / Unspeakable: Speech on Stage

153 MAURICE MANNING / POETRY / Birds of America: Or, Tell Me a Story about Farming, Haunted Houses, and Poetry in Motion

171 JILL McCORKLE / FICTION / Haunted

182 RICHARD BAUSCH / FICTION / Why Literature Can Save Us

193 ANDREW HUDGINS / POETRY / Inside "Out, Out—"

204 **ALLEN WIER** / FICTION / Technique Makes Imagination Matter More

216 **SIDNEY WADE** / POETRY / Metaphor: The Fundament of Imaginative Writing

227 **CHRISTINE SCHUTT** / FICTION / The Directing Sentence

234 **WYATT PRUNTY** / POETRY / Rationed Compassion: Philip Larkin and Richard Wilbur

247 Contributors

251 Index

As We
Were Saying

Introduction

The pieces in this collection represent the Sewanee Writers' Conference as it gathers every summer for readings, craft talks, and workshops. During that time someone driving into town might ask, "Whose house party is this?" In fact writers willing to carve two weeks from their lives to gather in Sewanee to attend the Sewanee Writers' Conference are not present for parties but for each other by means of workshops, close line-by-line responses to texts, readings, talks, individual meetings over manuscripts, and formal and informal opportunities to meet editors, agents, and publishers looking for new talent. Some essays in this collection focus on one or two writers, some focus on texts; others cast their regard more broadly yet. All are written in response to one or another question generated by the process of writing. The immediate benefit to others from these essays derives from masters of a craft candidly reporting issues they confront as they begin, pause, worry, resume, stop, despair, resolve, revise, finish. Revise again.

An instance of the above is Alice McDermott in workshop or after workshop and in conversation, and then finding herself in yet more conversation, instructing and celebrating one good story after another. McDermott's contribution to these pages comes from a folktale she tells about a man being turned down for a drink of water for his dog. At play in this is Horace's injunction that literature should teach and delight. McDermott does both with grace. On the way to that she makes a point about the "mobs," not McDermott's name for violence, just "middle-of-book-syndrome." Her solution is change. In fact her solution for all—dog, man, *and* writer—is "change." And change is what occurs, as the man in the folktale stops at a second place, a quite different place, and asks again for water for his dog and this time is given just what is needed. Read Alice McDermott to learn the address for that.

Adrianne Harun uses architecture to think about the structure of fiction. Discussing the imagination's use of metamorphosis to transform space to narrative, she cites the way her childhood home always stands behind but never appears in her work. "*Not the frame itself,*" she says of this dynamic, "*but the animation of the frame.*" Stories are "energy confined in space." The spatial part of Harun's thinking riddles the workings of word, place, and event as these appear in the imagination's refusal to abandon the past even as it hurries toward the future. Harun's highly polished discussion of this dynamic focuses on some of the most fascinating aspects of fiction, especially the ways the mind melds things physical and imaginative. Harun is as original in her insights about fiction as she is with her own writing. There is an elegance of mind here that expands the implications of every detail discussed.

Randall Kenan's essay, "The Character of Our Character," reviews the mixture of "Reality, Actuality, and Technique in Fiction and Nonfiction" as he asks the question, "How do you create a human being in ink and paper?" No one addresses this question better than Kenan himself does with his own writing, but also does here as he surveys fiction's strength to outlive nonfiction. Such creations as Daniel Defoe's character Robinson Crusoe and Herman Melville's whaling ship the *Pequod* have far outlasted their factual origins, the Scottish castaway Alexander Selkirk and the whaling ship *Essex* out of Nantucket. Praising things human, or our brilliant "mess of it all," as Kenan says, he reminds us what fiction can always give and what the evening news will always lack. The former is what we need and remember, as there we are not given scarred fragments ourselves but stories of full character.

Charles Martin's essay about plot's contribution to character notes literature's movement from oral to written preservation and the way this change enabled interiority to surpass "heroic unreflectiveness." The "unreflective hero of an earlier day" was replaced by a "consciousness" based on "literacy" that brought "not only time [with it] but space." New patterns emerged to organize the space and time of "conscious contrivance." Chiastic structure was one. Martin continues with a discussion of chiasmus that ranges from Catullus to the evangelist Matthew (Ariadne's abandonment by one lover then being "sought after by another"; Christ's birth, his rebirth). Martin also provides a fascinating discussion of plot as used by Edgar Allan Poe in "Murders in the Rue

Morgue" and then Robert Browning's employment of it in "My Last Duchess." Other highlights range from Dylan Thomas to Sappho to Philip Larkin, Father Ong to Hugh Kenner as "the plot of a poem is [seen to be] the revelation of . . . character," persona or poet. Martin ends his mischief with the written text, with its plots and characters, *and* with the sly conclusion, "Texts are inherently contumacious."

Naomi Iizuka begins by saying "playwrights traffic in the possibilities and . . . limitations of time and space" amid which they "work with . . . language" but also with so much more than language. She adds, "theater is ultimately less about ideas, and more about body" as a play brought from the page becomes "actors in real time." They become us. They sweat the way we do. Their struggles move us by being like ours. We grieve when grief fits, laugh when funny *is* funny, and we know fully—that is, emotionally—why, because we the audience are part of the living world the theater creates. The question often asked is, how can all this happen? Only the brilliant members of an almost-occult embodiment seem to know. And they laugh with the pleasure of having a knowledge outsiders cannot quite grasp. Sometimes they grieve that way too. The play on the page is a fragment of the "ineffable." Most of us grow up being introduced to plays by anthologies and school productions. Iizuka's example for that is *Arsenic and Old Lace*. Her ideal, on the other hand, is something closer to Sam Shepard's *True West*, of which she has much to praise despite the rough spots she notes. In fact roughness in a play can be just the right thing, she says, just as props can give "associative tendrils" that are wonderfully "multivalent and idiosyncratic." The word "multivalent" is applicable to Iizuka's vision as to what a play can bring about, and how the playwright's mind must operate to create that.

William Logan identifies Donald Justice's "middle style" as deriving from his "discretion" and "principled reserve." It is by this, Logan says, that one finds "the only artifice" in Justice "is at times the seeming lack of artifice." Justice "inched" his way "toward meaning," Logan says, such that in reading him one learns only a little about Justice but "a great deal about the manners of language." There is "a mildness that by hiding nothing seems to hide all." I would argue that Justice's style is at one with the durable honesty of emotion found in the guarded argument of his poetry. Logan says as much and more, making the point that Justice has been a major influence on the generations that have followed him thanks first of all to the distilled style of his poetry but secondly due to his having taught so many poets who have gone on to achieve much and in turn to teach their own students. Mark Strand's poem "Nostalgia" is dedicated to Justice, for whom nostalgia is a major figure different from but related to Richard Wilbur's "marchlands" and to Philip Larkin's "bog." Asked by a young reader why Strand had dedicated his poem to Justice, Strand replied, "Because Justice is the *King* of nostalgia." The humor of this reply was part of the friendship the two enjoyed but also the affinity they shared as writers.

Mary Jo Salter opens her essay on Mark Strand with a distinction Strand made between two poetic realties, "visionary" and "confessional." Strand's perspective left him with the pious belief in neither as he held the door open for something more, what Salter calls a "void." Like his elder in the Iowa Writers' Workshop, Donald Justice, Strand wrote with a spare style. In his case this served a tongue-in-cheek take on things. There was economizing here, a limited investment of assertion—the "void" Salter finds in Strand, and others. In Strand such emptiness invites humor and with that an increased sense of humanness, no matter how contradictory situations may seem. "I'd really like to be alive after I'm dead," Strand says at one point, turning the corner on Mercutio and smiling—also leaving those who knew Mark personally rereading with a smile. He was great company. Salter's discussion only adds to our sense of that. Her piece is a fine example of the sympathetic imagination by which writers write and readers read. She captures Strand as the friend who speaks to us with tact and charm about things that empty into the sky of a winter night. Yet with Salter's insights concerning Strand, readers find themselves feeling not empty but included.

Margot Livesey's "The Train Stops Here: The Optimism of Revision" gives us what she believes to be "the three stages of writing." First, "finding a voice and creating characters, setting, situation, and plot," then "revising," then last "editing." She uses James Baldwin's "Sonny's Blues" as a basis for asking ten questions about composition, each of which she then answers. (Once you finish reading Baldwin, then read Livesey's *The Boy in the Field.*) Livesey's questions work as guides for one in the process of revision. Her first question asks what the main character wants, and what prevents getting that. Then there are other considerations, one of which is, "What is the most important thing missing from the story?" Here Livesey tells us "finish the story." At the same time she acknowledges "writers parse the verb 'finish'" the way "the Inuit do 'snow.'" Writers learn these principles by one idiom or another, though here Livesey focuses matters on editing, observing that "to edit prematurely" will be "to sail a half-built boat." On the page Margot Livesey is a master shipwright. Her discussion of such topics as "voice," "character," "setting," "situation," "plot," and "then revising" and "editing" is as lucid an introduction and/or reminder as any writer could wish to find. Livesey's ten questions ought to be posted on the refrigerator door, for every morning's blank white page.

Steve Yarbrough considers the mystery of writing to be like a footrace the writer must run with himself against himself for something important and yet unknown. That writer keeps running thanks to fascinating "characters" along the way. The runner's sense is that what is happening is real. This generates conviction without conclusion—the tipped angle of a runner just off-balance but still upright thanks to momentum and therefore continuing to the end. The origin of all this may be a shy recess of the imagination, but the process is something to celebrate outright. Yarbrough records what he does with unfailing accuracy and generosity. Seeing matters not by analogy, or small excerpt, but by the arc of the act that grows to become one's story or novel. He maps that way ahead, especially in terms of the writer who begins (and for a long time continues) with a vivid population encountered over an unseen geography. Here Yarbrough speaks of practice more than mystery. But practice *is* the mystery, and ultimately it resides in others. They are realized along the way in the faces and voices of those characters who appear in the story's passing. Yarbrough is about an endeavor much more nuanced than a footrace, and more taxing. He is about others, not just the runner or the person telling the story. Read Yarbrough's fiction and learn to run eyes straight ahead yet seeing every face on either side.

Early in his essay, "Unspeakable: Speech on Stage," Dan O'Brien remarks that "When we write speech we are really writing behavior. For what we say is arguably the most conspicuous thing we do." Shortly after that O'Brien adds, "people still like to advise young writers to 'find their voice': for me the practice of playwriting has always involved doing everything I can to lose my voice." Meanwhile metaphor is the mode by which the "unspeakable" best can be said. For O'Brien metaphor is a mode of discovery as much as it is a mode of expression. This is especially so within "speech on stage," which is "compressed and precise" so that "each line, sometimes each phrase or each word," can introduce a "new, subtle or dramatic" step in "plot or characterization or theme" and by that generate "laughs and gasps and utterly airless points of apprehension." O'Brien summarizes these elements as being the "unspeakable dimension of well-written speech." Figurative language is effective thanks to the theater of our surrounding world. O'Brien's language brings that outside in to where it magnifies on stage.

Maurice Manning's essay on Robert Penn Warren's *Audubon* is about reverie, craft, art, interactions with the world's provisions for life and its brutalities against life. Manning describes what he calls "the rudimentary and raw coagulation of art." This is a must-read for anyone interested in capturing idioms of the American romantic imagination. Manning sees poetry as "the tool we have to go back and forth between" the basics of "landscape and mind." Elaborating on this leads him to the utopian "Pantisocracy" Samuel Taylor Coleridge and Robert Southey envisioned for America. Manning ranges from the "live off the land" scheme of Coleridge and Southey to Warren's sometimes terrifying *Audubon*. In Warren there is a "sense of *self* beyond itself," whereas for Manning such change occurs in the ways "literary composition" can "resist stasis." Our writing enables our "Disposed Garden" a second chance at its "flawed promise." Woven through this understanding there remains the imagination's longing for return, encouraged by the ways artistic "form defines the within." In sum, all is as if "the poem" (Coleridge speaking here) "is going to . . . 'caverns measureless to man'" but not ending there. Manning's argument expands upon what Robert Penn Warren discovered through the character created in John James Audubon's account of his spending a fearful night on the American prairie. Audubon experienced what he did. Contradictions between his account and other records indicate imagination was at work in Audubon's version. Katherine Anne Porter ran across Audubon's account in the Library of Congress and gave it to Robert Penn Warren, telling him here is your poem. Warren wrote that poem. Now with these details known and Manning's reading before us we can travel back for a second look at the ways imagination and experience will coagulate to leave us greater understanding.

Jill McCorkle's essay, "Haunted," explores art's compression of human possibility. Her advice is selecting the right object to study, considering its implementation over time, and using that object to tell the course of a life, or lives. McCorkle reads an older house as an extended self, or family perhaps. How can a house represent a life, one's own aging, say, or duration in death? A house is a dwelling. To dwell is a verb, but a dwelling is a noun. With age a house can become both. And such doubling can haunt the imagination. Jill McCorkle feels that way. A house can be read in reverse and by that become an extended record of the past. Our seeing it offers us a suggestion that has outlived those it implicates. We are haunted by what we imagine might have happened once, or some uncompleted action we should complete or might repeat were we to enter. If that is the case, then it is better to write of the house while passing by outside, or while looking back. Either of these perspectives seems safer than writing from within. But Jill McCorkle ends her essay saying, "such hauntings are what keep us [as writers] in business as we work to build and rebuild our houses." We are within. Read Jill McCorkle to see where the key is kept.

Richard Bausch's humor is prismatic. His essay captures the hilarious half-finished feats of a Catholic boy discovering something new about his body and then in the confessional telling the priest he has committed adultery. Bausch captures innocence, self-discovery, and a Church-packed head primed for guilt. For the boy the mystery is the difference between discovering something good but then wrong as he understands the teachings of the Church to which he confesses. As the boy's confession proceeds, the priest has trouble breathing—bad asthma or laughter? The latter. Bausch is interested in the ways "a good story," as he says, "*breaks down the walls between people,*" even a confessional's screen. Another way for thinking about this is the linguist's "triadic event" that simultaneously links and divides. Operating in the triadic way that so interested Walker Percy, art avoids the failure of the modern/postmodern mind that sees two parts to a moment rather than three brought to the event by language. The point Bausch wishes to make about writing is contained in the funny story he tells. Storytelling can reverse the mistake we make by separative thought, and it does this by increasing the sides of the event as it is recounted. Bausch illustrates this by opening with his own story—boy and priest—and then continues, managing to include his readers seated all sides too.

Andrew Hudgins gives a close reading of Robert Frost's poem "Out, Out—" that is valuable to anyone in any genre. He focuses closely on the choices Frost made with diction to give dramatic power to every detail. Meaning, phoneme, and etymology magnify each other so that the poem's language multiplies its action and its argument. Hudgins reads Frost, as he says, "inside out," giving the reader a tour de force where aesthetic considerations apply. As Hudgins demonstrates in his own work, he is a master of pace. His poems show an unerring sense of how much detail is required and when it should appear. As Hudgins says of Frost's poem, "what is left out of the narrative after the boy loses his hand" is critical to the effect of what is included. (One imagines a poet during revision.) The boy's first utterance is "a rueful laugh," not a cry of terror. The reader is already supplying the terror, which Frost's understatement guarantees will build to the very lonely end of the poem, with the boy now dead and others having "turned to their affairs." Frost's poem makes use of description, idiom, setting, and allusion. His poem might be regarded as "a low mimetic fairy tale," or one may see the dust the saw kicks up as an echo of the expulsion from the Garden of Eden. But Hudgins convinces us with two facts—that he was "first drawn" to "Out, Out—" for what it had to report, but over time it was "the way" the poem said things that really held him. By the end of his essay Hudgins pins this difference down to one word, "performance." And by that he means "the complex intellectual and emotional richness" the poem displays, what we might say are its precisions operating as witness to human value.

Allen Wier argues that "technique—is the shape-shifter imagination couples with" as it "constructs and counterfeits" a piece of fiction. Wier says doing this can seem "mystical" thanks to the "compelling voice" involved that creates "its own authority." In part Wier has in mind Samuel Taylor Coleridge's understanding of the imagination constituting "a synthetic magical power." Related to this he quotes Joseph Cottle's remark that narrative's goal "is to convert a series into a Whole." Wier adds that for writers "if something *moves* us, we want to understand how *it moves*." And, once again, technique is at the center of doing this. Technique as thought of here is a mode of discovery—"the difference between anecdote and story." "Rules" (not just discoveries) also exist, and in turn these create occasions in which the writer can "break" the rules and by that say something in a new way. "What we care about, we name," but by naming "We do not solve so much as 'rediscover' the mystery." The ability to do this (the "Talent" Wier says, quoting Thomas Mann) stems from some "permanent dissatisfaction." Wier shows us how that initial dissatisfaction of the restless imagination can be the wellspring of writing to the satisfaction of many.

Sidney Wade's essay on metaphor as the "Fundament of Imaginative Writing" is an elegant treatment of what she calls the "queen of the tropes," the "writer's . . . giver of life . . . the magic wand" capable of making "a brave new world spring out of a handful of words." Wade reminds us the Greek meaning of metaphor is "to carry over." Out of that forthright term Wade moves to the complexities poetic thought creates, the fact that likening is always provisional yet when successful creates more than existed before. Wade sees metaphor as something close to what Albert Einstein meant by the term "combinatory play." Wade's piece is particularly helpful for the ways it makes the point that poetry is a physical art, "The abstract . . . understood in the context of the concrete, the metaphysical in" terms "of the physical, the emotional in the context of the biological." She seals that argument with an excellent reading of Sylvia Plath's "A Winter Ship," using Plath's description of boats docked in winter, which includes, "the water slips / And gossips in its loose vernacular." Wade's example here pits human idiom against a physical vernacular, and it offers insight into the figurative thinking by which Plath held her suffering closely clarified.

In her essay, "The Directing Sentence," Christine Schutt says, "it is subtraction that shapes stories." As part of this principle she urges we consider the ways a story's guiding sentence "has been recalled and rewritten." Her first example is taken from Flannery O'Connor's "A Good Man Is Hard to Find." In her opening O'Connor introduces the main character, a grandmother who wants her family to vacation somewhere other than where they are going. Pursuing this she mentions news of an escaped murderer known as "the Misfit" and says, "*I wouldn't take my children in any direction with a criminal like that aloose in it.*" This statement, Schutt tells us, "directs the story." All that follows grows out of it. Schutt goes on to discuss the same process of development in stories by John Updike, Stanley Elkin, and Leonard Michaels. Here is Updike's opening sentence: "*In walk these three girls in nothing but bathing suits.*" Schutt reminds us that this opening directs what follows. The checkout boy at the register listens as the store manager objects to the way the girls are dressed, and in support of the girls the boy quits his job. The point here is no one notices. More memorable as a directing sentence, Stanley Elkin's "A Poetics for Bullies" opens this way: "I'm Push the bully, and what I hate are new kids and sissies, dumb kids and smart, rich kids, poor kids, kids who wear glasses, talk funny, show off, patrol boys and wise guys and kids who pass pencils and water the plants—and cripples, especially cripples. I love nobody loved." Elkin's language magnifies everything it touches. Meanwhile, Leonard Michaels's "Murderers" does things in a different but equally memorable way, setting the story's tone by the narrator's early statement, "I wanted proximity to darkness, strangeness." Following that the character gets what he wants. So does the reader. The most fascinating element of Schutt's piece is her demonstration that "Pronouncements made in opening paragraphs must be overturned and returned to." This is "the recursive gesture" she recommends that in turn "makes for profounder meaning." I would argue that, the stronger the directing sentence, the more significant the recursive moment can become. Just as important as this, however, there is Schutt's principle of subtraction. That practice will also magnify a story's implications.

"Rationed Compassion: Philip Larkin and Richard Wilbur" is a reading of the ways limit and inclusion give each other meaning. Philip Larkin's tough-guy poesie (his "Old Fools," his "toad *work*," his "uncle shouting smut," or dinner party with a "*crowd of craps*") brings compassion just as he takes away assurance. By this Larkin recaptures romantic ground even as he reignites our doubt. In comparison to Larkin, Richard Wilbur's responses to experience are generally affirmative. Larkin was the master of bog, Wilbur the master of praise. How different these two writers seem. And yet how very much alike. Both used astringents, and both rationed compassion for the sake of meaning. Larkin's bog was what Wilbur called his "marchlands." How did each write beyond the limits of these restricted landscapes? Wilbur said he strove "to have objects speak" so they freed "the devout intransitive eye." Larkin did so too, in his own way, by his use of a diction that could characterize and comment in one breath. Whether immersed in the details of a train ride ("The Whitsun Weddings"), a tomb ("The Arundel Tomb"), or the indifference of institutional windows ("High Windows"), Larkin turned one's expectations into condemnation, then back to something kinder. Richard Wilbur wrote the same small odysseys. But his events—a bird trapped in a room ("The Writer"), the ironies of New Year's Eve ("Year's End"), or a person who carries "roses always in a way that says / They are not only" hers ("The Beautiful Changes")—concluded in more openly affirmative ways than Larkin's grumbles. Even so, both poets reached similar findings—the challenges of time and mortality, love and separation, our tendency to abstract things yet having the ability to see beauty, moments of humor and sorrow, insight and opacity. The list goes on—art rationing emotion to make room for compassion.

Sewanee, 2020

Story

ALICE McDERMOTT

An old man wakes up one morning, calls to his dog, and heads out on a lovely walk down a familiar country road.

As the two go along leisurely, enjoying the scenery and the fine weather, the old man slowly begins to recall that the dog at his side died many years ago, when the old man himself was just leaving his boyhood. Delighted as he is to see his dog again, the man can't help but conclude that if this friend of his youth has returned to him, then he, too, must have died. And indeed, as he walks, the old man remembers his own peaceful passing.

Soon enough, man and dog come to a turn in the road that leads up a steep hill. At the top of the hill, the man can just glimpse a towering white arch lit up with the sun. As he and his dog approach, the old man sees as well high, alabaster walls inlaid with mother-of-pearl, and then two golden gates, and, behind them, a street paved with gold. There's a handsome man sitting at a beautiful desk just inside the gate.

"Is this heaven?" the old man asks.

"Yes, it is," the man at the desk says. "Would you like to come in?"

"I would indeed," the old man replies.

Smiling warmly, the gatekeeper rises from the desk. "And is there anything we can get for you?" he asks as he comes forward to open the gate.

"Well, I've been walking a long time," the old man says. "I'd love a drink of water."

The man says he'll gladly have a glass of ice water sent right up.

"And have you got a bowl for the dog?" the old man asks.

The gatekeeper pauses behind the gate, his hand frozen on the latch. "Oh, the dog can't come in," he says. "Pets aren't allowed here."

The old man looks at the handsome fellow behind the gate, and the streets of gold beyond him. He looks up at the sunlight on the beautiful arch and down at his dog.

"I'll be going along, then," the old man says, and turns and walks back down the hill and out onto the road.

The man and the dog continue in the direction they had been going.

After another long walk, they reach the top of another steep hill, where they find a dirt road that leads through a farm gate. There's no fence, and the gate is wide open. So much grass has grown up around the gate that it looks as though it's never been closed. Just beyond the gate, there's a man sitting in a rickety chair in the shade of a tree, reading a book. The old man calls to him, "Excuse me, sir. Sorry to bother, but I've been walking a long time and I wonder if you've got any water."

The man looks up from his book. "Oh sure," he says. "There's a pump over there," and he points to a place beyond the gate. "Come in and help yourself."

But as the old man approaches the farm gate, he hesitates. "What about my friend here?" he asks, gesturing toward his dog.

The man returns to his book. "Not a problem," he says pleasantly. "There's a bowl beside the pump."

The old man and his dog pass through the gate and, sure enough, they find the water pump. The old man fills the bowl for his dog and then takes a long drink himself.

The two return to thank the man. They find him waiting for them in the shade of the tree.

"This is a very nice place," the old man says.

"Yes, it is," the man under the tree says. "It's heaven, in fact."

The old man and his dog exchange a look. "Well, that's strange," the old man says. "There's a place down the road that calls itself heaven as well."

The man under the tree smiles. "You mean the place with the alabaster walls and the golden gates?"

"That's right," the old man says. "It's very beautiful."

"It's hell," says the man.

"Is it now?" the old man asks.

"It is," the man says, laughing. "Though they're always after calling themselves heaven."

The old man considers this for a moment. "That must make you very angry," he says.

But the man with the book shakes his head. "No," he says. "We don't mind at all. They do us a great favor." And he leans to pat the old man's dog on the head. "They sort out for us all the people who can't be loyal to their friends."

I found this little story in an Irish magazine.

I read it—as I do a great deal of my magazine reading on a busy day—while walking up the driveway from the mailbox, the rest of the serious mail tucked under my arm and Rufous, our labradoodle, watching my progress up and back with his big black nose pressed to the sidelight window beside our front door. I usually take Rufous for a midday walk after I get the mail, so if I linger too long on the driveway with an opened magazine, he'll give a polite bark to remind me of my more pressing obligations.

I have, in fact, quite often had to make a choice—much like the old man in the story—between reading a magazine piece in its entirety, right there in the driveway, or putting it aside in favor of my shaggy friend. More than once I've entertained the notion that the fiction editors at the *New Yorker* should be informed each week of how well the opening paragraphs of the current short story have withstood Rufous's brown-eyed charms. If the opening paragraphs are good enough—vivid, lyrical, intriguing, funny (how many ways can a story seduce you into reading it in its entirety in one standing?)—then poor Rufous will have his walk delayed. Chances are that if the story is by the likes of Alice Munro or William Trevor or Tessa Hadley or George Saunders, poor Rufous will have his walk delayed.

Far more often, however, he will give his polite bark and then that wonderful, anticipatory whole-body shiver that dogs do to convey their gratitude for what you haven't even done for them yet, and the story loses out. Call it the Rufous test. Do you choose the story of post-adolescent angst in the life of a Brooklyn or L.A. hipster, or the tail-wagging dog? Do you finish reading this ironic tale of emotional catatonia in the overeducated, or do you put the stupid magazine down and pick up the leash?

One of the first writing classes I took was taught by a mad Scotsman who would read our weak opening paragraphs out loud and then, glaring, ask us why in the world anyone would want to take time out of his day to read any more of this? People have lives, he'd shout, people have things to do, people want to go out and have a drink.

Fortunately for Rufous that day, the little story in the Irish magazine was short enough to read in its entirety as I walked up the driveway. It was titled "Animals in Heaven," and it was placed as filler, a narrow, unsigned sidebar, in a magazine devoted to the Irish music scene: results of various competitions, impossibly adorable photos of Irish dancers, and group shots of impossibly stereotypical looking (that is, they all look like my relatives) festival organizers and sponsors.

The magazine contained as well the usual (for the Irish) number of memorial essays—"we'll not see his like again" accounts of humble and generous fiddlers or pipers or singers who lived their lives dedicated to traditional Irish music. Obscure names, of course, known only to the community of Irish musicians—a community of artists, by the way, for whom fame and fortune play almost no part in their ambitions for their art. Kind of like poets.

There's a whole other lecture on what fiction writers can learn from practitioners of the obscure traditional arts, especially now as literary fiction is becoming one of them, one of the obscure traditional arts.

For instance: We hosted three "famous" Irish musicians at our house—incredible players all, marvelously talented—and after playing a couple of particularly wonderful tunes around our kitchen table, one of them wryly proclaimed, "Jesus, lads, there's *hundreds* to be made with this music! Hundreds!"

Billy McComiskey, a great Irish box player from Baltimore, one of the finest musicians on the scene, and a high-school facilities manager in his day job, was asked by an adult student if he, the student, would ever learn to play as well as Billy. Billy asked him, "Do you like your job?" and the student said yes, he liked it very much. "Then you'll never play as well as I do," Billy growled. "I hate mine."

Perfection of the work, not of the life, as Yeats might note. Obscurity a small price to pay for the pleasure of indulging our passion, pursuing our vision, for the great gift of a life spent in service to the art that we, God knows why, cherish above all others.

And lest you think the novelist's pursuit, with all its possibilities of fame and fortune, movie deals and grand prizes, is of any more value than the homely pursuit of the obscure traditional arts, consider something else Yeats had to say:

> Last night I went to a wide place on the Kiltartan road to listen to some Irish songs. . . . The voices melted into the twilight and were mixed into the trees, and when I thought of the words they too melted away, and were mixed with the generations of men. Now it was a phrase, now it was an attitude of mind, an emotional form, that had carried my memory to older verses, or even to forgotten mythologies.
>
> I was carried so far that it was as though I came to one of the four rivers, and followed it under the wall of Paradise to the roots of the trees of knowledge and of life. . . . Folk art is, indeed, the oldest of the aristocracies of thought, and because it refuses what is passing and trivial, the merely clever and pretty, as certainly as the vulgar and insincere, and because it has gathered into itself the simplest and most unforgettable thoughts of generations, it is the soil where all great art is rooted.

". . . refuses what is passing and trivial, the merely clever and pretty, as certainly as the vulgar and insincere. . . ." I love that.

But back to the story.

I don't need an Irish musician's self-awareness to understand why I felt compelled to read the whole of "Animals in Heaven" right there in the driveway, despite Rufous's adorable face at the window. For one, the piece was very short. For two, it had a dog in it—always a draw for me. I was one of those kids who lost sleep at night worrying about whether or not dogs could go to heaven (until a wonderful young nun assured me that taking care of the animals in heaven was the very task for which St. Francis of Assisi had been created). And it was about death—always a favorite subject. And it was sentimental. So am I.

But what I didn't understand, after I read the story and left the magazine with the rest of the mail on the table in the hall and took old Rufous for his walk, was how much I wanted to repeat it.

I had no idea what compelled me. It wasn't a joke—it didn't have one of those great punch lines you can't wait to deliver to someone else the moment after it's been delivered to you. Nor was it one of those bizarre or tragic Internet stories that it seems we're always trading: *did you read about that bride who . . . did you see that story about the shark . . . apparently there's a teenager in Memphis with . . .* stories we repeat for no more complex reason, it would seem, than our childish delight in the weird or our rubbernecking curiosity about other people's bad luck.

I can't say that I found "Animals In Heaven" a particularly astute little story, and I knew its charms were hackneyed and unsophisticated enough to make me aware of how poorly they might reflect on the literary taste of the teller. And yet I knew that if I had run into a neighbor on my walk with Rufous that day, I would have told her the whole tale as soon as I could work it into the conversation—which would have been easy enough to do, *dog* being the operative, single-word preface, and Rufous himself being the obliging narrative segue.

I know I repeated the story to my husband as we put dinner together that night. (He reacted with a tolerant "Ah, cute.") I know I told it again to my daughter as I drove her to work the next morning. (Polite smile on her part and no assurance on mine that she'd listened to a word of it.) The semester at Hopkins was over, but I'm certain I would have told my class—my most reliable depository for stories I want to tell whether or not anyone wants to hear them.

Mired as I had been for the past few years in two separate novels-in-progress, I'd been thinking a lot about the wrong turns, the blind alleys, the mistaken goals that seem so much a part of the long march that is the composition of a novel. So it's possible this little story appealed to me because it's a kind of metaphor for the writing process itself. Not the waking-up dead part—but the whole up and down the steep hill thing, the trudging toward some recognizable, and then unrecognizable, goal.

And then, some weeks after reading the story, I heard, in Sewanee, John Casey's wonderful craft lecture on Aristotle's *Poetics*. And when John mentioned Aristotle's simple, *easy-for-you-to-say* injunction that every story have a beginning, a middle, and an end, I began to wonder if what had compelled me to repeat this silly little story of the man and his dog was not that deep, sentimental flaw in my own literary sensibilities, but merely the fact that the story itself is a perfect Aristotelian whole with not merely a beginning, middle, and end, but pretty damn good ones.

Consider:

A beginning is that which does not itself follow anything by causal necessity, but after which something naturally is or comes to be.

An old man wakes up one morning, calls to his dog and heads out on a lovely walk down a familiar country road.

> As the two go along, leisurely enjoying the scenery and the fine weather, the old man slowly begins to recall that the dog at his side died many years ago, when the old man himself was just leaving his boyhood. Delighted as he is to see his dog again, he can't help but conclude that if this friend of his youth has returned to him, then he, too, must have died. And indeed, as he walks, the old man remembers his own peaceful passing.

A perfect beginning. Well, maybe not the "an old man wakes up" part. Anyone who has taught fledgling fiction writers knows the bane of those "The alarm clock rang" opening lines—although Kafka and Katherine Anne Porter, to name just two, pull it off pretty well.

What makes this beginning so perfect is the magical moment when the old man, walking *leisurely* along in a familiar landscape with his dog as—it is implied—is their morning routine, *slowly begins to recall* that the dog has returned to him from a time long past. What a surge of joy is implied in those simple, and amazingly understated, lines—a resurrection, a return of what was lost. A hint of magic.

The storyteller's art is, always, the conjurer's art, and what we look for in beginnings, whether we know it or not, is the first hint of that magic.

For many Sewanee summers now, I've taught with my brilliant friend Tony Earley. Once, hoping to illustrate the idea of a reliable or unreliable narrator, Tony told the workshop a story from his childhood. On a vacation in the country, his parents, it seemed, wanted some peace and privacy in their cottage one afternoon, as parents of small children are on occasion inclined to do, and so they locked the screen door while little Tony was playing outside. As small children of amorous parents are inclined to do, Tony, of course, sensing they wanted him out, demanded to be let in. He rattled the screen door and made various entreaties and was rebuffed by his father each time until little Tony finally got the terrific notion to tell his parents, through the screen, "I saw a snake out here."

This, of course, brought his father outside. As father and son made their search around the property, Tony's father asked him to describe the snake. Delighted by the excellent result of his lie, Tony became increasingly more explicit in his descriptions until he added, "It's got two heads," going immediately, as far as his father was concerned, from reliable to unreliable narrator.

It's as good an illustration of getting the details right as any I've ever heard, but Tony's story also says something about magic. The magic not in little Tony's credulity-straining lie, but the magic in the moment he said "I saw a snake out here" and his father, in his imagination—and despite more pressing and appealing real-world distractions—saw the snake too. The magic, the storyteller's magic, is contained in those moments in which both son (the author) and father (the reader) saw that snake out there in their minds' eyes and went about trying to find it. During those moments, until the spell was broken by the wrong detail, the snake *was* there, conjured by the storyteller's words.

Whether we're aware of it or not—and there's no reason for readers to be aware of such things—we look for that magic in every opening of every story, a conjuring of a place, of a voice, of a way of seeing that shows us both the material world of the story and the shimmer of the artist's skill.

Of course, I'm not just talking Harry Potter magic here. Not even magical realism, although Gabriel García Márquez's well-trampled opening paragraph in *One Hundred Years of Solitude* is as good an example as I can think of:

> Many years later, as he faced the firing squad, Colonel Aureliano Buendia was to remember that distant afternoon when his father took him to discover ice. At that time, Macondo was a village of twenty adobe houses, built on the bank of a river that ran along a bed of polished stones, which were whole and enormous, like prehistoric eggs. The world was so recent that many things lacked names, and in order to indicate them, it was necessary to point.

But consider, too, the perhaps less heralded magic of Virginia Woolf's opening paragraphs in *Jacob's Room:*

> "So of course," wrote Betty Flanders, pressing her heels rather deeper in the sand, "there was nothing for it but to leave."
>
> Slowly welling from the point of her gold nib, pale blue ink dissolved the full stop; for there her pen stuck; her eyes fixed, and tears slowly filled them. The entire bay quivered; the lighthouse wobbled; and she had the illusion that the mast of Mr. Connor's little yacht was bending like a wax candle in the sun. She winked quickly. Accidents were awful things. She winked again. The mast was straight; the waves were regular; the lighthouse was upright; but the blot had spread.

The magic here being the way the writer, the great prestidigitator, utterly changes the visible world—now you see it, now you don't—by passing it through the transforming prism of Betty Flanders's tears.

And here's Dickens, the great conjurer himself:

> My father's family name being Pirrip, and my Christian name Philip, my infant tongue could make of both names nothing longer or more explicit than Pip. So, I called myself Pip, and came to be called Pip.
>
> I give Pirrip as my father's family name, on the authority of his tombstone and my sister—Mrs. Joe Gargery, who married the blacksmith. As I never saw my father or my mother, and never saw any likeness of either of them (for their days were long before the days of photographs), my first fancies regarding what they were like, were unreasonably derived from their tombstones. The shape of the letters on my father's, gave me an odd idea that he was a square, stout, dark man, with curly black hair. From the character and turn of the inscription, "Also Georgiana Wife of the Above," I drew a childish conclusion that my mother was freckled and sickly. To five little stone lozenges, each about a foot and a half long, which were arranged in a neat row beside their grave, and were sacred to the memory of five little brothers of mine—who gave up trying to get a living, exceedingly early in that universal struggle—I am indebted for a belief I religiously entertained that they had all been born on their backs with their hands in their trousers-pockets, and had never taken them out in this state of existence.

Language becomes incantation, and the conjured world is both a real and an imagined place, an authentic *and* an enchanted landscape. The voice in our ear is both a voice we know as well as our own, and one we have never heard before. It shows us the bleak image of the five small graves and, simultaneously, the dear, adorable shape of five children with their hands forever in their trouser pockets.

Inundated as we are by story—Internet story and television story and gossip and horror and mass murder everywhere—it is this shimmer of magic that remains the province of the fiction writer alone. To see, to recognize, what we have never seen before. To marvel at the familiarity of the conjured world even as we glimpse the never-before-seen enchantment of it all.

> As he walked along, the old man slowly recalled that the dog at his side had died years ago, when he himself was just leaving his childhood. . . . Walking along, he remembered he too had died peacefully. . . .

A beginning that gives us character, situation, movement forward and above all magic. No wonder it passed the Rufous test.

Middle:

A middle is that which follows something as some other thing follows it.

> "Pets aren't allowed here."
>
> The old man looks at the handsome man behind the gate, and the street of gold beyond him. He looks up at the sunlight on the beautiful arch and down at his dog. "I'll be going along then," the old man says, and turns and walks back down the hill and out onto the road.

I have a writer friend who calls the point at which she has reached the middle of a novel-in-progress "middle-of-book-syndrome." "Mobs," she says. "Rhymes with sobs."

The world has been created, the voice established, characters sent out along their path. All the creative energy spent on the initial conjuring, the beginning, all the high hopes the writer has for the imagined end, now sag a bit, flag a bit, as the middle of the book approaches.

That simple story-driving engine, And then what happened? And then what happened? becomes in the middle of a story a slightly more impatient, Now what? Now what?

And, as the "Animals in Heaven" story shows us, the answer is, Now things change.

Now, Gatsby's house goes dark, and the parties end.

Now, Emma Bovary returns from the marquis's ball with the viscount's lovely cigar box in hand, and her boredom suddenly becomes unbearable.

Now, Cathy is brought back to Wuthering Heights after her stay with the Lintons, and poor Heathcliff hardly knows her.

Now Marlow is convinced he will not find Kurtz alive:

> For the moment that was the dominant thought. There was a sense of extreme disappointment, as though I had found out I had been striving after something altogether without a substance. I couldn't have been more disgusted if I had traveled all this way for the sole purpose of talking with Mr. Kurtz. Talking with. . . . I flung one shoe overboard and became aware that that was exactly what I had been looking forward to—a talk with Kurtz. I made the strange discovery that I had never imagined him as doing, you know, but as discoursing. I didn't say to myself, 'Now I will never see him,' or 'Now I will never shake him by the hand,' but, 'Now I will never hear him.' The man presented himself as a voice. Not of course that I did not connect him with some sort of action. Hadn't I been told in all the tones of jealousy and admiration that he had collected, bartered, swindled, or stolen more ivory than all the other agents together? That was not the point. The point was in his being a gifted creature, and that of all his gifts the one that stood out pre-eminently, that carried with it a sense of real presence, was his ability to talk, his words—the gift of expression, the bewildering, the illuminating, the most exalted and the most contemptible, the pulsating stream of light, or the deceitful flow from the heart of an impenetrable darkness.

The antidote to "mobs," then, is, quite simply: change. Our narrator becomes aware. (*Now I will never hear him.*) Our hero/heroine gets what he or she wants and then discovers it's not what was imagined. She changes her mind. Reconsiders. Loses heart. Turns away. Continues along on the road, or finds another road, climbs another steep hill toward another, less certain, goal, despairs, resolves, walks on air—to borrow from Seamus Heaney—against his better judgment.

And the End:

An end, on the contrary, is that which itself naturally follows some other thing, either by necessity, or as a rule, but has nothing following it.

The satisfaction "Animals In Heaven" provides results, no doubt, from its modest cleverness: a cleverness—we recognize only at the end—that the teller of the tale was aware of all along, from the first words. Had the story begun, "An old man dies one night and finds himself at the pearly gates," our sense of delight at the end of the tale might not be so keen.

But when we reach the end of the story, we can look back at that offhanded and seemingly inadvertent phrase, "called to his dog"—a phrase that we, naive, new to the tale, barely notice on first reading—and see now how cleverly it was planted, how cleverly it hid its role as the essential element of the story, for out of it blossoms the old man's realization that he has died, his rejection of the first heaven, the revelation of the nature of the second, authentic one and, finally, the story's whole reason for being. No dog, no story—no plot, no happy resolution.

We're probably more accustomed to praising the cleverness of jokes and comedy sketches and small children, but it's not a bad element to consider even in the headiest of literary novels and stories. I think of cleverness as that pleasant satisfaction we feel when we understand that what the novel has revealed to us at its end *the author knew all along.* I don't mean by this a surprise, or a piece of information previously withheld—that's the province of stories whose endings leave us feeling deceived, not delighted. Rather, I mean the sense that from its first sentence, the novel has been, inevitably, heading toward this conclusion.

A good ending also sends us forward, much as a good beginning does, into what Isak Dinesen in her short story "The Blank Page" calls the "silence at the end of the story." (If the storyteller has been true to the story, she says, the silence will speak.) But a good ending also casts a light back through the novel, back to the first chapter and scene and word. Naive as we were when we first encountered these words—just following along, asking, And then what happened? And then what happened? Or, further along, Now what? Now what?—on a second reading we can pause to appreciate the author's design. We can appreciate the story's cleverness.

Cleverness, wholeness, an appreciation for design—but a good ending does something more. It says something. It says something about us.

Years and years ago, when I was writing one of my first reviews for the book review section of a major newspaper, I mentioned to the editor that I thought a certain novel was ultimately unsatisfying because it lacked a moral vision. The editor didn't like the term. "I have no moral vision, either," she told me.

I thought of suggesting she might want to make an appointment with a metaphysician, but that was only hours later. *Staircase wit,* as the French say.

Moral vision. The modern reader, and critic, recoil a bit at the phrase—it seems, these days, to portend a scold; it seems to be the province of religious tracts and right-wing politics—but I think it's as much a part of what we look for in the ending of a novel or a story as cleverness, magic, and Aristotle's consistent whole. Put simply: We look for what the novel says that's true for us all. We look for us.

Consider *The Great Gatsby*'s famous ending, "And so we beat on, boats against the current, borne back ceaselessly into the past. . . ."

Now hear the difference the slightest pronoun change, the slightest change in perspective, can make:

> And so I beat on, a boat against the current, borne back ceaselessly into my past.
>
> And so he beat on, a boat against the current, borne back ceaselessly to his boyhood in St. Paul.

Or, postmodernly:

> And so you beat on, you boat against the current, you, borne back ceaselessly into wherever it was you came from. . . .

The ending of "Animals in Heaven" doesn't try to convince us that loyalty to our friends is a good—it simply acknowledges a truth universally known: that loyalty *is* a good. But in doing so, it acknowledges that there *are* universal truths to be known, that there are in human experience elemental notions of good (and bad) that we, being human, share. A novel about loyalty—*Billy Budd, Beloved, Great Expectations, The Quiet American, Remains of the Day, A Gathering of Old Men*—will show us the complexity, drama, rewards, and difficulties of this truth—but the truth, the *we* of it, is there.

Of course it can be argued that there are no unassailable notions of elemental good. That another version of "Animals in Heaven" might just as well prove that loyalty to friends, to dead dogs, for instance, is a foolish burden that will result in the loss of wealth and beauty—the kind of wealth and beauty only selfishness can buy. An ending in which an old man is stuck for eternity on an overgrown tract of useless land where he has to pump his own water and endure the company of smug people who read books just because of his blind loyalty to an old dog might also illustrate some universal truth. But not one I'd have felt compelled to share with my dog-walking neighbors or the people I love.

It didn't occur to me, of course, that day on the driveway, that the little Irish story was a bit of Aristotelian perfection. (Although it may have made Rufous—who is of a philosophical bent—feel better about having his walk delayed.) And I'm quite certain that the original author of the story—and I've since learned that versions of this tale appear in a variety of cultures—had no idea of this either. I like to think the story was first conjured for a child who worried about whether pets go to heaven. Or maybe it was a loving dog owner who'd been betrayed by a friend. Whatever its origins, it was a good tale, with its nice beginning, middle, and end, and because it was a good tale whoever first heard it felt compelled to tell it to someone else, who told it to someone else, and so on, right on down to this moment, when I have found my excuse to tell it to you.

Narrative Architecture and the Inhabitation of Story

ADRIANNE HARUN

Nearly every story I've written has originated in memories of my childhood home, a place that does not, in fact, appear in any work I've written. I remember it as a sprawling English Tudor on an oak-lined street. The families who lived on the street, for the most part, were large like my own, and in the late afternoons and on weekends, you could not walk outside without hearing the sound of children. Children playing. Children wailing. The industrious, subterranean hum of children scheming as they claimed yard after yard, house after house.

Our house had four porches: a front porch we never used, an enclosed "rainy day" porch where we played board games, a back raised deck that, again, we did not use (my parents did not much like the outdoors), and a sleeping porch off my parents' bedroom that also remained empty. One of my older brothers and I used it for the sole purpose of spying on our next-door neighbors with binoculars. (We watched them watch television shows, often the same ones that played in the next room at our house.) The house had two living rooms separated by pocket doors, a long corridor that led from the kitchen to the dining room, along which lay a nook with a generous red leather booth where all five children ate every meal. My parents regularly dined alone in the dining room since my father's medical practice rarely saw him home before seven or eight at night.

There was a front staircase with two landings and a narrow curved back staircase that led from the kitchen to the upstairs hall and was always a trial to negotiate since the vast quantities of medical samples my father received were stacked there. On the second floor, we had a television room, where truthfully our lives were spent. We did homework there, our eyes skittering between workbooks and the screen, only pausing to change into pajamas which were kept on shelves in that room's closet. My younger sister and I slept on the second floor, across the hall from our parents, near that television room, so I often stayed up late to sit close to my cracked-open bedroom door and read by the hall light or listen covertly to Johnny Carson or puzzle out the scraps of my parents' late-night conversations. Two of my brothers slept down the hall, and the third brother was on his own on the third floor in a long, low-ceilinged room between a vast cedar closet and an attic I can honestly say I never entered. That attic had an enormous fan that took up half the room and functioned in every way like a family monster we must never visit or acknowledge. The attic's very door, like Mr. Rochester's, always locked, terrified me.

I could go on and on. The house was endless to me: the cellar with a furnace larger than my mother's Rambler station wagon, the second-floor family bathroom with a deep cupboard in which I locked myself when I was five, crawling well back from the shelves and into secrecy until I lost consciousness from lack of oxygen. My grandfather broke down the bathroom door, which I'd also been careful to lock, and then took the cupboard door off by its hinges to rescue me and carry me outside where eventually I sipped the air and came awake again. I only remember I'd been telling myself a story, one that required me to leave the world and become part of the house itself. Early on, I was clearly the kind of child who longed to hide away and continually needed to be warned against stepping into abandoned refrigerators or against crawling through brambles into the hobo caves beside a nearby creek.

When we moved from that house, I was eleven, and I cried for nights, missing it with a deep, physical pain. Sometimes now I wonder if during those weeping nights, I was actually bringing the house into me in a way that guaranteed I'd never lose it again. While shorn of the kind of dramatic event that etched, say, William Maxwell's own childhood homes into the riveting *So Long, See You Tomorrow,* the house held all of my childish stories, my early shames, my deep delights—endless horrific puzzlements—and I relived them, night after night, in a strange new bedroom, one without the built-in cupboards or the deep closet that smelled of cedar. In short, the old house provided a center of my psychic universe. It burrowed into and shaped a formative part of my consciousness, and it's never left me. I visit a version of the house in dreams. I walk through it in every story that mentions a kitchen, a staircase, an attic, a sleeping porch, love, desire, mistakes, fear, and deep embarrassment. It has provided a template that has yet to be replaced, and while I might build onto that template, the animation of that house remains. It inhabits me. And ultimately, what I hope to do in any piece of fiction is recreate a similar, enduring feeling of inhabitation for a reader.

In *The Golden Bough*, one of my all-time favorite reference books, Sir James Frazer describes two principles of primitive magic, both grouped under the title "Sympathetic Magic," so-called because "both assume that things act on each other at a distance through a secret sympathy . . . to explain *how things can physically affect each other through a space which appears to be empty.*" That "secret sympathy" is a terrific description, I think, of what took hold of me with my childhood house and also what takes place between a reader and a story when all is working as it should. To engage and transfix through the construction and inhabitation of a nonexistent, but "real" world. To "*physically affect through a space which appears to be empty.*"

As fiction writers, we have a slew of narrative tools for this job, and most of us are fairly adept at constructing. The real trick, the magic, comes in the forms of inhabitation, the emotional being that takes shape alongside, within, and through that construction. And although it may be the most obvious and workmanlike, the choice of structure, the melding of shape and subject, may be, it seems to me, at the heart of creating that secret sympathy.

When we first begin to write a story, we tend to hold the bits and pieces in our heads, proceeding intuitively until story events begin to happen in a coherent fashion and our characters reveal themselves in ways that make sense of or clearly instigate those events. If we are really lucky, we have the voice, which may very well guide all. At some point, we realize we have a draft, and then the fun begins as we work toward creating something that comes alive on the page. It's the rare writer about this point who doesn't soon become aware of the need to shape the material at hand, to acknowledge what Madison Smartt Bell in his insightful and highly instructive primer, *Narrative Design*, calls "the need for scaffolding, the interdependence of plot, character, tone, *and structure* into one whole Design."

As I became more aware of the need for shaping in my own work and the possibilities that might emerge from being more consciously aware of design,

I began looking more closely at the fictional forms in front of me, not just the forms themselves but the reasons behind them. At the same time, I was reading a bit about architecture and mulling over architecture's blatantly obvious parallels to story-writing as well as other less-explored shared territory between the two fields. My simple hope—and you will note how lazy I am—was to glean something from architects about how to *shape* a story, tuck that something in my pocket, and use it ever after as my own bit of primitive magic. Overlaying interesting structure on content seemed both sensible and inspired, a basic technique to invest and direct meaning, and I imagined correlations between the two fields unfolding in the most obvious ways: a framed story, perhaps, or a story manufactured in levels. I was also interested in exploring more esoteric versions of basic engineering in story form: how circulation, for instance, might translate or how narrative walls, so to speak, might be positioned for the best effect.

Unlike poets, it seemed to me, fiction writers lacked the endless intriguing possibilities offered by clear formal structures and at times, especially those hours early on when I scoured my bookshelves for a real rule book, I have felt that loss keenly. How grand it would be to know that every family story should contain, say, six scenes interspersed with one long passage of exposition or that a particular kind of love story must only be told in second-person, interior monologue.

Reductive, of course. And, okay, fiction writers are clearly not without structural choices. We learn early on about the classic underpinnings of a story, the three-part narrative arc of beginning, middle, and end. That familiar Freytag triangle of exposition, climax, resolution. A storywriter dedicated to a particular genre soon becomes trained, too, to grab hold of the useful fail-safe of schematics, and a more literary writer steals and translates as much as she can from those genre-proven effects when possible. Yet despite those basic guidelines, a fiction writer often finds a story or novel refuses to fall in line with any notion of standard shaping. Certain chapters or scenes—highly *necessary* chapters and scenes, we believe—may seem to derail a story or, at the least, feel clunky and *out of place*. A crucial organizing principle appears to be missing or unworkable and, as a consequence, our early readers scramble or struggle to make either logical or emotional sense of the narrative at those points, and the work never fully comes to life. So one begins a desperate game of shifting tenses, juggling scenes, cutting characters, praying for the appearance of that organizing principle. Sometimes but rarely, we get lucky and this approach works toward a truly satisfying result. Yet one—*me*—still persists in hoping a more strategic structural solution might exist.

To peruse the last century's theories of architecture, even in my cursory, dabbling way, is to discover not simply dynamic discourse on how to structure environments, but also a boatload of philosophical thoughts on how to inhabit space. And this may be one of the more interesting links between the arts of architecture and fiction writing. Architects enjoy a history of evolving forms to contextualize problems that mirror many of the novelist's dilemmas and, even better, they have a habit of developing credos that might bear much in common with the goals of fiction writing. Take this twentieth-century dictum attributed to Louis Sullivan:

> It is the pervading law of all things organic and inorganic,
> Of all things physical and metaphysical,
> Of all things human and all things super-human,
> Of all true manifestations of the head,
> Of the heart, of the soul,
> That the life is recognizable in its expression,
> **That form ever follows function. This is the law.**

Sullivan's proclamation—how strong! how enticingly definitive!—was later nuanced by Adolf Loos, who called the premise and raised it with "form follows function; ornament is a crime," a concept Le Corbusier placed close to heart as he designated buildings as "machines for living." Then along came Mies van der Rohe. His improvement of the Law—the Hemingway-esque motto, "Less Is More"—was more or less kicked across the room by Robert Venturi, who famously came back with "Less Is a Bore." In their book *Learning from Las Vegas*, Venturi, Denise Scott Brown, and Steven Izenour took that rebuke further, presenting ornamentation as more or less intrinsic as with their famous example of "The Duck," a Long Island poultry store designed in the shape of the bird. Or ornamentation as application, as in signage, a form called "The Decorated Shed." Think here of the Vegas strip, a long line of businesses, each declaring its purpose through eye-catching signs. Or you might simply think of a ubiquitous "decorated shed": your nearby McDonald's. In either manifestation, ornamentation is necessary. Meaning, the architects maintained, could evolve

The Duck (© Beth Savage/Wikimedia Commons)

from an iconic shape ("The Duck") or could be lathered on with well-chosen embellishments ("The Decorated Shed").

I have to admit my first attempts at translating these architectural dicta into fiction-writing technique garnered results that felt contrived and facile. What I thought might be witty, even powerful—a mighty fine Duck of a story—felt flat and trite and merely confused. A duck-shaped store that sold eyeglasses. I'd missed more than a step, I decided. And too—a bit of a side road—about now I began to have doubts, to worry that, by experimenting with story forms, I'd end up with a potentially clever premise embedded behind an inscrutable structural barrier, one readers would have to vault to get to the story itself. Readers, most writers tend to believe—and I've been among them—need the familiarity of form to enter and accept the fictional world. They need the fiction equivalent of a center-hall colonial.

Fiction is not reality and, to entice readers to believe, we offer the illusion of similitude. In choosing a traditional story frame, that linear design, we reinforce this with a recognizable form. We say to the reader, *here is a story,* and so, in effect, believe we have removed one obstacle between the reader and the entrance to the story. Here is the hallway; the stairs are straight ahead; living room on the right, dining room to your left. Here is the situation entryway; the first conflict is to your right; second to your left; resolution at the end of the hall. Welcome again to the familiar house of story.

In the linear story, in that three-part narrative arc, we have expectations:

expectations that events will follow laws of cause and effect, that time will "make sense," that something or someone will change *dramatically* from the beginning (our entry) to the end (our exit). A fine plan, yet . . . yet stories appear that won't fit well inside that form. Truculent stories, expansive, wandering stories. A center-hall colonial taken over by a tribe of unemployed brothers-in-law with only a day-old newspaper to entertain them. Or, perhaps, not a center-hall colonial, after all.

Maybe it's because I didn't want to feel trapped by that need to remove obstacles for the reader, but it seemed clear about now that a writer also needs to remember that readers—all readers, not even especially good readers—inhabit two worlds simultaneously. Cars drive by, children call out, the teakettle sings while the reader hangs desperately onto the screen door that separates her from Joyce Carol Oates's Arnold Friend, or with Jane, must climb the stairs and stand watch in Rochester's attic, or perhaps race recklessly on a snowy day through the Old Forest with Nat and the soon-to-be-missing Lee Ann.

Yes. A reader inhabits two worlds simultaneously. Enclosure within enclosure. Right away, the frame is not what we think it's been or assume it needs to be. It is not simply a clear and familiar separation from the world. The frame goes beyond form alone—beyond rudimentary engineering. A dialogue is already underway between at least those two simultaneous realities: the one in which the reader exists *physically* and the one in which the story exists. I was cheered by this conclusion, and I went back to the architects to slow down and try again.

Architects begin the design process by assembling the program, a kind of brief from the client detailing needs. Once that is in hand, they *design* by developing a building's narrative partly using that program. Put in the simplest way, the purpose of the architectural narrative is to translate the program—the engineering, aesthetic, cultural, even historical demands—of a building as determined by its potential use, the desires of both the clients and the building's future occupants, and the constraints of the site into something productive. That narrative sum is crucial and an entity all its own, one that might be speculative in all the best ways. The narrative determines both form and function and leaps past both, becoming a third configuration altogether, a kind of intangible response to tangible needs. In other words, the eventual design, which must hue closely to the original program, refers not to the structure itself but to all the ways in which the structure will be inhabited. *Not the frame itself but the animation of the frame.* And the two, animation and frame, are inextricably intertwined.

Assembling the narrative can be extraordinarily straightforward. Architects can use a standard program template as guide, plans that rely on familiarity. Remember, at its most basic: program = needs. A bank, for instance, usually must have a central lobby, a line of teller stations, a separate vault, and areas for automated transactions and elevated financial dealings, a ranking of private offices. And we are all familiar with the needs of a library. A library should have a desk for checking out books and rows and rows (stacks) of bookcases and a public area for reading on-site and so on, with a few more specified areas to accommodate kids and technology, and so forth. Following a standard program design template is a common and recognizable path for many architects, and given the persistence of modern architecture's form-follows-function mandate, most of our libraries—viewed narratively as work spaces—are utilitarian in character and direct in organization. Think here, for instance, of your high-school library.

Yet, in previous eras, ornamentation and reverence might have been seen to supplement the pursuit of knowledge, as in the main reading room of the Library of Congress, which illustrates not only the basic form-follows-function of library needs, but a greater response. The Library of Congress implies a grand scale, a *national* library, *and* an emphasis on public access, both in play here.

Or take the Long Room in the Old Library at Trinity College in Dublin.

The Library of Congress (© Carol M. Highsmith/Wikimedia Commons)

Again, form clearly follows function. However, anyone entering or viewing this library experiences a clear emotional response as well. The space offers an echoing of forms, an elevation that suggests an expansion as well, both concepts—elevation and expansion—also wonderfully twining with "learning." And, too, there is a sense of daunting enclosure—and enclosure that, again, feels rather endless. All this connects with the concept of knowledge, the life of the mind—a concept that comes alive with the design.

The Long Room of the Old Library at Trinity College Dublin (© David Iliff/Wikimedia Commons)

In more recent times, some architects, Rem Koolhaas and his firm OMA, for instance, while still hewing to form-follows-function, also revel in "reprogramming," taking the traditional program—for, say, a library—and scrambling its familiar components, revising them so that they adhere closely to the form/function dictate and yet create a new dynamic.

Remember, a program coordinates the needs. If we could look closely at the series of programs and templates the architects developed from the librarians' initial floor-by-floor inventory, we would see an evolution, as those stated needs are worked into kind of a hierarchy of importance and use inside the building

Inside Seattle Central Library (© Peter Alfred Hess/flickr)

and, importantly, *outside* as well. The OMA architects first took stock, separating out the old library's usage into categories—for example, space for books, staff areas, reading, and workspaces. The architects then began to shift the spaces around to create a certain kind of movement through the building, one that proceeded both vertically and laterally. They designed for orientation, sun and shade, and views, keeping in mind the vistas of Mount Rainier to the south, the Olympics and Elliott Bay to the west.

Koolhaas's firm ultimately ended up with a result that hardly resembles any other library. The building is sheathed in glass and steel, creating aspects of reflection that guide the visitor/user/worker from floor to floor. The library is light-filled and even mutable on some levels.

The design represents a rather blunt approach, but it works spectacularly. Although the library fulfills the functional programmatic needs, in the process, however, how that library is used—or animated or experienced—is also somewhat altered from any other. We feel differently in that library from how we might, say, in the Library of Congress or the Trinity University Library—less cloistered but still immersed in those qualities of reflection and learning.

The bottom line here is that the narrative design defines how the architect intends to invent or control or dramatically direct the energy of the building—its

Seattle Central Library (© Bobak Ha'Eri/Wikimedia Commons)

thematic meaning and actual use or import—through its narrative structure for an effect that's most likely an emotional reaction. Story shape, too, I reckoned, needs to be less about the possibilities found in formal constraints than about that oft-missing crucial dialogue between animation and frame, between problem and solution, and crucially between reader and text. With that, I turned to novels I admired to take a closer look.

Yuri Herrera's novel *Signs Preceding the End of the World* follows one character, the intrepid Makina, on a border-crossing quest to find her brother, a story containing characters and tropes well-known to such narratives: a coyote or trafficker, a wide treacherous river, vigilantes, an assortment of enablers and villains. One could say that the "program" for this novel must have included a dangerous journey, crossing borders and cultures, requiring an extraordinary central character and easily imagine, too, a narrative design then that hews closely to a standard story arrangement, much like that found within Joseph Campbell's *The Hero's Journey*, with sections divided into "The Call to Adventure," "The Acceptance of the Call," "The Gifts of Supernatural Aid," "Crossing the Threshold," and so forth, all the way to "The Final Return to the Known World." And, guess what? Herrera does make great use of this template.

The novel opens with what feels like the end of the world, the sudden appearance of a sinkhole, the gaping earth opening beside Makina. While others disappear around her, Makina seemingly retains solid ground. She scrambles to her feet and swiftly moves on to accept a dangerous errand from her mother. Her journey begins with visits to three gangsters in succession, a trio of questionable "godfathers," to ask for help (1) crossing the border, (2) finding her brother, and most importantly, (3) returning home. One of the gangsters demands she perform a favor for him in return, handing over a small bundle for Makina to transport to the other side.

As with Campbell's template and, too, those of fairy tales and Greek myths, the narrative proceeds in a linear progression, a sequential series of events linked together causally and advancing mostly chronologically through time. The narrative allows no room for rest. No real backstory in this novel. No lengthy sections of exposition. Challenges appear and are addressed. A very strict sort of linear design is in play, one that allows the reader to travel through events, comfortably aware that the story shape, at the very least, promises to be contained, all of a piece, one cogent whole.

When I visualize a linear design like the one Herrera employs, in fact, what comes to mind is an enfilade of rooms, something like one of these:

Enfilade (© Kovacs Daniel/Wikimedia Commons)

The reader traverses that enfilade of story events. She might pause on a threshold, but the narrative shape doesn't allow for digressions or explanations or much in the way of secondary or tertiary threads. The reader leaves one room and is immediately in the next. The reader—this reader!—is propelled. And, of course, that's partly Herrera's emotional aim for us. We live Makina's unstoppable, inevitable journey *forward.*

But there's more, of course, to this novel. Imagine for a moment you are the novel's architect, and you have that original border-crossing program in hand. The novel's structure—linear design—addresses the function or story need—that urgent push forward. It's recognizable much like the standard bank or library template might be. But, like Koolhaas, you'd like the building to do more than simply accomplish its function. You note there's a twist in this classic Hero's Journey, one that addresses transmigration and the brutal "skinning" of identity. One that will require a revisioning, not of the familiar frames and scaffolding that comprise the Hero's Journey, but of the way in which the Hero's movement will be perceived and experienced by the reader.

Until the mid-eighteenth century, most buildings were designed as enfilades of rooms—one room leading directly into another, front to back. The door became the big signifier, providing a single point of view from room to room. In *Signs Preceding the End of the World,* Makina signals her overt assumption of this role early in the novel when she's given that bundle to carry over to the other side in exchange for the gangster Mr. Aitch's help. This task is, of course, replete with danger, but Makina doesn't—she can't—hesitate.

> You don't lift other people's petticoats.
> You don't stop to wonder about other people's business.
> You don't decide which messages to deliver and which to let rot.
> You are the door, not the one who walks through it.
> Those were the rules Makina abided by . . .

And so she *is* the Door, opening and ushering the reader through each room in the enfilade of scenes that compose this narrative. Not surprisingly, the upshot of that familiar linear shape is that the novel resonates first *as a fairy tale,* easing the reader into the narrative. But it's not long before subtle moves simultaneously undermine and ratchet up the expectations of a fairy tale. The reader begins to comprehend what Makina's role as "door" will mean, and the distinct language choices—richly incisive and cleverly layered—that Herrera and his excellent translator, Lisa Dillman, utilize become more visibly integral to the story, creating unexpected texture and vistas in each of those enfiladed rooms. Language enters the architectural narrative, shaping story on the micro level of word choice, and twines with that fairy tale resonance in deeply unexpected and visceral ways.

Here is just one small example of many made throughout the novel: Herrera makes use of the Spanish verb *jachar* to mean "to leave," not usual *dejar.* It seems perhaps a minor shift, but the usage signals a deeper intent, one Lisa Dillman explores when she talks about her decisions in translating *jachar* to English. The origin of the word *jachar,* she writes in an afterword, lies in a Mozarabic word that means "exit"; more specifically, it referred to the verses tacked onto the "*end of longer Arabic or Hebrew poems written in the region we know as Spain. Mozarabic being a kind of hybrid that was not, of course, yet Spanish.*" She goes on to note that "*On one level* Signs *is just that—a book about bridging cultures and languages.* Jachar *too is a noun turned verb.*"

In other words, the word has crossed borders, as Herrera well knows.

Understanding Herrera's intent, Dillman takes the two: the noun, meaning "the exit line of the poem" and the verb meaning "to leave" and translates "*jachar*" as "verse." So, when a character leaves a scene, they "verse," or, say, when Makina picks up her bag and goes, she "verses." As *we* move through this enfilade of scenes, *we* verse. It's a usage, Dillman notes, "that's easily understood in context," and while a reader doesn't have the explanation of the translation in hand, the word choice pierces and amplifies the familiar fairy tale structure, that vibrating inner framework of the processional. The combination defamiliarizes a situation to which many have become emotionally immune, creating a story that is not only understood and animated, but urgently and beautifully felt.

Let's consider, for a moment, another architectural example: the Bunny Lane House, designed and built by Adam Kalkin.

The outer frame of the Bunny Lane House is built from what looks like a Butler building, a manufactured steel building that resembles a large shipping container. From the outside, it appears as a beautiful, light-filled airy box—more object than dwelling. Inside, however, Kalkin has done something different. He has placed another full house—a real farmhouse that once stood on a corner of

Bunny Lane Exterior (© Peter Aaron/OTTO)

Bunny Lane Interior (© Peter Aaron/OTTO)

his property—into the center of the new house. So, if you stand in the center of Bunny Lane House, you can turn in one direction and see an older, iconic form of home, or you can switch directions and enter a modern rendition of a house, room upon room in the redefined container.

Now why would he do this? Here's what Kalkin has to say: "The container is a purpose-built object. When you recontextualize it, put it in a residential context, use it for architecture proper, you both destroy the original context and create a new context. This is a form of upcycling, taking modest storage . . . and using it for a higher purpose. You get a beautiful dialogue between the old and the new. And between one set of ideas and another and you get a certain kind of vitality that resonates . . . ."

Note those phrases: a "*dialogue between the old and the new*"; "*a certain kind of vitality that resonates.*" Kalkin is, as he says, revisioning space with space, recontextualizing, using familiar connotations to create a conversation, an exchange then between the elements of the house and, by extension, between the house and the occupants, the house and visitors, the house and the viewer.

Kalkin's approach is not entirely alien to fiction writers. We are familiar, of course, with framed stories, which often seem like a sensible answer to narratives that occupy different time frames or places yet somehow depend upon each other for meaning. Yet one might take the concept of a framed story and interrogate that shape even more according to a story's intent for more meaningful effect.

Take, for example, Olga Tokarczuk's novel *House of Day, House of Night*. The novel is built in titled sections. At times, these sections resemble chapters; at times, interstitial poetic fragments. The sections are linked by their characters' connections to place, the mountain village in the Polish province of Lower Silesia where the unnamed narrator lives for a part of each year and, too, by the narrator's own preoccupations, practical and philosophical. Although individually the sections read holistically and possess their own internal integrity, the novel does not read as a linear narrative. That is, within the disparate sections, the story threads move through their separate time frames, mostly driven by a kind of wondrous causality, but the overall design eschews those demands. Instead, built by the force of the unnamed narrator, the sections accrue and gain meaning through juxtaposition and reflection and thematic unity.

The novel opens as we are taught stories never should: with a dream. Yet this is no mere recounting of a nighttime wander, no fantasy, no gimmick to shoehorn in plot points; the narrator's dream boldly throws out a statement on being, on the dubious separation between waking and dreaming, on the fluidity of time and space and consequently, the ever-present possibilities of transformation, and also signals the supremely ambitious and marvelous intent of this novel. This first paragraph offers its blueprint:

> The first night I had a dream. I dreamed I was pure sight without a body or a name. I was suspended high above a valley at some undefined point from which I could see everything. I could move around my field of vision, yet remain in the same place.
>
> It seemed as if the world below was yielding to me as I looked at it, constantly moving towards me, and then away, so that at first I could see everything, then only tiny details.

One might say the intent of Tokarczuk's novel is to tell the story of a Polish valley, connecting present-time characters and gossip with historical incidence, past tales, and local myths. Why not simply move through time, offering the stories sequentially, perhaps throwing in yet another, *clearer*, narrative line—say, the effect of the Second World War, perhaps dividing the novel's stories into the periods of occupation visited on the valley throughout centuries? The valley began as Polish, then became part of the Prussian Empire, and much later, was given back to Poland as part of a postwar Soviet swap.

Well, perhaps the writer feels the valley's history is not past, but instead continually informs the present she wants to fully discover, and so the story calls for, let's say, a narrative movement that works in a multitude of temporal directions, forward and backward and even simultaneously, continually crossing the border between the real and the dreamlike, the visible and the felt. So how then does one create that necessary multivalenced effect, one that informs the story on every level, causing the reader to see a world that as the novel's opening sequence portends "is constantly moving" all at once or "in tiny details"—in other words, to *live* the world as a reality or a dream?

Layering the stories, using that fabulous device of white space, as if the chapters and fragments are separate dwellings on a broad field and the reader ambles along from one to the other, might provide one design choice. But that sort of structuring would also suggest separation, not continuity or connection.

Fun fact: The hallway or corridor is a relatively recent architectural invention. While the introduction of the corridor was reported as early as 1530, and a single external hallway shows up in the seventeenth-century manor houses of extremely well-to-do English families (primarily to keep the servants out of sight), hallways were not common in houses or public buildings until the mid-eighteenth century. Hallways brought about and are still used to "describe" and define social interaction. They offer possible routes through a building.

Most importantly, hallways provide resting spots and pathways between private and public spaces. I love that distinction between public and private spaces because it seems so damn relevant to stories where the visibility of and the balance and communication between action and meaning, between event and emotion, is crucial.

Bell Labs Hallway (© Elliott Erwitt/Magnum Photos)

To my mind, the narrator and narrative voice in *House of Day, House of Night* act as a kind of metaphorical hallway. Occasionally, the story resides in that hallway, in the narrator's own life and preoccupations. More frequently, the narration moves away that place into one individual story/time frame before returning to the narrator's present time, then into yet another time period or even from one mythic reality to another. Only the setting remains a constant, and of course, that too is a variable, given the valley's own history of different national guises.

If the unnamed narrator and her stories act as a hallway, the door into many of the disparate chapters is the narrator's neighbor, a wigmaker named Marta. Marta either knows and relays these stories or introduces the narrator to an opening into many of the tales. And within the hallway itself, valley life, Marta's and the narrator's, streams forward.

What is in these rooms? These sections, chapters, fragments? Stories of the valley's real and supposed inhabitants for one thing. Marek Marek, the suicide, consumed with loneliness and longing and an insatiable thirst for the alcohol that obliterates both, believes a large bird has taken up residence within him. A bank teller, Krysia, travels to a distant town to find the lover who whispered his name in her ear in a dream. Ergo Sum, convinced he is a werewolf, isolates himself. An ongoing, vital thread seems to come from a pamphlet relating the tale of a saintly nun, beautiful and virtuous, who resists her father's determined plans to marry her off and eventually is graced with the face of Christ, beard and all, horrifying her prospective suitor and incurring her father's deadly wrath. Fantastic enough, but wrapped around that tale is another: the breathtaking transformation of a boy into a monk into a nun, himself, as he writes (or, indeed, fabricates) the fantastical biography of the miraculous nun: a room of martyred triumph within a room of longing. Good lord, you *feel* this, and feel too the desired resonance with shared, unspoken dreams.

The reader—this reader!—is captivated by the wholeness and intrigue within each section and pulled through the novel by a suspense built less through action or event than by exacting ellipsis, the propulsion of curiosity, necessary context, the twanging line between what's suggested and what's visible, the many turns and shifts of fate as more stories, different inhabitants and histories appear in or near the same physical place now occupied by the narrator and *also* by the novelistic density of observation and analysis *and* the emotional resonance between the sections. Dream and myth sit right beside story and everyday anecdote.

Form certainly isn't the sole driver toward animation in *House of Day, House of Night*, but in concert with Tokarczuk's fierce intelligence and imagination, the effect of those enclosed sections, accessible via the hallway of the narrator's own exploration, is nearly three-dimensional. The reader feels time layered upon time upon time within this single valley. A little bit of Kalkin's magic as well.

Anyone can tell an anecdote, lining up events and characters like walls and furniture and load-bearing walls, but for an anecdote or situation to become a story, the tale must be willfully inhabited, not simply constructed. "Go to where the story's 'hot,'" we tell each other when revision seems stalled. "Go find the moments that are *alive* and build from them." As James Woods wrote in the *New Yorker*, commending Hillary Mantel's work: "She knows that what gives fiction its vitality is not the accurate detail *but the animate one*. . . ." Woods goes on to elevate Mantel over other writers of historical fiction, who, he writes: ". . . are intelligent, but they are not novelistically intelligent. They copy the motions but rarely *inhabit the movement of vitality*" (my emphasis). What is that moment of vitality? Well, it seems to me that, as with architectural animation, fictional animation relies on an emotional response.

I was excited (emotion!) when I first saw Kalkin's Bunny Lane House because it upended my notion of House yet also satisfied my notion of a house. It vivified and enlarged a possible conception of Home with that dialogue between the old and the new, which reads to me also as a dialogue between the thematic (house), the energetic (alternating feelings of home), and the structural (varying values of enclosure). It was also deeply, wonderfully *strange*. The house was alive in a way that was altogether new and also completely recognizable. Similarly, Tokarczuk's novel transformed my ideas of time and place and self.

Ultimately, a story's needs, its intent, offer the writer a kind of introductory program, and within that program lies the suggestion of a more necessary narrative design, one that will press beyond the page, and what's more, direct and include the reader in a way that animates both structure and story and allows the reader to simultaneously inhabit and be inhabited. A successful story does not emerge solely from the logical unfolding of words or events on a page. Such a story is, in essence, energy confined in space—in our case, an imagined world—and so depends not just upon the idea of narrative, some overarching theme, but the context and reasoning for that narrative and the emotional responses the writer hopes to elicit from the reader.

The Character of Our Character

Reality, Actuality, and Technique in Fiction and Nonfiction

RANDALL KENAN

How do you create a human being in ink and paper? On its face that is a ridiculous question. You can't. And yet, we try. And some of us believe it can be done. We say we have seen it done.

So much of what I'm about to say you already know. It's intuitive. And yet, I might ask, why do we fail? So often. You fail. I fail. We all fail, from time to time, despite the better angels of our nature. I think of Samuel Beckett's famous line: "Fail, fail again, fail better." I read many stories and novels every year, and often they fail. They—we all—tend to fail when it comes to creating living and breathing characters who are more than an idea, more than an archetype or a type. More than a placeholder for a character yet-to-come.

But more, I want to muddy the water, and get at the shared tactics and strategies that writers of fiction and nonfiction must use to achieve a similar goal—to create a person on the page with dark squiggles on white paper. In many ways this is a perverse exercise; this is something only a writer, a dreamer, a head case can become obsessed with. In the non-writing world—what my brother would call "the real world"—it is insane to suggest a real person has any parity with a made-up one. But we word-pushers know differently. We know what those unsuspecting word and image consumers don't. We know that in their minds Madame Bovary, Captain Ahab, Little Orphan Annie, and Atticus Finch and Sherlock Holmes and John Henry and Anna Karenina and Dracula are as real as Reince Priebus and Mother Teresa and Lindsay Lohan and Hillary Clinton and Johnny Depp and Anna Nichole Smith and Dean Smith and Jared Kushner—assuming Jared Kushner is an actual person. And let's not yet touch upon the subject of all those historical figures—George Washington, Hannibal of Carthage, Henry VIII, Elizabeth I, Queen Hatshepsut, Julius Caesar, Benjamin Franklin, Benjamin Banneker, Caligula, Jesus—all of whom have been reinvented in works of fiction, and all of whom our non-scribbling brethern and sistern consider they've come to know as flesh and blood, but who they have come to feel close to via the pens of David McCullum or Robert Graves or Doris Kearns Goodwin or Joe Ellis or Norman Mailer or the camera of Ken Burns et al.

Why do so many writers—of both fiction and nonfiction—fail to capture people on the page? A major culprit, I believe, is the seeming omnipotence and omnipresence of the image, both moving and still, in our current postmodern culture. No sentient being alive today can escape them. People are even making videos for cats, these days. As much as I love pictures and movies, they ultimately spoil us writer folk. "A picture paints a thousand words." When I work with student writers, often it feels as if they are writing screenplays, as if they assume the reader is fully capable of filling in the blanks, painting the picture him or herself; the sense that our readers have neither the time nor the patience to read description or background or mood—all things that Quentin Tarantino or Steven Spielberg can convey, well-done or poorly, in a mere frame or two of a movie. But this presumption on the part of the writer is an abdication. The reader is putting himself in our hands, asking us to fill in the blanks, to tell us a story in full, not to give us the basic skeleton. We are storytellers, not story-outliners.

Again, I'm not really telling you anything you don't already know. But I ask again: How is a character created?—What are the elements that knit together to live in the mind?

Over the years I have striven to break these elements down into bite-sized pieces:

Building Character (Physicality. We all have bodies.)

For many decades in the twentieth century, there was an idea in psychology that a person's personality was seated in their physical body type:

Ectomorph = tall and skinny
Endomorph = soft and round, tending toward fat
Mesomorph = athletic and muscular

In Anthony Storr's 1989 essay "Churchill's Black Dog," found in *Churchill's Black Dog, Kafka's Mice, and Other Phenomena of the Human Mind,* the psychologist makes a startling and convincing case that Churchill became a great leader by working so hard against his body type. Churchill was an endomorph pretending to be a mesomorph.

The psychological community has long since moved away from this type of thinking regarding the impact of physiology upon psychology; however, I defy you to read Dr. Storr's essay and divorce his notion from your way of thinking about Winston Churchill.

But even more, when thinking of a character's physicality, there are other matters to consider like fitness and health, eyesight, voice (Consider President Lincoln delivering the Gettysburg address in a high-pitched screech of a voice), hair, handicaps. . . .

History (Where do we come from, and who are our people?)

(Personally, I hate the term "backstory"—not just because it is essentially a film term, but because it seems to reduce the core of being to a trick, filler, a necessary evil—"Oh, we need to give this character a backstory." As if the fact that Abraham Lincoln was born in a log cabin is somehow simply a colorful detail, and not integral to understanding who he is, where he came from, and how it has influence on how he sees the world.)

Important elements of a character's history: place of birth and growing up; parents and family; friends (our choices in friends tell us oodles about ourselves); religious background; education; occupation; significant incidents, failures, successes, major disappointments. . . .

Personality (What is it?)

John Gardner in *The Art of Fiction* probably said it best when he said there is something *strange* about everyone. The writer's job is to find that something and point it out to the reader.

Though it is hard to define, we recognize personality more by its absence than by breaking down its constituent parts. Here are but a few elements that go into making a person's personality—along with the aforementioned elements of character:

Intelligence; likes and dislikes; hobbies and interests; dreams; degree of self-awareness/view of self; religious beliefs; political beliefs; cultural and social values; zodiac traits; taste and care in personal clothing; temper and ways of relating to other people; introverted/extroverted; sybaritic?—Loves relaxation, comfort, and food? Or ascetic—self-denying, self-disciplined? Is this character assertive and active? Is this character private and restrained and reflective? What is strange about this person? (For example: hypochondria, compulsions, obsessions, fears); Identify inconsistences in personality; that is, What a character wants, versus ways in which that character acts and behaves that are at odds with those goals. (For example: A person who wants to lose weight who keeps raiding the refrigerator at midnight; an otherwise devout minister who can't seem to give up seeing the wife of a parishioner); What is the most important thing in the world for your character? And so forth.

By this point most of my students are eyeing me skeptically. All this, frankly, sounds like a lot of work. Writing should not be work, they admit to me. Writing should be fun.

This thinking is the sort of character work a writer must do. Prior to writing, or after drafting. A writer does not trust short cuts, abbreviations, substitute brand names and hope by saying Gucci or Eddie Bauer or Lexus that the reader "gets it." Or rely on winging it. In a letter to his daughter, Scottie, F. Scott Fitzgerald wrote, "You should learn as much about your character as possible, even though you will probably only use one-quarter of what you learn, but the other three-quarters matter greatly."

These are the nuts and bolts of it. How it is done. The fundamentals of craft. The scary truth about fiction and nonfiction is that when it comes to writing—the difference is that there is no difference. Anyone who believes there is a difference in how we approach the actual craft of writing fiction and the craft of writing nonfiction is suffering under a cloud of illusion. And I have discovered of late that many people suffer from this misconception—but more on that later. Consider the way most folk think of the New Journalism.

There are several prevailing myths surrounding the New Journalism: One is that it was "New," and another is that journalism proper is meant to be devoid of any literary technique to be legitimate. The heyday of the New Journalism was the 1960s and gave us Tom Wolfe, Norman Mailer, Truman Capote, Joan Didion,

James Baldwin, Hunter S. Thompson, Willie Morris. They jazzed up their prose and structure with all kinds of literary technique most readers assumed was the province of novelists and short-story writers. They were what's happening. They were brand new: they were psychedelic, up-to-date, dangerous, with it. Hotter than Coca-Cola, cooler than the Volkswagen Beetle.

But those writers knew they were not really doing anything new: They were very well-educated children. Read Hunter S. Thompson's letters to Charles Kuralt and others. You will not find a more deliberate and hardworking writer. He knew how rooted his work was in the hijinks of Laurence Sterne and *Tristram Shandy*, more than James Joyce and *Ulysses* and *Finnegan's Wake*. In fact, the modernists get blamed for a great deal of the New Journalists' techniques and tactics. I would suggest the roots go much, much deeper. For Tom Wolfe, I would have us look to Don Miguel Cervantes and his Don Quixote. For Joan Didion and James Baldwin, I would point to the father of the essay, that irreverent Lord of Montaigne. For Norman Mailer and Truman Capote's outrageous mythologizing, look no further than Dr. François Rabelais and his outsized perversity and distortion and humor and style. This deliberate confusion of fact and fiction, the use of "fictional" methodology to write about factual matters, goes back to the beginning of Western literature as well. It is our nineteenth- and twentieth-century need for classification, nomenclature, and factual bias that truly created the confusion. Joseph Mitchell's genius, back during the Great Depression, is that he was applying those mythmaking skills once only reserved for kings and queens and prime ministers and generals for the common man and woman. He was democratizing mythmaking, if you will; but as a country boy, he already knew the power of story and myth.

Here is my true agenda: The confusion of the real with the actual. Those characters in both fiction and nonfiction who are based on actual flesh and blood people who become independent entities in their own right. Characters who outgrow any measurable actuality, and achieve a reality all their own. I think it pays for writers to examine that peculiar *transmogrification*. I think it contains an energy we all hope to tap into.

I am particularly interested in and fascinated by those characters with roots in historically or journalistically "real" people, or as my philosophical friends would call them, "actual" people, who attain another level of reality as either characters on the page, or as fictionalized versions of themselves that outgrow themselves.

There is a particular type of voodoo going on here that I feel the serious writer takes for granted at her or his own peril. What we are talking about on a fundamental level is mythmaking. And I fear too many of us contemporary writers feel that thinking about our characters—whatever their origins or inspirations—as mythological to be grandiose and outside our purview. I would ask you to rethink that self-limiting point of view.

Please consider Joseph Mitchell and Robert Penn Warren.

Joseph Mitchell was one of our most influential writers of nonfiction. His long tenure at the *New Yorker* created a fresh idea of what the profile could be. His topic was more often than not the everyday men and women: police officers, fishermen, ticket takers, circus performers, homeless people. Or as he once wrote: "the cranks and the misfits and the one-lungers and the has-beens and the would-bes and the never-wills and the God-knows-what." He wrote about actual people with the flair, the detail, the color and depth one would have expected from fiction.

Robert Penn Warren, Pulitzer Prize–winning novelist and poet, on the other hand, was attracted to history and real-life figures, and yet he chose to write about them more straightforwardly as fictional characters. *All the King's Men*'s Willie Starke is not Huey Long.

Despite the longtime admonition to "Show, not tell," exposition can be a powerful tool, and for some reason we are more accepting of exposition in nonfiction than we are in fiction. But fiction writers can learn a great deal from nonfiction writers' use of exposition—something nonfiction writers first learned from fiction writers, in truth.

Consider Mitchell's introduction to his best-known work, *Joe Gould's Secret:*

> Joe Gould was an odd and penniless and unemployable little man who came to the city in 1916 and ducked and dodged and held on as hard as he could for over thirty-five years. He was a member of one of the oldest families in New England ("The Goulds were the Goulds," he used to say, "when the Cabots and the Lowells were clamdiggers"), he was born and brought up in a town near Boston in which his father was a leading citizen, and he went to Harvard, as did his father and grandfather before him, but he claimed that until he arrived in New York City he had always felt out of place. "In my home town," he once wrote, "I never felt at home. I stuck out. Even in my own home, I never felt at home. In New York City, especially in Greenwich Village, down among the cranks and the

> misfits and the one-lungers and the has-beens and the might've beens and the would-bes and the never-wills and the God-knows-whats, I have always felt at home."
>
> Gould looked like a bum and lived like a bum. He wore castoff clothes, and he slept in flophouses or in the cheapest rooms in cheap hotels. Sometimes he slept in doorways.

Later: a description of the first time he saw Joe Gould:

> He was around five feet four or five, and quite thin; he could hardly have weighed more than ninety pounds. He was bareheaded, and he carried his head cocked on one side, like an English sparrow. His hair was long, and he had a bushy beard. There were streaks of dirt on his forehead, obviously from rubbing it with dirty fingers. He was wearing an overcoat that was several sizes too large for him; it reached almost to the floor. He held his hands clasped together for warmth—it was a bitter-cold day—and the sleeves of the overcoat came down over them, forming a sort of muff. Despite his beard, the man, in the oversized overcoat, bareheaded and dirty-faced, had something childlike and lost about him: a child who had been up in the attic with other children trying on grownups' clothes and had become tired of the game and wandered off. He stood still for a few moments, getting his bearing, and then he came over to Panagakos [the diner owner] and said, "Can I have something to eat now, Harry? I can't wait until tonight."

Note how Mitchell punctuates this long introduction and description with dialogue. Like the better writers of fiction, Mitchell understands that dialogue is first about characterization. And that hearing Joe Gould is of paramount importance, his voice, her personality.

Likewise, Warren understands the importance of voice in creating Willie Stark. Like Mitchell, the novelist is not afraid to tell and to describe. We see all the people around him—the driver, his son; we see the people's reaction when he comes to a small Louisiana town: "It's Willie!"

> The Boss kept walking straight ahead, his head bowed a little, the way a man bows his head when he is out walking by himself and has something

> on his mind. His hair fell down over his forehead, for he was carrying his hat in his hand. I knew his hair was down over his forehead, for I saw him give his head a quick jerk once or twice, the way he always did when he was walking alone and it fell down toward his eyes, the kind of motion a horse gives just after the bit is in and he's full of beans.
>
> He walked straight across the street and across the patch of grass roots and up the steps of the courthouse. Nobody else followed him up the steps. At the top he turned around, slow, to face the crowd. He simply looked at them, blinking his big eyes a little, just as though he had just stepped out of the open doors and the dark hall of the courthouse behind him and was blinking to get his eyes adjusted to the light. He stood up there blinking, the hair down on his forehead, and the dark sweat patch showing under each arm of his Palm Beach coat. Then he gave his head a twitch, and his eyes bulged wide suddenly, even if the light was hitting him full in the face, and you could see the glitter in them.
>
> *It's coming,* I thought.

Willie Stark v. Huey Long. T. Harry Williams's masterful 1969 biography gives us the man and all the "facts." That biography broke a lot of ground in the study of the American South and its history. The real Huey Long was much more like something out of Latin American magical realism. He is both more improbable and mysterious than Warren's much more reasonable rendering. Warren's challenge then was to make the improbable seem probable, perhaps even inevitable.

If we had world enough and time, I could talk at length about how Mitchell and Warren use so many of the same devices and techniques, how very like Joseph Mitchell the novel's narrator, Jack Burden, is; how the tone of these narrators affects the reader's view of the character; how dialogue—the chief weapon of characterization—is deployed over and over again, slyly and with force; how action—think of Stark's theater of stump speaking, or the minutiae of Gould asking for a cup of tomato soup—are both deliberate, chosen and illuminating of character.

Moreover, both Mitchell and Warren are first and last *storytellers.* They never forget the main thrust of their story (what does your character want?—in the case of Joe Gould it is to obscure the fact that his great idea, "The Oral History," was never completed, and in the case of Willie Stark he simply wishes to become president of the United States); Mitchell and Warren use how other characters view their main subject; they flirt and subvert stereotype, that mental baggage we all bring along with us; they exploit the unpredictable; and ultimately they give us that Aristotelian moment of discovery—learning, changing (and they are also aware of the fact that some people DO NOT CHANGE!). They use place ruthlessly and with great art—in the case of Mitchell it is New York, always a character in his writing; and in the case of Warren it is the entire state of Louisiana, a love letter to a landscape.

This, of course, you realize, is witchcraft. And witchcraft can be black or white.

"I Am Not the Potter, or the Potter's Wheel"

Fiction v. Nonfiction. Both fiction and nonfiction are made things. Writers, above all, must always be mindful of this bedrock truth.

Consider three powerful stories from our cultural history: *Robinson Crusoe, Moby-Dick*/"The Essex," *Mutiny on the Bounty.*

In the case of Alexander Selkirk, he did exist. He was the man, he was there, he suffered. He was a Scotsman who was castaway on a deserted island in the Pacific in 1703 and who was finally rescued in 1709. Years later several accounts, including accounts written by Selkirk, were published. But we remember Daniel Defoe's 1719 novel, *The Life and Surprising Adventures of Robinson Crusoe,* best. In fact, many people believe he was an actual fellow. Why?

Herman Melville spent many years at sea as a whaler, so it made sense that he would undertake to transmute the 1821 *Narrative of the Most Extraordinary and Distressing Shipwreck of the Whale-Ship Essex* into his 1851 masterwork, *Moby-Dick; or The Whale.* Owen Chase was the first mate and one of eight survivors, and his book was out of print at the time and essentially forgotten. But why do we remember Moby-Dick and Ahab and Ishmael, and not—until recently, with the publication of a wonderful new work of nonfiction—remember the *Essex?*

And lastly *Mutiny on the Bounty.* The books, the movies—three so far and counting. As a boy, when I first saw the Charles Laughton version, I had no idea there actually was a Captain Bligh and a Fletcher Christian, and that there was actually a ship called Bounty, and that Captain Bly actually did live through one of the most amazing stories of survival at sea—forty-seven days—to live and write about it, and to be written about. It is through fiction that we remember his tale most vividly.

There is much anxiety today, primarily from writers and lovers of fiction, over the newfound popularity of nonfiction. People worry that, by and by, the writers of nonfiction will supplant the centuries-old, hallowed ground of novels and stories. I submit to you that storytelling is older than Samuel Richardson and Lady Murasaki's *Tale of Genji;* I submit to you that the atoms of storytelling are essentially the same, and that ultimately, if well done, the story itself, even greater than the original flesh and blood, will live on—if it's told right; if it holds some nugget of truth.

"Where Does the Truth Lie?"—Eudora Welty

The Truth. Reality. Actuality. I am reminded of Mark Twain's advice: "Never let the truth stand in the way of a good story."

I think it is important in an era in which our leaders launch such weighty accusations as "fake news" about so carelessly, that it is only responsible to pick apart this notion of reality versus the truth. Philosophers make a distinction between reality and actuality. Reality is what we can measure. That which can be supported by evidence. Actuality is the more intangible truth.

I point to the masterful biography of George Bernard Shaw by Michael Holroyd. Four volumes long. Holroyd is a supreme scholar, and not a word in that volume goes unsupported. And yet there is the man, Bernard Shaw, and all we do not and cannot know about him. There is the real George Bernard Shaw and the actual George Bernard Shaw. Neither one is fake.

Writing around "real" people is always fraught with ethical problems. Especially when a writer dares to take an actual flesh-and-blood person into the realm of fiction—I point to the aforementioned *All the King's Men*, or we could look at countless novels, such as Anthony Burgess's novel of Shakespeare, *Nothing Like the Sun.*

License Taken, the Ethics of "Stretching the Truth"

I quickly add here that I am not advocating lying. Rather, I am pointing out that good storytelling, proper mythmaking, employs techniques and methods that go beyond mere reportage. That the quality and care not only to attention to creation of character, but to care and feeding of story, go beyond "just the facts." That the very warp and woof of the narrative go into the formation of the mythology. Wise storytellers are always aware of this. Call it manipulation if you will. Call if fabrication. To fabricate means to make, not to lie.

Alchemy of fiction: Case in point: Toni Morrison's novel, *Beloved*, and the sad but true story of Margaret Garner—an example of the ultimate triumph of fiction, not over reality, but in its ability to live long, longer than our memoirs, and longer than reality. Garner's tragic story had been told, written about. And yet as a young editor at Random House, Morrison happened to read what was then essentially the detritus of journalism—what has been called the first draft of history—and that story stuck in Toni Morrison's mind, for over a decade, before she digested it and. . . .

I leave you with this paradox to ponder: Character is more than the sum of the parts; And yet you get no character without knowing all the various and sundry parts. You can't leap over those constituent ingredients, and yet the making of a woman or a man on the page transcends that catalog. This is the rub.

In one of his lectures at Cornell, Vladimir Nabokov sums up a writer's job as to Educate, to Entertain, and to Enchant.

The danger today of nonfiction supplanting fiction—anxiety of the reification of the real over the imagination. I do not share that anxiety, though I recognize a lot of nonfiction writers are out-writing a lot of fiction writers these days. I think what happened is that, in the wake of the aforementioned New Journalism crest in the 1960s, writers like John McPhee discovered how to mythologize places like the Pine Barrens, learned from Joseph Mitchell how to make the truth rise up to mythic proportions, how to make fishermen and truck drivers and grocers loom in the imagination the way warriors and Holy Grail chasers once did.

I think some fiction writers abdicated their birthright, and got lost in the weeds of literalism and quotidian fact and burdensome logic and lost sight of those things about the human condition that most excite our imagination: mystery, the intangible, the mess of it all, the human spirit.

But that's just a theory. What do I know?

I just believe in the imagination.

"Is There a Plot in This Poem?"

CHARLES MARTIN

I want to begin with a few acknowledgments: I have borrowed a good part of my title from Stanley Fish. I have enclosed my partly borrowed title in quotation marks in the manner of Leslie Fiedler, whose essay "Come Back to the Raft Ag'in, Huck Honey" got many people to think of the relationship between Jim and Huck in a way that they had probably not done before. And so, for a moment perhaps, you may believe that "Is There a Plot in This Poem?" is a real question, one that may have been asked by an actual student. It is not, but I like to think that it could have been, since my thinking about the relationship between these two words, "plot" and "poem," began when I was working with a pair of students whom I was teaching in a low-residency MFA program. Every month, they would send me poems, and I would comment on the poems and send them back to the students. I found myself baffled by the work of one of these students, Student A, unable to figure out her intentions for her work, and unable to offer her the help she was eager to receive. At the same time, I had no trouble with the work of Student B; whenever one of her poems went off the rails, I could help her get it back on again. I was able to offer her advice that she told me was useful to her. I began, naturally, to wonder what the difference was between my responses to these two students, and eventually the word "plot" sprang into my mind: I seemed to be able to understand the "plots" of Student B's poems, but not those of Student A.

When I say "plot" here, I have to admit that I wasn't really sure what I meant by the term. I couldn't summon to mind any discussion of the word in relation to the kind of poetry that my students were writing. Do lyrical (for want of a better word) poems even have plots? As usual when I am stuck like this, I went to the OED for help. Once I had whistled my way past the graveyard, the OED offered this by way of definition for "plot": "The plan or scheme of a literary work; the interrelationship of the main events of a play, novel, film, etc." The absence of a specific reference to plot as a feature of lyrical poems reinforced what I already knew: plot was not generally taken into account in any discussion of the kind of poetry most commonly written today.

The one discussion of plot in poetry that I was aware of was Aristotle's in his *Poetics*, but of course Aristotle was discussing dramatic and epic poetry, rather than the lyrical poetry that my students were writing. Nevertheless, Aristotle offered a beginning. You will recall that Aristotle lists six essential components of tragedy: plot, character, diction, thought, melody, and spectacle. Aristotle asserts that plot, the structure of the events of the play, is the most important of these elements, "the life and soul, so to speak," of tragic drama. The least important elements of the six are melody and spectacle, the musical and visual aspects of tragic drama. He is especially dismissive of spectacle, which, "though an attraction, is the least artistic of the parts, and has the least to do with the art of poetry." Aristotle moves tragedy even farther from the stage by asserting that "the tragic effect is quite possible without a public performance and actors." But how could the tragic effect be conveyed to an audience without performance? Why, in the same way that Harold Bloom receives his Shakespeare: by solitary reading.

As an undergraduate reading Aristotle's *Poetics*, I attributed his denigration of spectacle and his lack of enthusiasm for dramatic performance to a philosophical preference for theory over practice. It never occurred to me that one of the reasons why Aristotle privileges plot and nonperformance so highly was that they were relative novelties in his time. For Aristotle's discussion of these subjects comes after the first great transformation of consciousness in the West, the change that occurred with the passage from the spoken to the written word, from a world of orality to a world of literacy. The poems of Homer, we now know, were composed orally for spoken performances. As such, they were inevitably episodic rather than tightly plotted. As Walter J. Ong points out in his *Orality and Literacy;*

> Persons from today's literate and typographic cultures are likely to think of consciously contrived narrative as typically designed in a

> climactic linear plot often diagrammed as the well-known "Freytag's Pyramid." . . . an ascending action builds tension, rising to a climactic point, which consists often of a recognition or other incident bringing about a *peripeteia*, or reversal of action, and which is followed by a denouement. . . . This is the kind of plot Aristotle finds in the drama (*Poetics* 1451b–1452b)—a significant locale for such plot, since Greek drama, though orally performed, was composed as a written text and in the west was the first verbal genre, and for centuries was the only verbal genre, to be controlled completely by writing.

Ong goes on to contrast dramatic plot with plotting in the epic: "In his *Ars Poetica*, Horace writes that the epic poet 'hastens into the action and precipitates the hearer into the middle of things.'" Hastening into the middle of things leaves little room for the ground floor of exposition that leads to the ascent in Freytag's Pyramid. The "conscious contrivance" of plot is not possible for the orally composed epic poem.

However, once poets began composing their epic poems to be read, consciousness changed, and new organizational patterns—plots, we might call them—appeared to receive new thoughts and emotions. In an aphorism that should be as well known as McLuhan's "The medium is the message," Ong says, "Writing is a consciousness raising activity." Coming out of the oral tradition, Homer's heroes, especially in the *Iliad*, are famously unreflective. In Book XVI of that poem, Achilles's soulmate Patroklos borrows the great hero's armor and sallies forth to frighten the Trojan enemy by pretending to be Achilles. When he learns that Patroklos has been slain and his own armor has been captured by the enemy, Achilles has what appears to be a nervous breakdown. He collapses and rushes off to the seaside in tears, where he meets his mother, the goddess Thetis, who promises him a new suit of armor fashioned by the divine armorer Hephaestus and orders him to wait there for her return. Achilles does not hypothesize any other solutions to his problem. It does not occur to him, for example, that he could borrow another's gear as Patroklos borrowed his, suit himself up, and plunge into the fray, where he might have a very good chance of changing the situation for the better. That lack of interiority led the psychologist Julian Jaynes to posit a time in human development when our brains were bicameral, divided between a plodding diurnal left side, which didn't really require much to keep it going, and a superconscious right brain, which we experienced as a divine voice when the situation became dangerous and required correction. So Achilles, in a funk after the death of Patroklos, experiences his divine mother's voice, giving him his orders. Vigorously wielding Occam's razor, Ong sees this heroic unreflectiveness as nothing other than the way in which preliterate people routinely experienced their world.

When Odysseus descends to the underworld in Book XI of the *Odyssey,* he meets the prophet Teiresias and his own mother, who are both able to tell him what will happen to him on the rest of his way home. He also meets some of his colleagues who did not survive the Trojan War, and they can describe for him the circumstances surrounding their own deaths. But of the dead from generations earlier than those he has known, or of the living to follow his own generation, Odysseus learns nothing: if, as one of Robert Frost's characters opined, "the dead are holding something back," we do not learn what that something is in the *Odyssey.*

With literacy, however, comes an increasing interiority in which the representation of time expands greatly. In the *Aeneid,* an epic written in the first century BC by the Roman poet Virgil, the hero Aeneas, before he can found the city of Rome, must descend to the underworld even as Odysseus did. There he meets his father, Anchises, who proceeds to give him a grand tour that ranges from the mythical past to the historical present, explaining to him not only the economy of reincarnation, but displaying for him the entire history of Rome, the city that Aeneas has not yet founded, from the reign of the hero's posthumous son Silvius to the untimely death of Marcellus, the nephew of Augustus, the ruler of Rome in Virgil's time. Beyond that, of course, neither Virgil nor his characters can see.

Writing raises consciousness, and with literacy not only time but space opens up. Interior spaces now appear behind the eyes of characters in written epics, and those spaces are filled with emotional depths. Characters are able to feel passion for other characters, to tell their own stories, and to reflect on alternative possibilities for the situations in which they find themselves. In Virgil's *Aeneid* and in Ovid's *Metamorphoses,* it is principally female characters who display these traits: Virgil wants his hero Aeneas to be, like the characters of Homer's epics, not overly burdened with subjectivity, and Ovid probably wanted to poke a little subversive fun at the unreflective heroes of an earlier day.

Though these epics are the product of writing, there is only one episode in either of them where we see a character take pen in hand. This occurs in Book IX of his *Metamorphoses*, where Ovid tells the story of Byblis and Caunus, daughter and son of the eponymous founder of the city of Miletus. Byblis (whose name sounds like the Greek word for book, *biblios*, but is etymologically unrelated to it) falls passionately in love with her brother. Ovid leads her through carefully detailed stages of erotic entanglement, from unacknowledged desire through conscious resistance to unconscious acceptance:

> Often, however, when relaxed in sleep,
> an image of her passion came to her,
> an image of her lying with her brother,
> that made her, even sleeping, blush with shame.

When Byblis awakens from her erotic dream, she argues with herself and with the fates that have made impossible the satisfaction of her incestuous passion. She first thinks of suppressing her feelings and finally decides to confess them in a love letter to her brother Caunus, written in her boudoir:

> Still in her bed,
> she lifts herself up and leans on her left elbow:
> Now let him see, she says, my decadence!
> What slope am I beginning to descend?
> What fire is conceived within my heart?
> Her shaking hands set down the practiced words:
> She grips the iron stylus in her right
> and holds the blank wax tablet in her left.
> She starts and stops. Sets down—and then condemns.
> Adds and deletes. Doubts; finds fault wit; approves.
> She throws the tablet down, then picks it up!
> She cannot say what she is striving for,
> and every tack she takes displeases her,
> who sometimes seems ashamed and sometimes bold.

Even at the beginning of literate self-expression, we see the kind of behaviors common to writers of any time. After more erasures, inscriptions, and corrections, Byblis finishes her letter and immediately sends it off to her brother, who furiously spurns her advances. Byblis now considers a revision:

> So swiftly set down upon the page
> what should have been concealed! I should have tried
> to understand his feelings for me first,
> with speech that hinted but did not commit. . . .

Her attempt at revising her passion fails: Caunus, still horrified, flees Miletus to found another city; maddened, Byblis pursues him and ends up transformed into a flowing spring.

In making a connection between literacy and the expression of incestuous desire of one sibling for another, and in illustrating the catastrophic effects of that expression, Ovid may have had quite another point in mind. Nonetheless, in illustrating the way in which literacy aids, for better or worse, the expansion of subjectivity, he shows us the single most important difference between orality and literacy: words spoken can be blown away by the wind, misheard, misunderstood: "Did he say 'Blessed are the pacemakers, for theirs is the Kingdom of Devon?'" Words inscribed on a receptive ground however have a permanence quite unlike that of speech, as Byblis learns to her sorrow. It is fitting then, that she have the last word on this issue:

> Nothing I do now will regain his trust,
> since he has read the letters that I traced
> desire revealed may never be erased.

Whatever plot an epic has is revealed in the time of its oral performance by the voice of the poet or the reciter; in drama the plot is similarly revealed by the actors speaking on the stage. But with literacy the plots of epic and drama are also revealed to the eye of the reader, and are less dependent on time: the reader can stop, go back in the text, or jump forward to see where a foreshadowed event comes to pass. The new interiority that came with literacy needed new patterns in which it could be displayed. One of these patterns may go back to the oral culture; on the other hand, it is possible that it did not appear in poetry until poems were written down, as it is predominantly a visual way of organizing either individual lines or blocks of text. It is called "chiasmus," and Greek and Latin poets were very fond of it. Somewhere before 55 BC the Roman poet Catullus wrote an epyllion, a short epic of 409 lines, arranged in eight mythological, thematically organized tableaus. These tableaus form a chiasmus, a pattern that may be represented like this:

A B C D (E) D C B A

In the first A section, Catullus evokes the heroic age when gods and mortals mingled on earth freely and happily. It was then, he says, that the hero Peleus first burned with desire for the goddess Thetis, and Zeus consented to their marriage.

The first B section describes the preparations for the marriage feast in Thessaly, culminating in a description of "a couch fit for the goddess" in the center of the hero's palace, "one made of polished Indian ivory draped with a purple / coverlet steeped in the crimson dye of the sea conch."

The first C section is an ekphrastic description of the scene on the coverlet, one in somewhat questionable taste for a wedding: we see Ariadne, abandoned by the hero Theseus on the island of Dia, after she has helped him slay the Minotaur and run away with him, expecting fidelity and marriage. Catullus explains the situation that brought her to this dire condition.

In the first D section, Ariadne delivers a soliloquy complaining of her abandonment, at the end of which she summons the vengeance of the Furies, begging that "just as Theseus carelessly left me to die here, / may that same carelessness ruin him and his dearest."

The E section, the shortest of the whole poem, consists of five lines; in the third of them "the ruler of heaven assented, majestically nodding," and thus sets in motion the actions of the second half of the poem. (While the first five sections vary in length, as do the last four, the third line of the fifth section is the exact center of the poem.)

In the second D section, the carelessness of Theseus results in the death of his father, and the hero's subsequent lamentation is parallel to that of Ariadne.

In the second C section, we return to Ariadne and see Iacchus searching for her: true love is on the way.

In the second B section we return to the culmination of the wedding feast of Peleus and Thetis.

The second A section provides us with a conclusion in which Catullus expresses his regret over the separation of gods and mortals; owing to the corruption of the latter, the heavenly gods no longer come down to mingle with them on earth.

The plot of Catullus' poem would surely have struck Aristotle as episodic, though certainly it can assume the shape of Freytag's Pyramid, with the gods' assent to Ariadne's prayer poised at its peak. Catullus was not the only writer to employ chiasmus in this fashion, nor was it only used in poetry. Somewhere around the year 85 AD, the figure we know as the evangelist Matthew composed the gospel bearing that name. Matthew's gospel is not written as a chronological narrative; rather, its plot forms a chiasmus. Catullus wrote in Latin verse, Matthew in Greek prose. What they had in common was that their texts were written, were meant to be performed by a reader or by a speaker. The plot of Greek drama reveals itself either to the ear or to the eye, by the actor on stage or the reader in his chair, but the plot created by chiasmus reveals itself only to the eye. Chiasmus is also inseparable from the medium on which the works that employ it were composed. The Catullus and Matthew were both inscribed on papyrus rolls. If you want to experience them as their first audience did, just imagine yourself reading columns of vertical text from something about the size and shape of a roll of paper towels, an experience well described by Franca Arduini in *The Shape of the Book From Roll to Codex:* "To read the text, one would hold the roll in his right hand, using his left to unwind it and simultaneously rewind the part that had already been read. When the reader was done, the roll would be completely wound in his left hand, so that to read it again, he had to unwind and then rewind it to return to the beginning of the work."

Now if this sounds a bit more cumbersome than turning on one's Kindle, with a little practice you could no doubt arrange the papyrus roll so that the two A sections at either end were placed side by side. So with the B, C, and D sections. A cultured young poet in ancient Rome would have had a sophisticated mythological poem which could be read either straight through from beginning to end, or thematically, with related sections placed together for comparison and contrast: here we see Ariadne abandoned by one lover, there you see her sought after by another. If you were the Evangelist hoping to persuade your audience that, even though Jesus had come to an ignominious end, he was nonetheless the Messiah, the patterns revealed by chiasmus—here is His birth, and here is His rebirth, or resurrection—would help you to make your case.

Chiasmus and the plots it generated disappeared sometime in the third or fourth century of our era, when papyrus rolls were replaced by the codex, a precursor of the book, usually made of vellum, the leather made from the hides of calves. Chiasmus must have seemed no longer useful as the plot of a long text imprisoned, whether verse or prose, in the unyielding pages of a book, so it disappeared and was soon forgotten. Not entirely, as it turns out. In the "Author's Prologue" that Dylan Thomas wrote for his *Collected Poems*, the poet arranged 102 brief lines so that they rhymed chiasmically. The poem begins:

> This day winding down now
> At God speeded summer's end
> In the torrent salmon sun . . .

and ends with:

> My ark sings in the sun
> At God speeded summer's end
> And the flood flowers now.

Thomas was said to be greatly disappointed that no one noticed what he had done, but why should they have? His plot, spread out over several pages, is neither audible nor visible. More recently, James Merrill used chiasmus much more successfully in a late poem called "Pearl," an irregular ode that employs chiasmus to meditate on the various forms which loss reveals in a lifetime. Because "Pearl" fits on a single page, we can take in its chiasmic structure. Its beginning, middle, and end lines ("Well, I admit . . ." "Of grit . . ." "Shuts on it.") should give some indication of its impressive skill. The only large-scale use of chiasmus that I know of in a recent literary work is the novel *Cloud Atlas*, by David Mitchell, in which the plot unwinds through five different literary genres (Journal, Letters, Mystery, Parody, Science Fiction) to be stopped by an apocalypse and then unwound again in the opposite order to its conclusion.

Father Ong argues that with increasing literacy (more solitary writers creating works for solitary readers) came increased consciousness: "Though inspiration continues to derive from unconscious sources, the writer can subject the unconscious inspiration to far greater conscious control than the oral narrator. The writer finds his written words accessible for reconsideration, revision and other manipulation until they are finally released to do their work." The plots of novels become less episodic, more tightly wound, until, in 1841, Edgar Allan Poe brings the "pyramidically structured narrative to its peak in his 'Murders in the Rue Morgue.'"

Generally regarded as the first western detective story and the first sealed-room murder mystery, Poe's classic tale contains elements repeated or developed in later examples of the genre: an elaborately constructed mystery solved by a hyperrational detective—in this case, one C. Auguste Dupin—and narrated by an anonymous and less intelligent roommate who lives with him in a symbiotic bromance. The detective's ability to find significance in seemingly unimportant clues leads to the surprising denouement. Ong describes it so: "In the ideal detective story, ascending action builds relentlessly to all but unbearable tension, the climactic recognition and reversal releases the tension with explosive suddenness, and the denouement disentangles everything totally—every single detail in the story turns out to have been crucial—and, until the climax and denouement, effectively misleading."

Inevitably one wonders whether, as this was happening in fiction, a similar process was not occurring at the same time in poetry as well, for after all, the poets too were increasingly solitary writers writing for solitary readers. One might expect in poetry a development similar to that of Poe's great invention, the modern detective story. Interestingly, only a year after Poe's publication, Robert Browning published "My Last Duchess," a poem with a plot as tightly woven as Poe's—in fact, something of a detective story—and one that has given birth to a literary genre as enduringly popular as the mystery story: the dramatic monologue. The term "dramatic monologue" has two applications: one of them is to a verse or prose soliloquy in a play, and the other is to the kind of poem generally regarded as the invention of Robert Browning: his "Duchess," or his "Soliloquy of the Spanish Cloister." In *A Glossary of Literary Terms* the critic M. H. Abrams describes three features of the Browningesque dramatic monologue:

> A single person, who is patently *not* the poet, utters the speech that makes up the whole of the poem, in a specific situation at a critical moment [. . .]. This person addresses and interacts with one or more other people; but we know of the auditor's presence, and what they say and do, only from clues in the discourse of the single speaker. The main principle controlling the poet's choice and formulation of what the lyric

speaker says is to reveal to the reader, in a way that enhances its interest, the speaker's temperament and character.

When Browning's poem begins, its unnamed speaker is showing someone a portrait that he had commissioned of his "last duchess . . . / Looking as if she were alive." We realize that the sitter is now dead, but we have no reason to suspect anything untoward about her death, and the speaker presents himself as a genial, accommodating host, eager to display a valued possession to someone whom he thinks will clearly appreciate it:

> I call
> That piece a wonder, now: Fra Pandolf's hands
> Worked busily a day, and there she stands.
> Will't please you to sit and look at her?

The guest will be sure to wonder not only at "the pictured countenance" but at Fra Pandolf's ability to capture "that spot of joy upon the Duchess' cheek," a sign, we realize, of a nature spontaneous, attractive, and courteous. As the speaker continues, we come to learn that these qualities are precisely what he found objectionable in his last duchess. The tension builds as the depth of his revulsion becomes increasingly apparent, until, "I gave commands / Then all smiles stopped together. There she stands / As if alive." The murder is revealed, but of course there is more to come: one further revelation about the reason for the guest's presence:

> Will't please you to rise? We'll meet
> The company below then. I repeat,
> The Count your master's known munificence
> Is ample warrant that no just pretence
> Of mine for dowry will be disallowed;
> Though his fair daughter's self, as I avowed
> At starting, is my object.

The genial host is revealed as a murderer, potentially a serial killer, and his auditor will have to decide whether or not he wishes to be the Duke's accomplice. As with Poe, every detail turns out to have been both necessary and misleading.

There is, however, one great difference between Poe and Browning. In Poe, the function of plot is to reveal the murderer, thus solving the mystery. Character as such is unimportant in Poe's story: neither the Orangutan who has committed the murders nor the nameless narrator have any character to reveal. Nor does the denouement reveal anything of C. Auguste Dupin's character that we did not already know. But for Browning, the purpose of the plot is, as Abrams says, to reveal for us the character and temperament of the speaker. This is, of course, the difference between the detective story, which effectively ends when we learn whodunit, and serious literary fiction, where the function of the plot is the revelation of character. This is not to say that character is wholly unimportant in the mystery genre, but that such character as is revealed to us is generally revealed before the solution of the mystery and is pretty much independent of it. We are usually presented with the character of the detective wholly formed before the action starts, whether it is M. Dupin, Sherlock Holmes, Nero Wolfe, or Nigel Strangeways, and any subsequent engagements with the solver of the mystery usually repeat what we know already about them, rather than offering us any real surprises about their character or temperament. Like Poe's "Murders in the Rue Morgue," Kafka's "Metamorphosis" is a locked-room mystery, but one in which there is no detective, and one in which we never learn whodunit. We are left at the end with an insoluble mystery, but with all sorts of interesting revelations about Gregor Samsa and the members of his family.

Whether written in prose or poetry, the plot of serious literary writing serves to reveal character. But to move our discussion back to poetry, does it matter whether the speaker of the poem is employing a person or speaking in his or her own voice? Samuel Maio tells us that it doesn't, in his *Dramatic Monologues: A Contemporary Anthology*. Maio argues that dramatic monologues are much older than Browning and ignores Abram's first point, admitting to his anthology poems that would appear to be written in the poet's own voice. In justification of this practice, he cites Browning himself, in his introduction to *The Letters of Percy Bysshe Shelley*, "where he distinguishes between two types of dramatic verse: the 'objective' and the 'subjective.'" The objective monologist is the one who writes the persona poem; the subjective monologist "does not look externally but internally; a character is not created nor a persona used, but a speaking voice seemingly aligned with the poet's own." This too, in Browning's view and Maio's, may be considered a dramatic monologue.

At this point, though, the issue of how we know whether a poet is speaking in his or her own voice may seem to be far more unsettled than otherwise. How confident can any of us be that John Donne, even in his love poems, is writing in his own voice? The early modern French poet Christine de Pizan wrote heartfelt elegies for her beloved husband and also wrote a ballade complaining about the irrational jealousies of a spouse she despised; we may think of this as a persona poem, or that she was only lending her own voice to another woman's situation. In any event, one suspects that neither Donne nor Christine would have given much thought to authenticity. It is even more difficult to say whether the voice of the speaker of a poem read in translation is that of the original poet or that of his or her translator, a difficulty that seems to increase as we go back further in time. What we know about the speaker is that he or she is in some sense imagined, a persona. As Hugh Kenner once put it, in a collection of his essays entitled *Historical Fictions*, "To make speech course through verse means imagining, impersonating a speaker." Ong strongly believed in a fictionalized reader, without whom the writer cannot proceed. But isn't the writer also a fiction too?

If we accept the fictional status of both writer and reader, there cannot be much objection to the idea that there is very little difference, if any, between dramatic monologue and the kind of lyric poems we (and many of our students) write these days. It seems to be described fairly clearly in this modification of Abrams's description of the dramatic monologue:

> A single person, who may or may not be the poet, utters the speech that makes up the whole of the poem, in a specific situation at a critical moment [. . .]. This person addresses, and may interact with, one or more other people; but if so, we know of the auditors' presence, and what they say and do, only from clues in the discourse of the single speaker. The main principle controlling the poet's choice and formulation of what the lyric speaker says is to reveal to the reader, in a way that enhances its interest, the speaker's temperament and character.

If we go back to the source of the lyric tradition in the West, we find Sappho, as translated by Aaron Poochigian in his Penguin Classics version of her poems:

> That fellow strikes me as god's double,
> Couched with you face to face, delighting

In your warm manner, your amiable
Talk and inviting

Laughter—the revelation flutters
My ventricles, my sternum and stomach
The least glimpse and my lost voice stutters,
Refuses to come back

Because my tongue is shattered. Gauzy
Flame runs radiating under
My skin; all that I see is hazy,
My ears all thunder.

Sweat comes quickly, and a shiver
Vibrates my frame. I am more sallow
Than grass and suffer such a fever
As death should follow.

But I must suffer further, worthless
As I am. . . .

The issue of whether Sappho is speaking in her own voice seems both insoluble and unimportant. Sappho might be writing a persona poem or she might not be. We can never know for certain. A single speaker who may or may not be the poet utters the speech that constitutes the poem, confessing her passion for another woman whom she addresses directly, and what we know about her auditor we know only from the speaker. The purpose of the plot of the poem is this revelation of the speaker's temperament and character to the auditor and to the reader, who, in a sense, stands in for the auditor.

A straight line could be drawn from Sappho's ode to Larkin's "Aubade," the one an erotic poem haunted by death, the other a premature elegy haunted by Eros. In either case, the plot of the poem is the revelation of the poet's character, in the hope that a lover (in Sappho's case) or the audience for poetry (in Larkin's) will find the poet's character attractive and be persuaded to remain in the poet's presence until the poem's conclusion.

The plot of such poems serves to reveal some aspect of the speaker's character, and to return briefly to the students I began with, it seems to me that Student B probably had a more mature sense of her own character, a greater degree of self-consciousness than Student A, as well as a better understanding of the ways in which information of that nature can be communicated to another.

Once it has been set down on the page, such information continues to address others in that culture where it is embedded. It does so even in the absence of a speaker, who, as Hugh Kenner reminds us, is an imitation or impersonation, a fiction whose words are engraved onto a supportive surface, an approximation of permanence. In the words of Father Ong, "There is no way directly to refute a text. After absolutely total and devastating refutation"—the deaths of Sappho and Philip Larkin, for example—"it says exactly the same thing as before. Texts are inherently contumacious."

What Makes a Play a Play?

NAOMI IIZUKA

What makes a play a play, as opposed to a novel or a poem, as opposed to a movie or an op-ed piece in the *New York Times*? What is it about the form of theater and the theatrical event that is singular? What is it about actors performing on stage in front of a live audience that is like no other experience in the world? Maybe another way of saying this is: What can plays do differently from poetry and fiction? How can playwrights write plays that are not only striking works of literature on the page, but also, as the playwright Suzan-Lori Parks writes, "blueprints of an event"? For that is what we are in the business of doing as playwrights. We are tasked with writing vivid, evocative blueprints of theatrical events, fleshy blueprints for actors to embody and perform. As playwrights, we traffic in the possibilities and also the limitations of time and space. Time and space are the raw material that we work with as much as language. As playwrights, we know that the play on the page is not an end in and of itself. In fact, the play on the page is just a fragment of something larger, far more unwieldy and complex, and ultimately ineffable. The story is important. The dialogue and stage directions are important, but it is only when you combine language with actors, lights, costumes, a set that a play is truly complete. And it's only when all the stars align in space and time, when everything works in serendipitous synchronicity that your play can be fully realized.

I should confess to you that I came to theater and playwriting rather late. I know many playwrights who developed a love of theater when they were children, and so all the questions I have about what makes a play a play, and what makes a theater event so mysterious and unique were answered for them at a very young age. They take many things for granted that I still find curious and novel. I have playwright friends who can trace their desire to be playwrights back to skits they put up in their backyard when they were children. For them, theater began with directing their younger brothers and sisters on cardboard sets with curtains made from sheets and costumes borrowed from their parents' closet. That was not my experience. I did not read many plays growing up. My knowledge of playwriting extended little beyond what I read in school: Sophocles, Aeschylus, Euripides, Shakespeare, Chekhov, and Molière. I read the classics of the Western canon and not much else. I read these plays as literature. I had no real sense of them as living, breathing performance texts. I also knew nothing about contemporary American plays growing up. For me, theater was an old art form where actors spoke in an ancient vernacular and wore hoop skirts and pantaloons. My family simply did not go to the theater. My dad watched a lot of football while I was growing up. My mother watched a lot of evening news. She would occasionally take me to the Kennedy Center to see the ballet or the symphony in a dutiful expose-your-child-to-culture kind of way, but I don't remember ever seeing a play except for very humble, somewhat creaky school productions of plays like *Arsenic and Old Lace.* I had no conception that one could even be a playwright. If you had asked me then, I would've said being a playwright was akin to being a cobbler, a glassblower, or a candlestick maker. In my mind, playwriting was a quaint, antiquated profession, and theater was a quaint, antiquated art form.

That all changed thanks in part to a play called *True West* written by Sam Shepard. Many may know Sam Shepard as an actor. He played Chuck Yeager in *The Right Stuff.* Some may know his play *Buried Child,* which won the Pulitzer Prize in 1978. Some may know *True West.* It was made popular by a legendary Steppenwolf Theater production featuring John Malkovich and Gary Sinise back in the early 1980s. *True West* is not the kind of play I write. I want to say that up front. It comes from a theatrical tradition different from the one I feel kinship to. And yet, *True West* was the improbable catalyst to my awakening to the possibilities of what a play could be.

True West, for those who may not know the play, is the story of two brothers locked in a primordial struggle over just about everything. You name it: power, money, what it means to be a good son, what it means to be a success. One brother, Austin, is an aspiring writer who has lived his entire life playing by the rules. He tries to be a good son. He's responsible and serious by nature. He's on a path to becoming a success in his chosen profession. The other brother, Lee, has spent a lifetime rebelling against those very same rules. He is a renegade and an outlaw. He's also a classic narcissist: bright, charismatic, and also wantonly destructive. There's a hunger that fuels Lee, a sense of outrage that he's somehow been cheated out of his rightful share of an American Dream, and he's very, very angry. These brothers are familiar archetypes. Their conflict is mythic. The story is ancient. In many ways, it's the story of Cain and Abel retold in the California desert in the latter half of the twentieth century.

The production of *True West* that I saw which cracked everything open for me was by a small company in San Diego called Sledgehammer Theatre. You've probably never heard of it, although they did fantastic work in their day. The theater was an old, abandoned church in downtown San Diego in a part of town known for its tattoo parlors and dive bars. People said the theater was haunted. There were holes in the roof and a cracked stained-glass window far upstage. The seats were rickety, and the lighting grid was very old. As rundown as the building may have been, it was the home to some great theater. Like many small theater companies, Sledgehammer eventually fell apart after a few years. They lost the lease on their space. Some of the founding members moved on to more lucrative careers in New York and Los Angeles. When I saw *True West* in the early 1990s, Sledgehammer was in its heyday, doing some of the most exciting, provocative theater I had ever seen.

It was at Sledgehammer that I was first introduced to playwrights like Mac Wellman and Erik Ehn, pioneers of American experimental theater. Their plays completely upended everything I knew or thought I knew about theater. I remember one of Wellman's plays I saw at the time was titled *Terminal Hip: A Spectral History of America Through the Medium of Bad Language*. The play was verbal collage and meditation on the difficulties of communication. It featured lines like: "Strange the Y all bent up and dented. Blew the who to tragic eight ball. Eight ball trumpet earwax and so forth." And: "Xerox the sea at Del Mar, lose radicals their jobs and pandas their pants." You get the idea. It was language untethered from any semblance of conventional usage. It was playfully and defiantly non-naturalistic. I would say Mac Wellman's plays were most reminiscent of writers like Gertrude Stein, but suffused with anxieties and preoccupations of a late-twentieth-century American sensibility. I remember I saw a series of short plays based on the lives of the saints at Sledgehammer called *The Saint Plays* by Erik Ehn. I remember the character of St. Joan racing across the stage on roller skates, and the character of St. Barbara scrambling above the audience on the catwalk. I seem to remember that there was someone walking across the stage playing the accordion at one point, and another character with an electric guitar screeching feedback. I also remember a naked man with reindeer antlers appearing out of the blue. I was a rather logical, sheltered twenty-something-year-old at the time, and I found these plays very disorienting and strange, but strange in a good way, strange in a way that made me curious to know more. I might not have understood everything that was happening, but I was pulled into the surreal exuberance of it.

I saw a lot of plays at Sledgehammer Theatre, but of all the plays that I saw there, it was their production of *True West* that sticks with me the most and stayed with me all these years. The two main actors were young, fierce, and explosive in their energy in the signature style of acting favored by the theater company and by many other small companies like them. It was vivid and unnerving, and also unlike anything I had ever seen before. I remember I walked out of that theater and I didn't know what had hit me. I had been through something. I had had an experience filled with a series of sensations and emotions I couldn't put into words. That was key. As someone who had spent much of her life up to that point putting things into words, this experience was impossible to paraphrase. My mind was racing. Something I couldn't yet name had clicked for me. I was quite honestly transformed in ways that it's taken me years to figure out. I think I'm still figuring it out.

In hindsight, I think what that production of *True West* gave me was a tantalizing taste of what theater and playwriting could be. It was such a muscular, raw experience. It was intimate and dangerous, and filled with mysteries that resonated long after the lights went down. *True West* is now over thirty years old. I have seen and read many other plays since then that are flashier and shinier, more innovative, more sophisticated, more artfully constructed, more linguistically daring, but on some very deep and visceral level, nothing quite compares to that first experience I had of seeing *True West*. Why is that? That's the question I've been asking myself on and off for decades. I think I've arrived at some answers, or at least some educated guesses, and those answers have coalesced into something approximating a theory about playwriting and theater. With that in mind, I want to share some things I know about what makes a play a play, and what makes an experience in the theater, when all the stars align and everything is working just right, like nothing else in the world.

1. The Best Theater (and What Theater Does Best) Is Fleshy and Human. It's Sweaty and Physical and Sometimes Bloody

One of the most striking memories I had of that production of *True West* was the sheer amount of sweat on stage. These actors were sweating profusely, in large part because they were in constant motion. They were pacing, they were stalking each other and shoving each other, they were fidgeting and making toast, they were pounding at a manual typewriter and eventually attacking that same typewriter with a golf club, they were wrestling each other, they were ripping phones from walls, and at one point they were even strangling each other. They were in constant motion. What this meant was that they were sweating a lot.

Sometimes playwrights forget the importance of sweat as well as blood and other bodily fluids in making a play. Some plays consist of characters talking in living rooms and motel rooms, around kitchen tables and on front porches about ideas. There's nothing wrong with ideas. Ideas are interesting and great, but theater is ultimately less about ideas, and more about the body. When we watch a play, we are watching actors in real time embody the human experience, and the human experience is filled with sweat and blood. Shakespeare knew this. Think about Hamlet's final duel with Laertes or the blinding of Gloucester. Centuries later the great American playwrights understood this as well. Think about Stanley's confrontation with Blanche in *Streetcar*. Think about Mary Tyrone's onstage descent into her morphine addiction in *Long Day's Journey into Night*. When we watch these plays, we are forced to grapple with the human body in all its power and vulnerability. The best plays are the ones where we are reminded of the physical experience of being human. While it's true that great plays often house big ideas and urgent debates about big ideas, ultimately the body, weak and fragile as it may be, is the center of the story.

2. Every Good Play Has a Secret

If a play is an engine, secrets are the jet fuel. Without a good secret at its core, a play has a certain flatness or lifelessness. And by secret, I don't mean a Who-Done-It kind of secret. A secret is, on the most elemental level, something a character doesn't say. It's the thing just beneath the surface that makes the story thrum and vibrate with life. Sometimes in plays, the secret is integral to the plot, but more often, and perhaps more interestingly, secrets are what give characters life and dimension. In *Oedipus,* the secret is the true identity of the king's parents. In *Streetcar,* the secret is Blanche's marriage and her life before coming to live in New Orleans. In Thornton Wilder's *Our Town,* the secret is what it feels like to be dead and how the dead see the living. In Caryl Churchill's play *Faraway,* the secret is the true purpose of the beautiful, elaborate hats that the characters are constructing.

In *True West,* the secret concerns what happened to Austin and Lee's father. In a larger sense, the secret that lives beneath the surface of the play is the origin story of these two brothers. Who fathered these two embattled brothers? What legacy of loss and rage and grief have these two brothers inherited? We learn the secret, or at least part of the secret, midway through the play when Austin tells us about his father losing his teeth: first his real teeth one by one, and then eventually a set of fake teeth which he loses in Juarez, Mexico. Austin's monologue gives a sense of the music of Shepard's language, the metabolic rhythms of his diction and syntax:

> Yeah, he lost his real teeth one at a time. Woke up every morning with another tooth lying on the mattress. Finally, he decides he's gotta' get 'em all pulled out but he doesn't have any money. Middle of Arizona with no money and no insurance and every morning another tooth is lying on the mattress. (*Takes a drink*) So what does he do? He begs the government. G.I. Bill or some damn thing. Some pension plan he remembers in the back of his head. And they send him out the money. They send him the money but it's not enough money. Costs a lot to have all yer teeth yanked. They charge by the individual tooth, ya' know. I mean one tooth isn't equal to another tooth. Some are more expensive. Like the big ones in the back—So he locates a Mexican dentist in Juarez who'll do the whole thing for a song. And he takes off hitchhiking to the border. So how long you think it takes him to get to the border? A man his age. Eight days it takes him. Eight days in the rain and the sun and every day he's droppin' teeth on the blacktop and nobody'll pick him up 'cause his mouth's full a' blood. So finally he stumbles into the dentist. Dentist takes all his money and all his teeth. And there he is, in Mexico, with his gums sewed up and his pockets empty. Then I go out to see him, see. I go out there and I take him out for a nice Chinese dinner. But he

doesn't eat. All he wants to do is drink Martinis outa' plastic cups. And he takes his teeth out and lays 'em on the table 'cause he can't stand the feel of 'em. And we ask the waitress for one a' those doggie bags to take the Chop Suey home in. So he drops his teeth in the doggie bag along with the Chop Suey. And then we go out to hit all the bars up and down the highway. Says he wants to introduce me to all his buddies. And in one a' those bars, in one a' those bars up and down the highway, he left that doggie bag with his teeth laying in the Chop Suey. We went back but we never did find it. (*Pause*) Now that's a true story. True to life.

What I remember most when I saw the play, even more than the words or story, was this feeling the story engendered in me as an audience member. I was being told a secret. I was being served up a truth about the human condition in a way that shook me up and filled me with a kind of wonder, a vertiginous hyperawareness of everything around me. In retrospect, it was one of those moments where you say to yourself: "I get it. I see." I see who this character is, but in a deeper sense, I see something about the human condition that I might have known intellectually, but now in this moment understand viscerally. Somehow Sam Shepard managed to capture the secret of a life with a handful of artifacts: a martini in a plastic cup, a set of false teeth, a doggie bag of chop suey from a Chinese restaurant in Juarez, which brings me to the next thing I know about plays:

3. Every Good Play Has Lots of Props

Props are so important. In *True West*, the props are abundant. There is a typewriter. There are golf clubs. There are whiskey bottles and beer cans and toasters, lots and lots of toasters. And that's just for starters. A stage direction towards the end of the play reads as follows: "Mid-day. No sound, blazing heat, the stage is ravaged; bottles, toasters, smashed typewriter, ripped out telephone, etc. All the debris from previous scene is now starkly visible in intense yellow light, the effect should be like a desert junkyard at high noon."

The right props when placed on stage become totemic objects filled with power. They bring with them a lifetime of associations. They evoke whole worlds. In *True West*, one prop that figures especially prominently is a toaster. Halfway through the play, the character of Austin steals every toaster in the neighborhood. The set becomes filled with countless shiny chrome toasters covering every surface. There are toasters everywhere. And Austin, in fact, even makes toast. In the production I saw, he actually made a lot of toast. There was a whole *lazzi* of toast making with that iconic sound of the toast toasting punctuating the dialogue for the better part of the scene. It's a peculiar, yet undeniably powerful, stage image. Perhaps there's something about a toaster that conjures up the optimism and the possibilities of a new day. It's as if, by stealing all the toasters he can lay his hands on, Austin is somehow trying to lay claim to all that optimism and hope, all those bright, sunny tomorrows. I'm not sure why the toaster works as well as it does. Like the best props, the associative tendrils are multivalent and idiosyncratic.

It's not just the prop itself that's so important. It's how the prop is used and presented to us. Least interesting is when the prop is used as it is used in real life. In fact, one of the writing prompts I give my students is to include an object or prop in a scene and use it in a way that it was not intended to be used. In other words, a shoe becomes a soup bowl. A spoon becomes mirror. A teacup becomes a hat. Shepard engages in this particular magic trick repeatedly in *True West*. In his play, a kitchen becomes a putting green. A telephone becomes a deadly weapon.

The best plays make us see the world in which we live through new eyes. One of the most effective ways they do that is by taking an everyday object, reframing it, and making that object strange and foreign in our eyes. As the scholar Bill Brown writes in *A Sense of Things:* "We begin to confront the thingness of objects when they stop working for us: when the drill breaks, when the car stalls, when the window gets filthy, when their flow within the circuits of production and distribution, consumption and exhibition, has been arrested, however momentarily." In *True West*, as in all the best plays, we experience "the thingness of things." Things break down. Things don't work the way they're meant to work. The familiar is rendered strange. And by experiencing the thingness of things, we are able to see the world anew.

4. In Every Good Play, Language Is Important, but It's Not the Only Thing, and It May Not Even Be the Most Important Thing

When I think back on what I remember from that production of *True West*, the language spoken is only one part of what made that performance so vital. There's no question that Austin's story about his dad losing his teeth and Lee's feverish, improvised cowboy story represent virtuosic moments of storytelling. To see a good actor take on that kind of language is one of the great pleasures of going to the theater. I was in Ashland, Oregon, not that long ago at the Oregon Shakespeare Festival where I had the opportunity to hear actors read through Shakespeare's *Richard II.* Even in the rehearsal room with its fluorescent lights and the linoleum floor, just sitting around a table, hearing that gorgeous language was thrilling. It was a meal unto itself.

Yet just as important, maybe even more important, than the language characters speak are the images or stage pictures that playwrights create. When I think of that production of *True West,* I think about Lee smashing a typewriter to smithereens with a golf club. I think about the sudden, shocking appearance of their mother standing backlit in the doorway in the final moments of the play. I think about the last image of the play where the two brothers square off in a final death match, and how the lights go down on that final tableau with violence all but a certainty. I think about the omnipresent sound of crickets and coyotes like a spectral chorus offstage. As playwrights, our job is to create these moments in the theater where many different layers of meaning can coexist simultaneously, and where that meaning is generated not only by language but also by the choreography of bodies in space, the frame or context that we've built around those bodies. As playwrights, we are writing with more than just words. The sentences that we compose with bodies, light, and sound have their own grammar and syntax, but you can't find the rules written down anywhere. You have to figure them out as you go. You learn by seeing a lot of plays. You learn by sitting in tech. You learn by observing great directors and designers work. You learn by making mistakes.

5. The Best Theater (and What Theater Does Best) Is Ultimately Unparaphrasable

The best theater, the most transcendent moments in theater, are very hard to explain. You can't sum them up. I could tell you the story of *True West.* I could give you a synopsis of the plot, but that wouldn't convey what it is to see the play performed live. In the best plays, there's an alchemy that happens when you take the script and give it to actors, when you add light and sound and the design elements of a full production, and when you invite an audience to be part of the event. It's a potent and mysterious chemical reaction that we, as playwrights, attempt with each play. We spend lifetimes trying to figure out how to make that alchemy happen. This is what I know:

> 1. The present is everything in theater. Playwrights need to be alert to every facet of the present moment and be nimble enough to respond to all the possibilities of the present moment in the stories they tell and the characters they put on stage.
>
> 2. Actors are the key. They make everything come alive. They sit at the center of that alchemical process. They are the conduits and the magicians. A smart playwright listens carefully to actors and watches every move.
>
> 3. A close attention to detail is necessary to pull off this alchemical reaction that I'm talking about. The light cue needs to be just right, as does the timing of the exit. The shade of paint on the walls and the count on the sound cue matter. The three words that you cut from that line make all the difference in the world.

6. The Best Plays Embrace the Human Condition in All Its Awkwardness, Its Messiness, and Its Inexplicable Strangeness

True West is chock full of moments where characters are not at their best. The play is the opposite of polite and refined. It's loud and rude and obstreperous. Characters speak at the wrong times and say the wrong things. They wear funny costumes. They make a mess. They sweat and steal and fight and tell stories. They fail spectacularly. There is some singing, a little dancing, and a lot of violence. Like all good plays, *True West* is unapologetic and unafraid to embody the human condition even when it's awkward and messy and strange, especially when it's awkward and messy and strange.

The playwright Anne Washburn says:

> I often feel like I'm the bastard child of the most old fashioned theater ever and maybe the weirdest. I love, just the fact of people on stage in

costumes, like children, pretending to be other people—I love all the things high art finds embarrassing about theater: the lurid story making, the grandstanding, and even just the super earnest desire to be looked at, to be seen, to please, which is part of the awkward heart of playmaking. But I also really love the possibility the stage has to capture the most tangential parts of our sensory and emotional world, and to expose the strangeness of being alive, the perishability of the bargain we've made with the world to stay sane.

7. The Best Plays Are Violent

The violence might be physical. It might be psychic or emotional. In *True West*, the violence happens to be both physical and emotional. The sibling rivalry is a battle to the death. I think the best plays contain a promise of violence, even if it's not acted upon, because violence by its nature is an indicator of high stakes. And the best plays have the highest stakes. They are indeed life and death. This is not hyperbole. The best plays invariably capture characters at a moment when they face circumstances in which their lives, everything they love and believe in, are under assault. The best plays concern themselves with the biggest appetites and desires. Will I survive? Will I prevail against my enemy? Who is my enemy? Who is my *real* enemy? Will I find love? What is the truth, and can I bear the knowledge of it? Will I weather this terrible loss? Will I get out of here alive? These are questions that playwrights have been asking from Sophocles onwards through Shakespeare and the Jacobeans, through Chekhov and Ibsen, through Williams and O'Neill. These are the questions that the best plays ask and continue to ask. We still ask these questions because these questions get at the bedrock of our time on this earth.

8. The Best Plays Are Strangely Shaped Because Life Is Strangely Shaped

While there are hints and nods to an Aristotelian structure, *True West* is not a well-made play in that sense. It starts with an interruption and ends in the middle of a fight. There is a nominal arc, there is a reversal, but really, the story doesn't operate like a well-made play. There are tangents and dead ends.

There are red herrings and non sequiturs. There's a compulsive circling around the same sibling rivalry with each scene replaying and refracting the conflict between the two brothers. The arrival of the mother feels almost like the arrival of Apollo at the end of *Orestes.* All this to say, *True West* has a strange, at times unwieldy, structure. And, in my opinion, that's a good thing.

The playwright and historian Chuck Mee writes: "I like plays that are not too neat, too finished, too presentable. My plays are broken, jagged, filled with sharp edges, filled with things that take sudden turns, careen into each other, smash up, veer off in sickening turns. That feels good to me. It feels like my life. It feels like the world." In an interview in the online journal *Howl Round,* Mee amplifies this idea: "Things just happen in life sometimes. When we talk about it, we think we can understand cause effect, cause effect, cause effect. And we think we can impose that logic on life or reconstitute a description of life that is rational and can be explained in that way. But sometimes Mount Vesuvius erupts and that's just what happens."

The best plays understand that human lives do not move in a neat linear fashion, and if plays are meant to reflect the human, plays cannot be structured in a neat linear fashion. Life is, as Mee writes, filled with sharp edges and sudden turns. The best plays reflect that existential condition in their form. The best plays are informed by an awareness of catastrophe, of how life can suddenly end without warning. Death and the consequences of death run through so many of our greatest plays, from Iphigenia's death in Aulis to the death of Hamlet's father in the garden. In *True West,* the absent father is a kind of ghost. It is the father's absence, in fact, that lays the groundwork for the sense of loss that fuels Lee and Austin's hunger and pain. Abandoned by their parents, the two sons struggle to make their way in a world that is haunted and incomplete. And in that way, we are all a bit like Lee and Austin making our way through a haunted landscape, struggling with wounds that never heal, wrestling with memories and dreams we can't quite shake, careening and sometimes dancing towards death whether we know it or not. So much of theater is preoccupied by death. In Kabuki, the actors stomp on the floorboards to summon the ghosts of the dead. In classical French theater, they knock three times before beginning to wake the ghosts. In theater, the ghosts are always in the room. We summon them. We acknowledge them. We listen to what they have to say. We embody them. We give them form and substance. We retell and relive their stories. On our best days, we figure out the alchemy to make the ghosts come alive and speak to us in ways that resonate long after the lights go down.

And with that, I want to leave you with one last quote. It's an excerpt from Sarah Ruhl's beautiful book *100 Essays I Don't Have Time to Write on Umbrellas and Sword Fights, Parades and Dogs, Fire Alarms, Children, and Theatre.*

> Have you ever seen a Tibetan monk make a butter sculpture? The monks sculpt flowers and temples with colored butter, intricate and lovely, knowing they will melt, knowing that eventually they will feed the sculptures to the monkeys. . . . Many Western traditions pin the arts against mortality; we try to make something that will abide, something made of stone, not butter. And yet theater has at the core of its practice the repetition of transience. We take something intricate and lovely and feed it not to the monkeys, but to each other.

Seven Types of Ambivalence

On Donald Justice

WILLIAM LOGAN

Si je mets bleues après pierres, c'est que bleues est le mot juste, croyez-moi.
—GUSTAVE FLAUBERT

We commonly use the word "aesthetics" in two ways knotted like snakes on a Celtic ornament. It's helpful to unpick that snarl at the start. When we speak of a poet's aesthetics (such aesthetics as he has, I'm tempted to say), we mean the program or philosophy to which he's declared allegiance (Vorticism, perhaps, or LANGUAGE poetry), else the little sum of twitches and habits that go into the writing of poems. These get tangled when, as is often the case, a poet's leanings or fancies become the tenets of a manifesto. Pound's "A Few Don'ts by an Imagiste" responded to some hint of private preference toward which he had long been tending. A manifesto does not have to be published or nailed to a door. There have been movements enough—the Movement, Confessional Poetry, the Cockney School—where some critic christened a group by noticing affiliations unrecognized by the poets themselves.

I make the distinction because Donald Justice was never a joiner, never entered a school or founded one. There was a principled reserve, but also a reserve according to inclination. Most art, good or great, is selfish—that is, made for the artist alone. As soon as you lead a movement other artists can join, you're engaged in the will to power. That doesn't mean the loner is necessarily uncompetitive. Art is not just selfish but sovereign in creation (and therefore, to the degree it does not recognize the past, narcissistic), even if the art itself is generous, even if the artist himself is generous.

That generosity includes, but is not limited to, the training of other artists different in character. Though it is not the subject here, when the history of poetry in the last century comes to be written, the two teachers of greatest influence may be Donald Justice and Richard Howard. Yvor Winters, John Crowe Ransom, Robert Lowell, and many another were teachers of great virtue; but the intelligence of far more poets was formed and structured in the workshops of Justice and Howard, both of whom had long careers in large writing programs. I mention this only as far as it bears on aesthetics, because the peculiar thing about good teachers is how varied, even how opposed and antithetical, their students become. Not unaffected, of course—Howard's students sometimes favor monologues and alliteration, and Lowell's often wrote appalling imitations of *Life Studies*—but the best students have drawn something beyond the surface features of a taste, have drawn some bearing toward language itself.

My consideration of Donald Justice's aesthetics is partly affected, even circumscribed, by my memory of him as a teacher. He parried his way into a poem, fending off false meanings where he could and calling attention to them when he couldn't. He inched toward meaning by niggling shrugs—I'm reminded of that phrase Eliot lifted from Webster for an epigraph, "two religious caterpillars." Justice was a religious caterpillar; and the formula or rite by which he explored his observations, even his objections, was forensic: "On the one hand," he'd say. Then, reconsidering, "On the other hand." At last, if you were lucky, he'd add, "But on the other hand." Each reading had its point, and the impaction and scatter—even reversal—of readings their point as well.

The fine discrimination and rueful suspension of judgment were, I think, characteristics deeply veined in the poetry. His poems seemed written line by line, their means in view but not their end, and toward the satisfaction of the line rather than the intention or design of the whole—yet, in the end, the design had a whole. Until each line had had its say, the poems often withheld their meaning. Justice was never an obscure poet, though I'd like to say that obscurely; but his gorgeous plainness, not always plain, was never entirely revealing and may be considered a form of discretion.

In "On the Porch," from the sequence "My South," the theme is the passage of time, but the subject, perhaps, the passing of the Old South.

> There used to be a way the sunlight caught
> The cocoons of caterpillars in the pecans.

A boy's shadow would lengthen to a man's
Across the yard then, slowly. And if you thought
Some sleepy god had dreamed it all up—well,
There stood my grandfather, Lincoln-tall and solemn,
Tapping his pipe out on a white-flaked column,
Carefully, carefully, as though it were his job.
(And we would watch the pipe-stars as they fell.)
As for the quiet, the same train always broke it.
Then the great silver watch rose from his pocket
For us to check the hour, the dark fob
Dangling the watch between us like a moon.
It would be evening soon then, very soon.

Justice was born in Georgia in 1925, when many Civil War veterans were still alive; his grandfather had been born at the outbreak of the war. The dreamlike cast of the land, as if the caterpillars and pecans and white-flaked column were eternal as sunlight, is a stasis slowly, gradually being lost. From the small boy's view ("And if you thought / Some sleepy god had dreamed it all up—well, / There stood my grandfather, Lincoln-tall and solemn"), the grandfather must seem immensely old, old as a god. When the train passes in the distance, he may simply be a man who every afternoon checks his watch against the train (or the train against his watch, depending on which he trusts, if either) or a god making sure his whole creation is running on time. Or seeing, perhaps, if time has stopped.

The association with Lincoln goes beyond height to the depth of a vanished age, an age not just when gods were tall but when great men seemed gods. Mention of the man who presided over the destruction of the Old South may suggest that the manners of the South were changing (though not, when Justice was a boy, the ancestral racism). The line may mean only that the defeated Confederacy had at least one rival for Honest Abe's magnificent bearing. Readers can go too far down that path—it's unlikely that the falling pipe-stars, the glowing embers, are an allusion to the Night the Stars Fell, the great Leonid meteor shower of 1833, which survived more than a century in the memory of slaves and their descendants. Perhaps in that white-flaked column, though, there's some trace recollection of the poverty of the postbellum South; but perhaps, only perhaps. The South always had hardscrabble farmers.

All that is fairly straightforward; but look how Justice has prepared the end as far back as the third line ("A boy's shadow would lengthen to a man's / Across the yard then, slowly"). Does the boy see his shadow in boyish pleasure, or with some dawning apprehension of the movements of Earth and Sun? The reader can't parse such a line until the poem has run its course; only then can he look back and see, not only the small signs of decay and vastation (the caterpillars, the flaking column), but the foreshadowed future where the boy's shadow will *be* that of a man, and at last, perhaps, of a man as old as his grandfather. This mortal contingency within a poem that looks fondly back to childhood is darkened further at the end ("It would be evening soon then, very soon"). The boy himself will die—soon, very soon, by the measure of seasons, however slowly the watch ticks out a life. Notice, as a grace note, how the watch rises like a moon from the grandfather's pocket.

No matter how beautifully and carefully rendered the description, you learn very little about Justice in Justice, though you learn a great deal about the manners of language. "On the Porch," for instance, probably recalls one of the summers Justice visited his grandparents in southern Georgia. Many poets write in a kind of sentimentality or fugue of form—they love the forms more than what form contains. In Justice you feel the form's identity as vehicle or medium, but the content fits the form without much overflowing. (This may be less a vice than a transforming virtue.) There's nothing in the verse loud or declamatory (if anything, you wish that sometimes Justice would overreach); but there remains what is otherwise difficult to obtain, an exactness of expression and purchase that takes the part for the part and the whole for the whole—in sum, a kind of anti-synecdoche.

Justice's strongest, most architectural work was not accomplished until late, only after he had wrestled through a number of styles and at last stopped resisting the subject always before him—his complicated, driving relation to memory, the memory he may always have feared would sink into nostalgia. The language grew richer and more implicating after *Departures* (1973), offering much greater range for the forms of ambivalence. His early books were tentative, half-grown, curious but never quite his—reviewers sometimes sensed the poet's failure to commit himself to the terms of the work but could not see how firm the sense of purpose, how tortured the ambition beneath. Indeed, Justice spent much imagination on surface, as if to deny the depths he could not yet embody.

It is in his exactness, his casting among alternatives for the most suggestive, the most philosophically or psychologically balanced (weighing possibilities for their moral as well as aesthetic densities), for the purest and most moderate of words that Justice defined and defended a middle style for American verse. Such a style was drawn, like hot wire, from two artists of antithetical densities—Wallace Stevens for the aesthetic, the superfluous, the ornamental, the woolly and philosophical, and William Carlos Williams for the domestic, the demotic and humdrum, no ideas but in things, things, things. Without this tension, an artist like Justice might have been held back by his delicacy, his modesty, his withdrawal; but instead the terms of his personality as an artist (the personality of the man may be different, just as his impersonality may be different) were engaged by the exactness required and the alternatives judged. This might have ended simply, if such things are ever simple, in the fetish of the Flaubertian *mot juste.*

The *mot juste* is sometimes strangely mistaken for the *bon mot,* a word that ends words, a snide remark by Oscar Wilde, the showstopper that poets of a gaudier tendency than Justice employ. What Flaubert meant, in the lesson of his style, is a word that fulfills its labor as no other word could have done, not a word that calls attention to itself (either by its triumph or in its latency)—rather, a word content to let the sentence move toward its undefined and unforeseen end, taking modest satisfaction in its contribution. Such words must possess, must embody, a complex tension in their origin suppressed in the moment of action. Words, like poems, mean not because but in spite of their ambivalence—that is, both in their local actions and in their action at a distance. The tremor of their meanings must be felt as we pass through them—their valences facing two ways, like Janus, the Roman god of doorways. Within such ambivalence, invited into the origin if suppressed in the action, I would isolate the chief characteristic of Justice's style.

What are the manners and contradictions, then, of this instability, these gathered tensions that might be called an aesthetics of ambivalence?

(1) That the poetry make no apology for addressing the literate, that it revels or roils in allusion, figures of speech, the modernist digestion of foreign and classical poetry (if not to the extent of Pound or Eliot), the desires and delights of form while employing a voice indirect, guarded, more or less plainspoken—if not homespun, certainly never tailored or bespoke. However much the art lies in the knowledge, the referential frame, of such poems, the only artifice is at times the seeming lack of artifice. Consider a poem that begins with a statue, or a man no longer one.

A Man of 1794

And like a discarded statue, propped up in a cart,
He is borne along toward the page allotted to him in history.

To open his heavy-lidded eyes now would be merely
To familiarize himself with the banal and destined route.

He is aware of the mockery of the streets,
But does not understand it. It hardly occurs to him

That what they fear is that he might yet address them
And call them back to their inflamed duty.

But this he cannot do; the broken jaw prevents speech.
Today he will not accuse the accusers; it is perhaps all that saves them.

Meanwhile his head rocks back and forth loosely on his chest
With each new jolt and lurch of the endless-seeming street:

Impossible to resist this idiot shaking.
—But it is hard after all to sympathize

With a man formerly so immaculate,
Who, after a single night of ambiguous confinement,

Lets go all pride of appearance. Nevertheless,
Under the soiled jabot, beneath the stained blue coat,

Are the principles nothing has shaken. Rousseau was right,
Of that he is still convinced: *Man is naturally good!*

And in the moment before the blade eases his pain
He thinks perhaps of his dog or of the woods at Choissy,

Some thought in any case of a perfectly trivial nature,
As though already he were possessed of a sweet, indefinite leisure.

The language is almost prosaic—everyday language, more or less, suited to the everyday event. The simplicity ignores where the cart is heading—and even the alert reader may at first miss the real destination, since the poem is mildly, resistantly titled "A Man of 1794." The poem has identified the when, not the where; if the reader is no student of history, the date and the "soiled jabot" will do nothing. Only much later have further clues been dropped like scraps of worthless assignats: the man is a speaker of note, has suffered a broken jaw, has accusers, and though once immaculate has abandoned "all pride of appearance." The "idiot shaking" ("With each new jolt and lurch of the endless-seeming street: // Impossible to resist this idiot shaking") is the cart's, not the man's; yet his shaking might be read by onlookers as fear. The narrator in these lines disappears into the victim.

Even given all that, given even the passing reference to Rousseau, a reader might be surprised, three lines from the end, when "in the moment before the blade eases his pain / He thinks perhaps of his dog or of the woods at Choissy." The reader might imagine that blade as a surgeon's blade—which in a dry way it is, for this is revolutionary France, and the man is Robespierre on his way to the guillotine. A reader without the benefit of reading might miss how much the poem perhaps owes, how two or three times it seems to tip its hat to, Auden's "Musée des Beaux Arts." The great man is at last just a man thinking of his dog. Justice might have made high-flown drama here, but as so often he plays in a minor key. That key gives more scope to irony.

"Appearance" is an ambivalent word. Drawn deep into the word, ambivalence is not, not just, ambiguity (a shudder in the meaning), but also a shudder in the aim and condition of feeling, the writer's toward the word, even the poem's toward the word. This is a speaker used to appearing, now about to disappear—and part of the poet's ambivalence is his wish not to have a stake in feeling, not to express any disillusion about a man merciless during the Terror he helped create.

The suspension of resolution, that wish to leave the reader in a state of unknowing as long as possible rather than giving him genial—or blaring—updates along the way, is what makes art of the rubbish of the past. Though the borrowing is from that magnificent artist, History itself, Justice makes each turn of the cartwheel nothing but ordinary until we realize that the business is the ordinary business of death. Ah, and isn't Death that renowned physician, that sweet easer of pain, that charitable dispenser of analgesics?

At the end, before the blade falls, the man has "Some thought in any case of a perfectly trivial nature, / As though already he were possessed of a sweet, indefinite leisure." "Indefinite" does furtive work here, indefinite because no man knows how long in retirement his lease will run—and isn't the grave also a place of indefinite leisure, whatever his religious belief? "Trivial," however, is the ambivalent word, the poet's judgment on a thought he has no access or right to—or is "trivial" Robespierre's own judgment?

The wretchedness of life may be made bearable through mild irony—and yet that fallen condition, that death shortly to arrive on the falling blade, has been there from the start, evident and yet concealed by the opening line, for the cart is a tumbrel. What does history make of discarded heroes but discarded statues? The language has little interest in something as emollient as style—if there is a whisper of the literary, it lies in the borrowing as well as in the syntax winding through the "mockery of the streets." (But is he mocked by the gathered crowds or by the streets of his own Paris?) The lines seem like free verse; but there is a rough, reliable accentual meter—between four and seven accents per line, between ten and nineteen syllables, never lapsing into prose, because entirely funded by iambs and anapests. That is the indefinite leisure of the form trundling along the path to the Place de la Revolution (now the Place de la Concorde). The tension rises from the very capture of the colloquial, the literary colloquial, in the hard service of fate.

(2) That the poetry at times be about poetry—and may speak to the reader, may lament the failure of earlier poems or the lost favors of the muse. The poet may even title a poem about a poem—what else?—"Poem," but one written in such a deliberate craftsman's way, with the delicacies and pleasures of a task well done, that the idea of the *mot juste* is refracted by the lens of the artist's quiet, absorbed pleasure. Thus an art about art never seems an art for the sake of art.

Justice's use of other poets was as much provocation as imitation or homage. In his essay "Tradition and an Individual Talent," Dana Gioia calculates that more than a quarter of Justice's poems subsist on literary borrowing, which should remind us again how close the poet lived to the precepts of the moderns. Like many of his generation, Justice was a modernist decades after the event; but he continued into a time when that became radically retrograde.

Recall a section from the sequence "American Scenes (1904–1905)," which draws on Henry James's sadly tinged return to the country of his youth, his half-forgotten and largely still unseen America. Justice's sequence consists of three sections of paired quatrains, followed by a sonnet. These quatrains seem little fragments of James's thought as he made the rounds of Cambridge, where his brother William lived, then turned south for the journey that forms the end of his melancholy memoir, *The American Scene* (1907). They seem fragments because they are taken partly from James's own words.

St. Michael's Cemetery, Charleston

One may depend on these **old cemeteries**
To say the one **charmed** thing there **is to say**—
So here the **silvery seaward outlook** carries
Hints of some other world beyond the bay.

The **sun-warmed tombs, the flowers.** Each faraway
Game-haunted inlet and reed-smothered isle
Speaks of lost **Venices**; and **the South** meanwhile
Has only **to be tragic to beguile**.

Justice inhabits the novelist here by borrowing phrases (in bold) from James's mild contents and deeper discontents:

> In the **old Cemetery** by the lagoon, . . . this influence distils an irresistible poetry—as one has courage **to say** even in remembering how . . . almost anywhere on the American scene, the general place of interment is apt to be invited to testify for the presence of **charm**. The golden afternoon, the low, **silvery, seaward** horizon, as of wide, sleepy, **game-haunted inlets and reed-smothered** banks, possible site of some Venice that had never mustered. . . . To what height did he rise . . . at no great distance from this point, and where the silvery seaward outlook still prevails. . . . [T]**he South** is in the predicament of **having to be tragic** . . . in order **to beguile**. . . . [I]n the sweet old church-yard ancient authority seemed . . . to sit, among the **sun-warmed tombs** and the inter-related slabs and **the** extravagant **flowers**.

By sly adjustments and distortions the poet has taken the novelist in a different direction. The old cemeteries in the poem have something to say, like the aged warriors along the wall of Troy—but the "old Cemetery" remains silent in *The American Scene,* though "apt to be invited to testify." "To say" therefore rests on a hinge of ambivalence. It's not just borrowing, it is conversion and creative mutation.

That other world beyond the bay (Justice's notion, not James's) suggests both what the South once was and what it had never been. We're not told what that charmed thing is that the cemeteries, with their burden of lost hopes, will say (they sound very much like antediluvian southern belles); but Justice's inlet and isle "speak of lost Venices"—that is, a glamour that once gone can never be revived and that in ruin draws the traveler with that Romantic disposition for lost things, like Byron roaming the weedy ground of the Forum. That other world, that sleepy Paradise, is now unreachable. Perhaps it lies across a southern Lethe in the dominion of death.

James does not go so far. For him that Venice of the South never existed, was never mustered or muttered into existence; but for a southerner there's an inescapable feeling of something lost and little gained in its stead. ("Game-haunted . . . and reed-smothered" sounds the postbellum dream of the antebellum.) For James, the South is forced to be tragic to beguile; for Justice, like Bernhardt in *Camille,* the South chooses to be. That's the mythic world of the Agrarians, on whom Justice did his master's thesis. He sees what the South never was, what some refused to believe it was not. James's words have quietly been maneuvered, or outmaneuvered, to different purpose.

Justice has concealed nothing—an afternote says "after Henry James"—but he has not only used James's worn clothing but tried on the novelist's impressions over his own, finding through them access to his own ambivalence about the South. (One of the epigraphs to "My South" is the doomed Quentin Compson's "I dont! I dont hate it! I dont hate it!" from *Absalom, Absalom!*) The penetration into the heart of Justice lies through the mind of James; and just that feeling, acquired secondhand, secures for the poet the necessary distance from his own mixed feelings.

(3) That poems drenched in the very inadequacies of their art often seem, by analogy, poems about the intermissions and intrusions of the poet's life. Justice never wrote in that mode we call confessional. As a poet, his most naked emotions were masked or concealed in the character of his art. His most affecting (indeed, until he was old his only) love poem was "Ode to a Dressmaker's Dummy."

To take a small example, the incidents in "On the Porch" might have come the summer Justice turned ten, when he was diagnosed with osteomyelitis, a bone infection often fatal before the widespread availability of antibiotics, still a decade in the future. It's not a necessary reading, because the poem reveals nothing about the year, though it probably lies in the thirties. The theme of the poem, the shadow on the shadow of life, would fit a boy already ill with a disease perhaps shortly to be diagnosed—yet the poem exists free of the fact, if fact it is. Curiously, in matters of taste and judgment, Justice was rarely ambivalent. He had strong preferences and delighted in making them known.

(4) That the poems most revealingly and nakedly emotional be based on translations, as if only in words that begin in the words of others can the concealment of emotion be abandoned. That consolation begins in disguise, that to be unmasked you must have masks to begin with. (The most personal and mortal of Justice's poems is "Variations on a Text by Vallejo.") If this tension is lodged within Eliot's notion of impersonality, the result haunts the poems, as it does *The Waste Land*, by seeming everywhere permeated by personality, with hardly a shred of the life in sight. You can read a lot of Justice without learning a thing about the consequences or conditions of his life and end by knowing that such facts would have taken you not deeper but further away.

(5) That many of Justice's later poems fix fondly on memories of childhood, but a childhood that seems to deny nostalgia its sentimental character, reminding us that "nostalgia" was first used of Swiss mercenaries who had fallen ill with the sometimes fatal condition known as homesickness. Justice's nearly stoic use of nostalgia finds no consolation, not because it is beyond consolation, but because it takes consolation in the mere partiality of the past. It is typical of his ambivalence, of his character of seeing as well as saying, that Justice could say, at a reading in his hometown of Miami, "I miss Miami when I'm away," and then, after a pause, "and I miss Miami when I'm here."

(6) That the poetry remain divided in its loyalties to free verse and form, as if within that division a higher loyalty was implied, a loyalty to what suited the subject, the tone, the instance of conception (because the reader should never discount whim)—loyal to form, then, but with the possibility of accepting, even worshiping, chance and contingency. Such a poet could not have undertaken a sequence of 150 sonnets or an epic poem, because his fundamental relation to his art was not obsessive. He knew when to let go. (The reader must be aware, to adapt a remark by Jarrell, that a poet who doesn't go too far may not go far enough.)

These loyalties divided even further, so that despite Justice's belief that one of the pleasures of form lay in obeying the rules, he did not hesitate to disrupt form when it suited him, or when what suited him suited the poem even better. The collusive refrains in his villanelles perhaps answer a need deep in this artistic psyche—yet what poet has written a villanelle truncated like "Women in Love" or jury-rigged and artfully demolished like "Variations for Two Pianos"? Justice loved the form well enough to spoil it when necessary—or for pure delight, or when he thought he could get away with it. Think of the, to my ear, metrically corrupt third line in "On the Porch."

One of the nuances of an artist is his devilishness. Consider "Mrs. Snow":

> Busts of the great composers glimmered in niches,
> Pale stars. Poor Mrs. Snow, who could forget her,
> Calling the time out in that hushed falsetto?
> (How early we begin to grasp what kitsch is!)
> But when she loomed above us like an alp,
> We little towns below could feel her shadow.
> Somehow her nods of approval seemed to matter
> More than the stray flakes drifting from her scalp.
> Her etchings of ruins, her mass-production Mings
> Were our first culture: she put us in awe of things.
> And once, with her help, I composed a waltz,
> Too innocent to be completely false,
> Perhaps, but full of marvelous clichés.
> She beamed and softened then.
>   Ah, those were the days.

Note the small craft, or craftiness, in the rare cross-rhymes between the octet's quatrains (*her / matter, falsetto / shadow*). The sestet is unusually a series of three couplets. That is very untraditional for so traditional a sonnet. The meter always hits the mark, but the rhyme scheme is delightfully awry, as the schemes of the Romantics sometimes were—think of Shelley's "Ozymandias." It might be too much to suggest that the contrivance is not unlike Mrs. Snow's plummy self-satisfaction. How ludicrous she is—and yet the rhyme is not what makes her so. At the least, such deviations and violations (almost brazenly concealed by the slant rhymes) call attention in their cautious bravura to the poet's controlling ambition, to make the form his own even in the sacrifice of form.

There are smaller matters that show the poet's delight in deviance. Justice avoids the self-conscious, rather Hudibrastic or Byronic feminine rhyme, except when there is something unusual to be gained. (In other words, it is not a sin committed merely for the hell of it.) The rhyme *niches / kitsch is* remains part of that mild and almost apologetic condescension of which his memory is composed. The poet knows the risk he takes employing feminine rhymes, but that seems just to make him bolder. There are other examples of farce withheld from such rhymes in "American Scenes (1904–1905)": "The wild frankness and sadness of surrender— / As if our cities ever could be tender!" ("Cambridge in Winter") and "Out of this little hell of spurts and hisses, / . . . Of open gates, of all but bland abysses" ("Railway Junction South of Richmond, Past Midnight"). In both cases, the rhymes refuse to take advantage of the dormant comedy of manners, partly by language that refuses the easy smile, partly by a tone so wry yet full of longing it passes for regret.

There's a related device, used by the artist with an instinct for small but telling import, in the second stanza of "Mrs. Snow":

> But when she loomed above us like an alp,
> We little towns below could feel her shadow.
> Somehow her nods of approval seemed to matter
> More than the stray flakes drifting from her scalp.

That bathos of the envelope rhyme, the art of sinking from the alp to the dandruff on her scalp (treated like Snow's snow), places Mrs. Snow at the minor end of the scale of things. She can no longer be Stevens's "Alp at the end of the street," the summit of ambition for the little piano students—yet, though displaying the self-knowledge that raised this one student beyond his teacher's limitations, the poem does not lack fondness. Indeed, the care with which the portrait is managed displays his debt. It would go too far to say that the rhyme, for a poet who cannot forgo such minor tours de force, is tainted with private sorrow (the portrait is devastating, though), yet in its rare address it cannot go unnoticed. To ignore it entirely would not go far enough. The lines introduce the nostalgia while undermining it.

(7) Last, to bring this list of ambivalence ambivalently to an end, that a poetry of ambivalence secure its very nature, perhaps even triumph over it, by admitting that every poem might be other, if only it could be written once more.

So Justice sometimes wrote a poem once more. A poet of this character is by nature dissatisfied, and by nature a reviser, leaving as evidence the slight, shy reworkings of some poems (at times restored or revised afresh when they next appear); the sudden and revealing change of face (like the removal of the *en face* notes in "Childhood"); and, at the extreme of ambivalence, offering in *New and Selected Poems* two versions of "Incident in a Rose Garden," or, in *The Sunset Maker,* two poems about Mrs. Snow, some images and a couple of lines shared between them, with a memoir as well. In such acts of mutilation and regard the resolution is confessed on the page—the resolution that begins in irresolution, as if to admit that the form of a poem is forever contingent, forever vulnerable, that we must take the poem as found, while realizing that it has come to being through processes vague, marbled with contradiction, by nature occluded and occult.

Justice's contribution, to his students as well as to his poetry, was not a style or even a method easily imitated. His influence lay in the very character—the balance and moderation and ambivalence—of his stance. If such tensions operate at all it is not to create an unalterable stasis, but to leave language coiled in its potential, fraught with the murderous mildness of its *mots justes,* a mildness that by hiding nothing seems to hide all. Think of Greek palimpsests, think of Poe's purloined letter. The lesson to other poets lies embedded in the artist's practice—not in his rush to judgment but in the slow crawl of judgment deliberated and even regretted, not through the rules of Solon but in rulings by Solomon, contingent and humane in their cunning. The lesson is, if this be aesthetics, make the most of it.

S Is for Something

Mark Strand and Artistic Identity

MARY JO SALTER

Those of us who got to spend time with the poet Mark Strand, summer after summer, at the Sewanee Writers' Conference, will recognize the tongue-in-cheek tone of the following remark: "It is sometimes—but not always—nice to think that people may be talking about you when you are not present, that you are the subject of a conversation you have not steered in your direction and whose evolution depends on your absence. This is what happens to the famous. And to the dead. They can be the life of the party and never show up."

Mark Strand was one of the least explicitly autobiographical poets of our time—he hardly ever revealed the literal, factual details of his life beyond the unsurprising backstory that he had some parents, a sister, some wives, and some children—but he was nonetheless always writing about his own sensibility, which accommodated knowledge of himself as the life of the party. On the other hand, he was obsessed with the idea of *not* showing up—with being one whose absence was noted, or who turned absence on its head. "In a field / I am the absence of field," he wrote in an early, over-anthologized poem, "Keeping Things Whole," which every newspaper reliably quoted when, to the sorrow of us all, he died in 2014.

Some of us were lucky enough to be at Sewanee in 2012, when Strand delivered something just for us—his craft lecture wittily called "On Nothing." In it he made a distinction between *nothing* and *nothingness*—the latter being something a little too big to count as nothing. Nothingness, in other words, was a concept, *a thing about* nothing rather than actually nothing. He wrote me a few times as he was composing this talk, and boasted amusingly about how short it was.

"Dear Mary Jo," one email went, "I wrote my talk and it is fairly peculiar. I had hoped for greater peculiarity, but I kept getting bogged down. Anyway, I can now forget about it until I give it." Forgetfulness was also big with Strand. He wrote a wonderful poem in the 1990s, called "Always," in which some people—"the great forgetters"—sit around a table forgetting things one by one: North and South America, the moon, the grass, the trees. Finally they forget down to absolutely nothing: a condition which occasioned, in the poem's concluding line, "the blaze of promise everywhere." Surely Mark Strand knew he would be one of the remembered poets of our age, that the "nothings" wouldn't include him. Why? One reason is that he was so entertaining on the subject of nothing.

If you read only one book of Mark Strand's beyond his *Collected Poems,* which came out in 2014, just in time for him to attend a publication party—and to be the life of it—before he died, please pick up his little volume of essays, *The Weather of Words.* It begins with a minor masterpiece, "A Poet's Alphabet," which gives an ABC of the concepts essential to his own poetics. Quite characteristically, Strand's "A" is for "absence," "O" is for "oblivion," and "X" is for "crossing out." Somewhat contrarily, "S" is for "something"—but wait. "Something" can mean "just about anything"—as in the remark, "I want to eat something." Strand seems to mean it more in the sense of "the *one* thing," the very opposite of "just about anything." His entry for S begins like this: "S is for something that supplies a vacancy, which I might fill. It has a verbal presence that my own immediate appetite or ambition subverts, misreads, or makes into an appealing void, a space only I can elaborate on." We'll return to that idea shortly—"an appealing void, a space only I can elaborate on." But let's go on to "T." "T" is for "Tedium"! Vintage Mark Strand—he wouldn't want to seem *too* invested in poetry, this art to which he devoted his life. And "W": "W is for what might have been or what I might have written. Can I be influenced by what I might have done but didn't?" He does a brilliant spinoff on this for several sentences, and then adds: "W is for Wordsworth, who wrote what I didn't and couldn't and wouldn't."

Strand does mention in his "Poet's Alphabet" a number of poets who influenced him: "K" is for "Kafka," "N" is for "Neruda"—and for "nothing"; "R" is for "Rilke," "S" is for "something"—and for "Stevens"; "V" is for "Virgil." But before we have any of these, we have the letter D. "D is for Dante," Mark writes, "who has not influenced me, which is too bad." That too was vintage Mark Strand. Whether as his reader or as his listener while he read aloud, one was delighted simply to be in the presence of *his* sense of humor, nobody else's—to see Strand creating, as he wrote elsewhere, "a space only I can elaborate on." The confluence of self-criticism and self-assertion in his lack of indebtedness to Dante, a nothing that gets listed as a something, in breezy, everyday language—what could be better? He could have written, "D is for Dante, who has not influenced me, which is my great failing." But no. As Strand and only Strand would put it, not having Dante in your head is simply "too bad."

But back to Wordsworth. Of the many clever essays in Strand's *The Weather of Words*, the brainiest is the one near the end, called "Landscape and the Poetry of Self." I, for one, am no writer of landscapes, and am sometimes bored by even the most beautiful poems, travelogues, and fiction that feature them. Furthermore, Mark's essay is mostly about Wordsworth, a poet who almost always bores me. But for the first time I began to see how similar in sensibility Strand is to Wordsworth, and this not only made me like Wordsworth better, it made me think much harder about what it is for me—for any of us—to be an artist.

I hope to get at some of the ways any artist might think about the ABC of what art is, and what signature contribution to art each of us alone is equipped to make. That is: we know we're somebody, walking around in the world; but how do we identify for ourselves and manifest artistically the "something" in ourselves, and ourselves alone, that is worth exploring, revising, rethinking? How can our art convey "something" without being confined, limited, to that something? Most of my thoughts here will be about literature, and poetry in particular. But I'll take some detours into visual art, partly because Mark Strand was a fine artist and art critic himself, and partly because a consideration of visual art might help us approach what we writers too experience, and hope to convey, beyond words.

In "Landscape and the Poetry of Self," Strand makes a distinction between what he calls "the subjective-visionary mode of Wordsworth and the confessional mode of Lowell and Berryman." Wordsworth probably wouldn't mind being called subjective or visionary. Lowell and Berryman never embraced the term "confessional," but such names for schools of poetry tend to stick. So let's use "confessional," since Strand does: "In most so-called confessional poetry, there is no governing vision of submergence or transcendence as there is in Wordsworth. Submergence occurs when the poet uses darkness as a medium and communicates with his own unconscious. It is through such process that the poet makes the universe internal until it takes on its form. Transcendence is the process by which the poet puts himself into the universe until he becomes identified, finally, with the divine light. Light is its medium."

Submergence and transcendence (in the first case, the dark descent into one's own unacknowledged experience, and in the second case, the illuminated ascent to what's outside one's own experience): these are Mark Strand's subjects. No wonder he loves Wordsworth. Strand goes on: "No matter how self-centered the confessional poet is, he is tirelessly sociable. If he does not live in the city proper, then he lives in a place where he seems surrounded by people. For it is social life that provides him with self-authenticating action. Unlike Wordsworth, the confessional poet can't bear to be alone. . . . In landscape it is important to possess nothing. One does not travel in a landscape with belongings. . . . His spirituality depends on his unencumbered spontaneity and his purity as a wanderer."

How interesting that Strand associates confessionalism with urbanization. By the time we come to Lowell and Berryman, the Industrial Revolution and urbanization are old news and have been internalized in the psyche of our culture. The confessional poet can't really be alone, and thus he "self-authenticates," in Strand's terms, by means of reporting and interpreting particular interactions with other people. As Strand writes about the confessional poet: "Nature is not part of his world. Perhaps because it seems too unified to reflect his internal disorder, perhaps because he has been so deeply urbanized, he can no longer imagine himself in its presence. Whatever the case, Nature teaches him nothing." You may object to this assertion. After all, most of us have read plenty of contemporary poets who versify their long walks in the countryside, name the wildflowers along the way, and use this familiarity with nature as an occasion to rise, if a bit predictably, above highly specified personal problems. But I can't be alone in catching a hint of inauthenticity in poems of this type. When poets of the twenty-first century, who spend their lives in the normal twenty-first-century way—in the classroom, on the subway, at the grocery store, and playing with their iPhones—give the impression that they spend a lot of time with nature, and owe everything they know to nature, we don't necessarily buy it.

And yet. There is a certain kind of modern poet—and Mark Strand is one—who manages to make us feel that although his poem originates in the twentieth or twenty-first century, with all of its recognizable urban underpinnings, it nonetheless reaches toward the eternal and the sublime. As Strand says with offhand accuracy, "One does not travel in a landscape with belongings." Yes, you might pack a canteen of water in your backpack, but the whole point of your (or Wordsworth's) hike in the French Alps is that your personal baggage, literal and figurative, doesn't matter as much as your "purity as a wanderer." Then again: in a landscape, having packed nothing, you can only be only and wholly *yourself.* As Strand writes, "The celebrated 'I' [in Wordsworth] . . . does not have to arm itself with a voice tailored to the event. It *is* the event. It is what it says, and as it speaks so it is born."

When I read this, I felt instinctively that it is true: that ideally, the poet's voice should be the event of the poem, and come into existence for the particular poem in question. Yet how should such an argument save us, and the poem, from the danger of narcissism, preciousness, or worse?

A few other Strand essays may provide some further reflections, if not answers. In his essay "On Becoming a Poet," he writes, "Of all literary genres, the lyric is the least changeable. Its themes are rooted in the continuity of human subjectivity and from antiquity have assumed a connection between privacy and universality." That is, human subjectivity accounts not merely for my narcissism or yours. It accounts for what we know we share with all humans since "antiquity"—by which Strand means, in this context, Western antiquity; he doesn't say, but obviously knows, that other terms might be more appropriate outside Western culture. We know, in what Strand calls our privacy, that what we are looking at is our universality. We may be very small, but if we don't act *from,* act *out of,* our unique and acknowledged limitations, we can't aspire to representing in artistic terms what is universal. Our common tools and techniques—a poet's wholly necessary practice in the conventions of meter or rhetoric, for example—lead not to yet more conventionality but ideally to idiosyncrasy. This isn't Strand's point, perhaps, but it's my takeaway in reading Strand: your ineffable idiosyncrasy, that unnamable something that makes your poem yours, is what your readers—if you're lucky enough to have them—universally long for. In another essay, "Notes on the Craft of Poetry," Strand defines craft itself in individualistic terms: "To a large extent, these transactions I have chosen to call craft are the sole property of the poet and cannot be transferred to or adopted by others. One reason for this is that they are unknown at the time of writing and are discovered afterward, if at all."

This seems the right moment to shift gears a bit and consider Strand's insights as a critic of visual art. I'm going to do this from a highly personal, if not quite confessional, perspective. Just under two years before he died, Mark asked me if I would serve as his literary executor. I knew he was sick, but he seemed mostly OK, and although I consented, I didn't want to ask a lot of questions. He seemed convinced nobody would want to collect his letters or write his biography. "Shouldn't be much work," he told me.

And so far it hasn't been. My first act as his executor was to read a handwritten draft of an essay, in what I believe was his last notebook, and transcribe it for publication. It was a review commissioned by the *New York Review of Books* of a 2013 exhibit of Edward Hopper's work. Mark had abandoned the essay when he got sick. He had published in the 1990s a little book about Hopper, one of his favorite artists. As I opened the 2013 notebook for the first time, in the spring of 2015, I wondered if Mark could have substantially more to say about an artist he had already understood so well.

My first instinct in confronting the notebook, bought in Madrid, where he lived near the end of his life with his partner, was to note its physical characteristics. It was a cheap spiral notebook with an orange cardboard cover, and it contained lined A4 paper—that is, pages slightly narrower and longer than our 8½" by 11" standard American paper. Mark's essay was written in pencil in a remarkably clear, somewhat large cursive. Even his insertions, crammed into margins and directed here and there by arrows, were highly legible. That this notebook was a *something*, a tangible object serving as the realized site of Mark's imaginings, moved me. I noted that, in just a few places, he hadn't chosen between two versions of a sentence, or between two places he might put one sentence; making these choices myself and adding a few commas were the extent of my editorial tampering. Nor did I want to do more. I was struck by how fluently Mark wrote prose on the very first try.

I remembered, too, a comment he had made in a *Paris Review* interview in the late 1990s—that he always wrote in longhand first. This writer, born in 1934, belonged to the last generation that might reliably prefer to write whole essays in longhand. In that interview he explained, "When I read a poem in longhand, I'm hearing it. When I read it in typescript, I'm *reading* it. A poem can appear finished just because of the cleanness of the typescript, and I don't want it to seem finished before it is. A poem has already been brought into the world to some extent when it's typed. I feel more like an editor than a poet after that." Looking at Mark's notebook, it occurred to me that his writing by hand was not merely an aid in hearing his own words. As with his collage-making, writing by hand was a process whereby the mind understood itself only by means of the body. In a sense, Mark was *drawing* his ideas about Hopper's process of drawing and painting. And he was drawing in a way only Mark Strand could draw.

Here's how the final essay of Mark Strand's life begins.

> Paints and scrapes, paints and scrapes to get something right, the something that is not there at the outset but reveals itself slowly, and then completely, having traveled an arduous route during which vision and image come together, for a while, until dissatisfaction sets in, and the painting and scraping begin again. But what is it that determines the success of the final work? The coincidence of vision—his idea, vague at first, of what the painting might be—and the brute fact of the subject, its plain obdurate existence, just "out there" with an absolutely insular existence.

Look at that first sentence—a fragment—again. "Paints and scrapes, paints and scrapes"—the artist at work is not merely putting paint on a canvas but scraping it off. Mark Strand studied painting under Josef Albers at Yale in the 1950s, and although he was grateful for the experience, he said it taught him he wasn't much of a painter. Strand's best work as a visual artist would emerge in the medium of collage. Nonetheless, he is to be trusted here, characteristically perceiving the act of painting as the creation of absence as well as presence. As he writes, "vision and image come together, for a while," but then "dissatisfaction sets in." I think we recognize here the poetry critic who told us that "A" is for "absence," "O" is for "oblivion," and "X" is for "crossing out." And what needs to be crossed out? Those artistic gestures in which the distance between the artist's imagination, his vision of what the painting ought to look like, differs somehow from the image on the canvas. Even the most accomplished craftsman, we have to assume, even Rembrandt or Shakespeare, feels this difference between vision and realization. There is something the painting ought to be, and although it doesn't yet exist, it nonetheless has a relation to the "brute obdurate existence" of the subject, a *something* in the world.

This is not too different a point from what Mark wrote about Wordsworth. Let me repeat it: "The celebrated 'I' [in Wordsworth] . . . does not have to arm itself with a voice tailored to the event. It *is* the event. It is what it says, and as it speaks so it is born." Clearly, Edward Hopper served Mark with a way to write from his own poetic aesthetic, whereby artistic success involves "the coincidence" or, ideally, the identity, of something within the self—something like the painter's unique vision; the poet's unique voice—with what he perceives to be "out there."

By the time I was typing out Mark's second handwritten paragraph into my laptop, I recognized I was having a bodily experience of art-making too. "T" is for "tedium," "T" is for "typing"!—but there's no question that typing an entire draft of what you already have in longhand helps you to take responsibility for the shapes of your sentences and your ideas. You begin to own what you write. As I typed from Mark's notebook, I began to have the illusion I had written Mark's sentences myself. My goodness, how I had improved! How intelligent I was as I composed the second paragraph:

> Until Hopper sees something about it as a possible subject for a painting, and this image with its possibilities lodges itself in Hopper's imagination and the formation of the painting's content begins—content being, of course, what the artist brings to his subject, that quality which makes it unmistakably his, so when we look at the painting of a building or an office or a gas station, we say it's a Hopper. We don't say it's a gas station. By the time the gas station appears on canvas in its final form, it has ceased being just a gas station. It has become Hopperized. It possesses something it never had before Hopper saw it as a possible subject for his painting.

The essay goes on insightfully for what turns out to be eight typed pages, but this second paragraph struck me from first reading as the most memorable aperçu, the key to everything else. If the *subject* is what is out there in the world, the *content*, Mark writes, is brought to the table by the artist and by the artist alone. To repeat that passage from his essay on the craft of poetry: "To a large extent, these transactions I have chosen to call craft are the *sole property of the poet* and cannot be transferred to or adopted by others. One reason for this is that they are unknown at the time of writing and are discovered afterward, if at all. . . ." Paints and scrapes, writes and erases. What the painter and poet do is discover, by sketching their subject again and again and again, the unknown content. Mark participated in that process, too, by writing about Hopper again and again, trying to pinpoint the family resemblances among the paintings that so haunted him. As Strand points out, we see a painting of a gas station by Hopper and we don't say it's a gas station. We say it's a Hopper. We recognize, without words (although we might resort to vague words), the soul of a Hopper. Strand calls this essence "the quality which is unmistakably his." This surely is the artist's property alone, and yet what saves the great painting from solipsism or tedium is that we recognize, as Mark writes about the lyric poem, the universality in the privacy.

How might these ideas intersect with Mark's distinction between the "visionary-subjective" mode of Wordsworth, which occurs mostly when the poet is alone but surrounded by nature, and the "confessional" mode of Lowell or Berryman, which occurs mostly in an urban, socialized setting? Hopper, to complicate things, is very often an urban painter. He gives us fields on Cape Cod, but also pharmacies and all-night bars and gas stations and bridges and trains. And yet he nearly always gives us aloneness—either the complete absence of humans, or one person alone in a room, or two or more people in a hotel room or on a train who are clearly not communicating. To live in an urban age is to be alone a little less voluntarily than Wordsworth; to look at a Hopper is often to be participating in a portrait of aloneness. Note that I don't use the word "loneliness." As Strand writes in his essay on Hopper, we tend to react to these mysterious paintings by sentimentalizing them: ". . . We lapse lazily into triteness when trying to explain their particular power. Again and again, words like loneliness or alienation are used to describe the emotional character of his paintings."

Having come this far, Strand takes an unusual turn—all the more effective to his fans because we know him to be definitely *not* a confessional writer. Partly, I think, because he knew he was ill, that his own future was shrinking, he dared suddenly to cast himself back into boyhood and share with us a simple anecdote—and interestingly, his confessional moment is entirely urban:

> My own encounters with this elusive element in Hopper's work began when I would commute from Croton-on-Hudson to New York each Saturday to take a children's art class in one of those buildings on the south side of Washington Square that were eventually torn down to make room for NYU's law school. This was in 1947. The same year that Hopper painted "Approaching the City," I would look out from the train window onto the rows of tenements whose windows I could look into and try to imagine what living in one of those apartments would be like.

> And then at 99th Street we would enter the tunnel that would take us to Grand Central. It was thrilling to suddenly go underground, travel in the dark and be delivered to the masses of people milling about in the cavernous terminal. Years later, when I saw "Approaching the City" for the first time, I instantly recalled those trips into Manhattan and have ever since. And Hopper, for me, has always been associated with New York, a New York glimpsed in passing, sweetened with nostalgia, a city lodged in memory.

It takes Strand only a moment to recover his deliberately alienated critical bearings, to make sure that we know he knows that Hopper himself isn't sweetening New York with nostalgia: "Subsequently, my feelings about Hopper have grown more complicated, their strangeness has increased, their curious unerotic character despite the prevalence of naked or near naked women in bedrooms, their inwardness. . . ."

Strand was by no means abandoning his "take" on Hopper's human figures as strange, and in fact as not quite human. He was just confirming briefly that he, Mark Strand, was human.

In that little 1994 book called *Hopper,* Strand comments about a painting called "People in the Sun" in which several figures, male and female, are lined up on chairs, heads tilted back. "But," Strand asks, "are they there to get sun? If they are, why are they dressed for work, or as if they were in a doctor's waiting room?" He wonders why these people in business dress are seated facing a field and some hills, and notes that the hills seem to be looking back. The quasi-surrealism of this moment certainly has its own logic: it accords with the strangeness and aloneness of urban life, and of art too. Strand writes of this painting, "Nature and civilization almost seem to be staring each other down. So odd is this painting that I sometimes think the painted figures are looking at a painting of a landscape, and not a real one, which of course they are." Similarly, looking at the Hopper painting "Automat," Strand writes of the woman pictured that "she cannot possibly be happy. But of course she does not think, she is the product of another will, an illusion, an invention of Hopper's."

If Strand's position here is helpful to you, as it is to me, then to some extent your Hopper is an invention of Strand's. The critic too manipulates the world out there until it is closer to his vision. In Strand's vision, the artist or the writer looks out to the world, to the "plain obdurate existence" of subjects out there in the world, to find a way to make it coincide with his imagination. And yet, once the art object—the painting or the poem—has been made from the subject, that object is entirely self-enclosed. It is about itself, and thus at least partly about art. In more conventional seascapes, where people in bathing suits are seen doing something normal like making sand castles, we tend to forget that they too live only in paint, or in words. Some artists make a greater claim on behalf of artifice than others; some of them view artifice as supreme. Hopper and Strand, as well as Strand's acknowledged lifelong master, Wallace Stevens, are numbered among that group.

If we look at a gas station and call it a Hopper—if it has become, in Mark Strand's term, "Hopperized"—what is it, I wonder, for a subject to be marked by the signature of a Mark Strand poem or essay? I can't help myself: I'm going to say that it is "Stranded."

What I just did was to make a play on words—something I do all the time, and Mark Strand did relatively infrequently. His poems do strand us, leave us hanging, and they do that partly by surrounding his entirely familiar, simple words—lake, cloud, moon, stone, snow—with (somehow) magical auras. Strand doesn't usually rhyme his words, nor does he play much on their etymologies. His best poems remind me not only of Hopper but often of Hitchcock, who strived for what he called "pure cinema." In *Suspicion,* Hitchcock showed shifty-looking Cary Grant bringing a luminous glass of milk upstairs to the bedroom of reluctant Joan Fontaine. Film aficionados tell us that Hitchcock actually put a lightbulb in the glass to make the milk glow. It's a simple column of white, a simple color so luminous it seems radioactive. Glass. Milk. White. In the *Paris Review* interview with Wallace Shawn, Mark said, ". . . I favor the immediacy of plain Anglo-Saxon words: monosyllables, you know, two-syllable words. My preference has always been for simple, declarative sentences, simple words. Of course, my poems have become much more elaborate."

The critic Willard Spiegelman wrote a superb review of Strand's *Collected Poems* which I wish Mark had lived to see. Spiegelman states baldly and rightly in his first paragraph that Strand's "poems have always had a generic quality." Strand knew, the argument goes, what he was doing: he was becoming, to the extent that any poet can be, translatable. Spiegelman points to an even earlier *Paris Review* interview of the 1970s where Strand said he was writing in "a new international style that has a lot to do with plainness of diction, a certain reliance on surrealistic techniques, and a strong narrative element." And Spiegelman says, too, what I wish I'd said first, that the generic landscapes and diction of Strand's poems are as abstract as his collages. Strand remarked with amusement more than once that his poems were more popular in Italy and Spain than in the United States. Even if that was an exaggeration, it is certainly true that you don't have to be schooled in English poetry to be moved by a poem translated into your own language about the cold, the snow, the wind, the clouds, the lake—as long as they've been revisited in a fresh, even a strange, context.

Maybe at this moment, a little more context is necessary. It will seem a detour, but as all artists know, no detour is really a detour. I had been thinking about Mark Strand in the spring of 2015, when suddenly a book I had been awaiting for years, Langdon Hammer's biography of the late James Merrill, was published. I had a mound of student portfolios to grade, and I postponed reading them all for a few days so that I could inhale this marvelous eight-hundred-page biography. I was interested for personal reasons, though not merely personal reasons: I had known James Merrill pretty well, or as well as I could, being who I was in the 1980s and early 1990s—a young writer dazzled by a brilliant, prolific poet who was almost to the day the age of my father, and who came from what seemed to me a very glamorous, elite world. He had been friendly and supportive to me, but his greatest gift then and now was in writing a model of the sort of poetry—packed with daily experiences but intellectually challenging, culturally engaged, rhymed ingeniously but with seeming ease, metrically turned on a dime, really funny but also moving—that I aspired to write. Probably his greatest shorter poem, and even his short poems tended to be on the long side, was called "Lost in Translation."

This famous poem is definitely not in the Wordsworth "subjective-visionary" camp. It's much closer to Lowell and Berryman: a confessional, urban poem with lots of people in it, a memoir in verse of being a lonely but extremely rich American boy, brought up in New York City by a nanny, Mademoiselle, who is apparently both French and German, and with whom the boy James is putting together a puzzle on a card table in—where else?—the library. In no time we see that the poem itself is a puzzle not ever to be solved, a rumination about what children glean of adult life, marriage, politics, and war. And the poem is also about the mature poet, who (in one of its subplots) is trying to translate a poem by Rilke.

There are so many layers to this poem that I'll direct you to it and to Langdon

Hammer's excellent analysis on your own time. For now, let me just say that in reading Hammer's biography of Merrill, coincidentally during the same period I was thinking about Mark Strand's poetics, the subject "out there" of the lecture I'd envisioned began to change. It had been—can I say this? Hammered?—No, I think I mean Saltered. Suddenly I had recognized, to borrow Mark Strand's phrasing, "a something, a void only I can elaborate." I hope it doesn't sound grandiose to say this. I only mean to illustrate that this is what we do when we make things. We have some sort of mental outline for what we think we want to express, and then some seemingly random subject "out there" claims us, and we adjust accordingly, shaping the subject to our internal content, content which we often didn't even consciously know was ours.

Once Merrill and Strand became roommates in my head, I began to see them as mirror images of what poetry can be. I mean a sort of Column A and Column B, within which each of us poets might live our unique poetics. (I should mention that Willard Spiegelman also used the mirror image to place Strand against Merrill—but in a different way.) One of these two writers, Column A, Strand, was composing poetry that actually could be translated reasonably well: simple words, simple sentences, simple and—this was his saving grace—idiosyncratic strangeness. The other poet, Merrill, Column B, was not only the author of the great poem "Lost in Translation," but he was, in most of his poems, almost completely untranslatable. He wrote rational, complete sentences, but they are complex. There's simply so much going on that the translator can have no choice but to water down the fun of reading it. There are brief passages in Merrill in which he's punning and rhyming across three languages at once. What really makes Merrill stand apart is his wizardry in sound and diction, achieved with a far wider vocabulary than Mark Strand chose to employ. Strand expressed his great refinement far more implicitly, far less theatrically, than Merrill.

Another way to put it is that, although all poets are word-obsessed, they might be said to go at words from two possible directions. Some of them begin with a strange feeling and attempt to get at it somehow with the most suitable words they can find. Mark Strand would be listed under this heading, Column A. Other poets (Column B) seem to begin with words and work with them almost as magical totems to help them arrive at whatever this strange feeling is.

Strand's 2006 lyric "Moon," about the celestial being most often scrutinized in his work, is a Column A sort of poem:

Open the book of evening to the page
where the moon, always the moon, appears

between two clouds, moving so slowly that hours
will seem to have passed before you reach the next page

where the moon, now brighter, lowers a path
to lead you away from what you have known

into those places where what you had wished for happens,
its long syllable like a sentence poised

at the edge of sense, waiting for you to say its name
once more as you lift your eyes from the page

and close the book, still feeling what it was like
to dwell in that light, that sudden paradise of sound.

Strand is practically versifying his theory of poetry here. The long sentence of "what you had wished for"—a deliberately vague phrase—is "poised at the edge of sense." It need not be entirely sensible, and in fact would lose its poetic magnetism if it were. But it "wants you to say its name"—that is, the poet has the feeling first, and the word second. And the search for that word leads to what Mark in his essay on poetry and landscape called "transcendence," which he associates with light.

If Strand is the quintessential Column A poet, what about Column B, the poets who start with words? In English poetry, the best seventeenth-century example would be George Herbert, who looked for signs within clusters of letters to see what God wanted him to write. He would spell out the word W-H-O-L-L-Y, for instance, and rhyme it with H-O-L-Y, and thereby arrive at some sort of link, in his mind and yours, between integrity and grace. In the nineteenth century, the best example of a "words first" poet would be Emily Dickinson. For her too, words are things, utterly concrete things. They're made of letters, which are at least as concrete as the bird singing outside her window. She rhymes words and off-rhymes them, she makes anagrams and near-anagrams out of them—"Giant," for instance, a word just one letter larger than "gnat"—and then, as if in a flash of lightning, meaning emerges.

In the twentieth century, the best example I know of a "words first" poet would be James Merrill. After all, he wrote a three-volume epic, *The Changing Light at Sandover,* based on the messages he received from the other world via the Ouija board's A through Z. You couldn't be more beholden to the alphabet than that. Sitting uncomfortably in church one day with his mother, the middle-aged Merrill scribbled the following heretical thought: "the great event was not when Word became flesh but when the reverse happened—when man emerging from animal life began to use the alphabet." And as Langdon Hammer writes about Merrill's wordplay: "the pun says it is language that uses us to speak, and not the other way around." I'd agree, and I'd make that statement even narrower: for such poets, it is *letters* that use us to speak, and not the other way around. Like Emily Dickinson, Merrill was brilliant at anagrams. He and his friends engaged in anagram games just for fun: throwaway genius never to be used in poems. Since we find ourselves in Tennessee, I'll share with you Merrill's anagram for Nashville: "Ill-shaven." Proust? "Stupor." And Neruda? "Unread."

And what do you know?—my detour has taken me full circle back to Mark Strand. The Strand essay I opened with, "A Poet's Alphabet," represents the closest this writer ever got to being a "words first" poet. He does use, as Merrill or Dickinson or Herbert would, the accident of our common alphabet to help him think through what matters to him most about poetry. Like Merrill, he is not just witty but downright funny in the way he does it. Strand's wit, though, resides in saying "N" is for "Neruda," which leads him to add that "N" is for "nothing." Both of these words that start with "N" are concepts—the concept of Neruda, the concept of nothing; not wordplay per se. Merrill's wit, on the other hand, makes wordplay essential, and his letters lead to a concept, to saying that "Neruda" = "unread."

I've lingered on this contrast between Strand and Merrill partly because reading them at the same time was an accident of my spring and summer of 2015. And accident, whatever is happening "out there," intersected with a particular writer's sensibility—mine, which was not thinking *about* itself but helplessly acted *like* itself anyway. Reading in Strand and Merrill, I recognized not merely that I came closer in my own poems to the confessional poets, like Lowell and Berryman, or the words-first ones, like Merrill, than I did to the visionary, concept-first ones like Strand. That was something I knew already. What was more interesting—for me, anyway—was that, by integrating them in my head for this essay, I widened my perspective, but I also became more myself. I became the person who would write the next poem or the next essay; I became more capable of sensing a void only I could elaborate on. I also realized that I would never have thought in these terms—of "a void," or the contrast between a "something" and a "nothing"—unless I had read Mark Strand. He was indispensable in how I became my most recent version of myself.

And finally, finally, I found myself ready to hazard a word of advice to writers: Don't think too much about what it is to be yourself. You can't help having your own sensibility, whatever it is. You're Column A, or Column B, or whatever Column Q stands for, and you will almost certainly shift positions somewhat over time. And certainly, you want at least one editor to like you, and you want to have readers. But please, please, don't waste precious time worrying about what other people might think you are. Even if you are a darling of Poetryland, blessed with great reviews, nobody cares how you "arm yourself" with a persona to sell; you still have to write a good poem "tailored to the event," as Mark Strand proposes. If you write that good poem, it will stand on its own, a closed system. And you will go on being yourself, which is to say, alone. Each of us is as alone as one of those figures in Edward Hopper's paintings. We are also as alone as Edward Hopper, painting and scraping, creating absence and presence. We're alone as Mark Strand, opening an orange spiral notebook in Madrid and writing his final essay, in pencil, about Edward Hopper, not sure anybody will ever read it.

In that 1998 *Paris Review* interview, Wallace Shawn said he needed to ask Strand

> One more personal question. Well, I don't have to, but I will, because I'm curious: do you care whether you're read after you're dead?
>
> *Strand:* Well, not to be funny about this, but I'm sort of split on the issue. I mean, I would like to be read after I'm dead, but that's projection.
>
> *Shawn:* You mean, because you're imagining . . . ?
>
> *Strand:* I mean, I'd really like to be *alive* after I'm dead.

That answer was a "something" that could only stand for Strand.

The Train Stops Here

The Optimism of Revision

MARGOT LIVESEY

A number of years ago I was teaching at Carnegie Mellon University when a graduate student asked if she could study me writing fiction; she was doing a PhD in rhetoric. Cautiously I asked what that would involve. Leah said she wanted to sit behind me, in my small office, for two hours each morning for a week and transcribe every mark I made on the screen. I was trying to write a new novel and, out of curiosity and affection, I agreed to this intimidating plan. Needless to say, Leah's presence changed my writing habits. I didn't fidget, or go in search of coffee, or check whether the water fountain was still working. During our two hours together each morning I did what Leah wanted: I typed. The following week I was still basking in my recovered solitude when she handed me a transcript of what I had written in her presence.

The week of her observation had been moderately productive. I had six new pages of my novel in progress. But the transcript Leah handed me was several times that length. Over and over I read sequences like this:

> The tabby cat sat on the mat.
> The tabby cat lolled on the mat.
> The mat that filled the doorway was currently occupied by a tabby cat.
> The cat, some kind of tabby, occupied the worn doormat with ease.
> The cat . . .
> The last entry read: The tabby cat sat on the mat.

Reading these pages, which I had in a certain sense written, was revelatory. I understood how often I fiddled around with a sentence, making it slightly better, then slightly worse, then slightly better again, before, more often than not, returning to the adequate first version. What I needed to do, I realized, was not make the sentence about the cat into a thing of beauty but to write the next sentence, and the next, until I found out where the story was going and what the cat's role in it was. The computer was pandering to my desire to edit prematurely in a way that I would never have done when writing longhand. "Edit," according to my *Oxford English Dictionary,* comes from the French verb meaning "to publish," and we use it, optimistically, to mean "make publishable." But to edit usefully, I would argue, one needs a complete text, or at least a good part of one—an act of a play, a section of a novel. I was trying to sail a half-built boat; no wonder I tacked so often and ran aground.

There are writers—the British novelist Tessa Hadley is one of them—who produce three or four hundred words a day, moving steadily forward, and end up with a manuscript that requires almost no revision, but my informal research suggests that most writers need to work through the three stages of writing—writing, revising, editing—to get their work to the highest level. I would also add that, while early editing can deepen our understanding of a text, it can make it harder to do the necessary work of compressing and cutting, not only because we're loathe to recycle our labor—kill our darlings—but also because the beautiful sentences act as a scrim, obscuring what we need to see.

Making art is fundamentally inefficient. In one of his prefaces the novelist Joseph Conrad suggests why this is so.

> (The artist's) appeal is made to our less obvious capacities: to the part of our nature which, because of the warlike conditions of existence, is necessarily kept out of sight (within the more resisting and hard qualities)—like the vulnerable body within the steel armour. His appeal is less loud, more profound, less distinct, more stirring—and sooner forgotten. Yet it endures forever. . . . He speaks to our capacity for delight and wonder, to the sense of mystery surrounding our lives; to our sense of pity, and beauty, and pain: to the latent feeling of fellowship with all creation—and to the subtle but invincible, conviction of solidarity that knits together the loneliness of innumerable hearts: (to the solidarity

> in dreams, in joy, in sorrow, in aspiration, in illusions, in hope, in fear, which binds men to each other, which binds together all humanity—) the dead to the living and the living to the unborn.

More recently James Baldwin in an interview remarked, "When you're writing, you're trying to find out something which you don't know. The whole language of writing for me is finding out what you don't want to know, what you don't want to find out. But something forces you to anyway." The writer, the artist, is working out of hidden parts of the self, parts that must be protected from the warlike conditions of existence. We approach that self tentatively, often reluctantly. We are only sometimes our own gatekeepers.

So, on the one hand, we have to negotiate the labyrinth of the self. On the other, we have to generate material. As writers, first we make the clay; then we shape it into a vase. We put words on the page, finding a voice and an occasion, creating characters, setting, and plot, figuring out the psychological arc, then we revise, finally the delicious task of editing. Most of us need to learn the valuable skill of revision, of looking again at what we have made, and seeing how it can be made better before we bear down on our sentences.

While some writers love revision—they've built the boat; now they can sail to Byzantium—many approach it with a sense of drudgery, and even hopelessness. Rather than make the story more seaworthy, they fear it will founder on the rocks. Revision is not a skill that advertises itself. By its nature, it is hidden from the reader. The works we love emerge on the page with an authority that conceals the labor that created them. Elizabeth Bishop's famous villanelle "One Art" took sixteen drafts to reach its final radiant form. Jane Austen wrote "Finis" on the last page of *Persuasion* only to return to the manuscript a couple of weeks later and radically rewrite the climactic proposal scene between Anne Elliot and Captain Wentworth. Scott Fitzgerald moved the history of Gatsby's past around several times before he put it in chapter 7. More recently we have the example of Flannery O'Connor, whose last story, "Judgement Day," is in many ways a revision of her first published story, "Geraniums," and Raymond Carver, who turned the minimalist "The Bath" into the much more expansive "A Small, Good Thing."

Of course, there are exceptions to the "write, revise, edit" rule. Sometimes the occasion of the story is just right; the characters, point of view, setting, and plot are working well; the structure is sturdy; and the climax reveals the inner life of the character. The writer in this situation can happily combine revising and editing, looking for better details, reconsidering syntax and subordinate clauses, working on all the elements of style that conspire to make a story vivid, resonant, and suspenseful. What she needs to do is write better sentences.

So why, given that it's so crucial, does revision often feel hard? James Baldwin helpfully says, "Rewriting is very painful. You know it's finished when you can't do anything more to it, though it's never exactly the way you want it. . . . The hardest thing in the world is simplicity. . . . You have to strip yourself of all your disguises, some of which you didn't know you had. You want to write a sentence as clean as a bone."

I am no stranger to the I-can't-do-anything-more feeling, but I'm often surprised by what happens when I put a story aside. I've reached the point of thinking every last semicolon is in place. Doesn't that mean the story is finished? As I reread the pages after even a few weeks away, my first thought is usually, "Who wrote this? Who thought this was a good paragraph? An interesting description? A complex character? An inevitable surprise?" In the case of my story "Gilbert in Arcadia," suddenly I can see that I don't need the opening description of the bull bellowing in the field. That the scene with the court officer is too brief, that two scenes between Gilbert and his brother are making the same point. I begin deleting and moving paragraphs, expanding a summary into a scene, moving a flashback. But as I work on the story day after day, my vision again begins to cloud. I've learned not to trust the I-can't-do-anything-more feeling until I've experienced it several times.

Another reason revision is hard is that, after months of work, we're often, as Conrad and Baldwin suggest, still not sure what our story is about at the deepest level. This seems ridiculous to nonwriters. We've assembled the ingredients; don't we know whether we're making a frittata or a crème brûlée? But when an editor from *The Atlantic* visited one of my workshops and asked the students what their stories were about, almost none of them could give a coherent answer. Often the writer is waiting to find out what happens just as much, perhaps even more than, the reader.

Putting aside the deeper reasons that blind us to our own work, here are some possible reasons why a story may not be working at the highest level:

- The main character is not sufficiently complex.
- The main character's outer journey is not revealing her inner journey.
- The minor characters are not working hard enough.
- A key event/scene/emotion is missing.
- The different elements/strands/plots are competing, rather than combining.
- We haven't chosen the best point of view.
- The plot isn't working and/or we have no turning point.
- We are in love with a scene or a character—perhaps for autobiographical reasons—in a way that distorts the story.

In the midst of our own confusion, we also often face the challenge of conflicting advice. One of the central premises of workshops is that the author, buoyed up by constructive criticism, will return to her desk ready and able to revise. She will take those insightful comments and use them to finish the story, although writers parse the verb "finish" as keenly as the Inuit do "snow." While working on my first novel, I had two editors: Cynthia in Toronto and Dawn in New York. Cynthia would phone from Toronto and say, "I was reading happily, until the beginning of chapter 4. Then you seem to get bogged down. Chapter 4 is much too slow. You need to cut as much as you can." Next day Dawn would phone from New York. She really liked what I'd done in the opening chapters. Celia's situation was much clearer. "But suddenly in chapter 4," she said, "you start rushing through the material. I couldn't follow what was happening. You really need to slow down chapter 4." I would replace the phone in Boston and wring my hands. But gradually I began to understand that Cynthia and Dawn were telling me the same thing: there was a problem with chapter 4. It was up to me to figure out what was wrong, and how to fix it.

In the workshops I teach I see this scenario repeated over and over. While there tends to be considerable agreement about what's working and what isn't, there is often considerable disagreement about the reasons. The scene where the main character makes Beef Wellington brings readers to a standstill. One doesn't believe the main character would make Beef Wellington. Another thinks the scene is too slow. A third asks why the Beef Wellington isn't given its due. Someone else argues that they don't see how the scene advances the story. Why was so much time devoted to the Beef Wellington? Only to be countered by another reader saying if anything the scene is overly meaningful. The author, listening to all this, diligently taking notes, wants to run away to Scotland, rather than roll up her sleeves and set to work. What she needs to focus on is that there is a problem with the Beef Wellington scene. How can she include most of her readers?

I say "most" because reading is an intimate activity. We read the words the author has written, but we bring our lives, memories, ideas, and perceptions to bear. When I was growing up, we had a Pekingese named Rollo, who accompanied us on long walks, bounding over the heather, and kept me company while I did my homework. Fifty years later any mention of a Pekingese brings beloved Rollo to mind. Whereas my husband, reading the same sentence, pictures a spoiled, short-legged dog given to yapping. When I gave a draft of my most recent novel to four readers—a parent, a fellow writer, a feminist philosopher, and an artist—they each found a completely different problem with the narrative.

So, we have a hard time figuring out what our stories are about, and our readers offer conflicting advice. How can we get a better handle on how to revise? Try answering the following questions for a story, and see what new doors open. I'm answering them for James Baldwin's "Sonny's Blues."

1. What does the main character want? What prevents he/she/they from getting what they want?

   The narrator, Sonny's older brother, doesn't want to believe Sonny has taken drugs and that he may have played a role in his doing so. He wants to believe he can make the world safe for his family. Sonny's musical ambitions and his going to prison prevent him from getting what he wants.

2. List the several elements or strands of the story.

   The narrator's role as an older brother, his daughter's sudden death, his uncle's death at the hands of a white man, the neighborhood where he lives—what Baldwin calls "the killing streets" of Harlem—Sonny's love of music.

3. What are some key emotions? Some key words?

Fear, a desire to escape, a sense of duty, frustration, love. "Safe," "darkness," "light."

4. Are there any symbols?

The darkness of the subway train and of the road where the narrator's uncle is killed, music, especially jazz, the glass trembling on the piano as Sonny plays in the final scene.

5. What does the first page promise? How does the last page fulfill that promise?

The first page promises a change in the narrator's relationship with his brother. On the last page he recognizes Sonny's gifts; there is a provisional moment of grace.

6. Who are the most important minor characters?

The young man who first told Sonny about drugs, the mother, Grace, the dead uncle, the other musicians.

7. What is the most crucial scene?

The one when the brothers talk about suffering.

8. What does the main character feel at the most important moment in the story?

Love, grace, awareness of the dangers all around.

9. Is the title a good ambassador for the story?

Yes.

10. What is the most important thing missing from the story?

In "Sonny's Blues," nothing. In my own work . . .

These answers reveal several things that are necessary to the success of most stories: the narrator has complex wants; he and Sonny are fighting a duel about their different ways of looking at the world; the elements of the story combine to bring us to the final scene in the bar; music functions as both action and symbol.

In addition to trying to answer these questions, I find specific writing tasks helpful. I've gone over and over the scenes, I've worked on the descriptions of the countryside, I've explained Gilbert's sense of being betrayed by both his lover and his business partner, but the story still isn't building to a turning point. When I get to this stage, I find writing outside the story liberating. (I am borrowing this idea from Pamela Painter and Anne Bernays's inspiring book *What If?*) I write a letter, or a series of texts, between Gilbert and his girlfriend. I write a scene that plays no part in the story: What happened when Lucy went to the museum? What happened when Carol took her first glass-blowing lesson? I write a dream for Gilbert's younger brother. I allow my characters, like prisoners, to make one phone call. I describe them shopping for a birthday present for an ex-lover, or a difficult stepparent. These paragraphs may not end up in the story, but they help to expand my thinking. The description of Lucy at the museum makes me reconsider her relationship with her composer husband. Over and above the new details I discover, just the act of writing freely about the characters, who have, for several drafts, been marching in lockstep, helps me to imagine new possibilities. In draft nine of "One Art," Bishop once again allows the poem to sprawl on the page.

Another helpful task is returning to a key scene and writing it from the point of view of the non–point-of-view character. Early versions of my scenes often suffer from the minor characters being pushed around. Gilbert is having a conversation with his brother. He is convinced Patrick can't wait for him to move out of his spare room and, from his point of view, everything Patrick says confirms that idea. Writing in Patrick's point of view, I discover that he's happy for Gilbert to stay as long as he wants; his anxieties are all around his partner's pregnancy.

Both of these tasks help me to deepen crucial scenes, but they don't always help with the larger questions of sequence and structure. To understand those, I map the story. I do this in two ways. I go through the pages marking:

- Scene
- Narration
- Summary
- Exposition
- Description
- Interior
- Exterior
- Memories
- Flashbacks
- Transitions
- How time is passing
- When each character is introduced

Suddenly I can see that the essential exposition is withheld until page 11, that I have flashbacks on three successive pages, that the opening scene is the longest in the story, that a vital minor character isn't mentioned until page 9.

Then I go through the pages again, making an index of the events. For "Sonny's Blues": page 1—the narrator's disbelief about Sonny's fate; pages 2–3—the narrator's day as a teacher and his meeting with Sonny's friend. I note how Baldwin sets a clock ticking and how he uses a long flashback to provide exposition and pass time while we wait for Sonny to get out of prison. These strategies help me to see, often for the first time, how the story is built.

Sometimes revision depends on many small changes, sometimes on a single large insight. In the case of my novel *Eva Moves the Furniture,* I wrote eight versions, each of which failed in a new way. What finally made a difference was realizing that Eva could tell her story from beyond the grave. I never believed García Márquez's claim that one need only find the opening sentence of a novel and everything else will follow, but in *Eva,* once I began to write in the first person, everything shifted. The novel I'd been trying to write for a decade emerged onto the page. More recently, while working on my novel *Mercury,* I realized that telling the story only from the husband's point of view was a mistake. As the wife behaved increasingly badly, showing her thoughts and feelings became essential.

It's helpful to remember how much readers do as they read the opening page. Within a few paragraphs they figure out whom they're reading about, when and where the story is set, the psychological territory, and the tone. They decide if they want to spend time with this narrator; they decide if they want to turn the page. One of my editors described reading my manuscript in his hotel room, longing to drop it into the wastepaper basket. Happily, a sentence on page 2 stopped him. All this means that we need to find just the right place to enter the story, just the right details to introduce the protagonist and her situation. Sometimes the first couple of pages turn out to be part of the scaffolding; we needed to write them, but the reader doesn't need to read them. A not infrequent workshop question is: Could this story begin on page 3? Or page 5? It's surprising how often the answer is yes.

Here is the opening of Daniel Orozco's short story "Orientation."

> Those are the offices and these are the cubicles. That's my cubicle there, and this is your cubicle. This is your phone. Never answer your phone. Let the Voicemail System answer it. This is your Voicemail System Manual. There are no personal phone calls allowed. We do, however, allow for emergencies. If you must make an emergency phone call, ask your supervisor first. If you can't find your supervisor, ask Phillip Spiers, who sits over there. He'll check with Clarissa Nicks, who sits over there. If you make an emergency phone call without asking, you may be let go.

Within a few sentences, we understand the implied speaker, the implied audience, and the occasion of the story. We begin to understand the unusual tone. By the time we get to the end of the paragraph, we realize there is no main character. Contrast this with the opening of ZZ Packer's "Drinking Coffee Elsewhere," when a first-person narrator is immediately at the center of a very different orientation.

> Orientation games began the day I arrived at Yale from Baltimore. In my group we played heady, frustrating games for smart people. One game appeared to be charades reinterpreted by existentialists; another

involved listening to rocks. Then a freshman counselor made everyone play Trust. The idea was that if you had the faith to fall backward and wait for four scrawny former high school geniuses to catch you, just before your head cracked on the slate sidewalk, then you might learn to trust your fellow students. Russian roulette sounded like a better way to go.

"No way," I said. The white boys were waiting for me to fall, holding their arms out for me, sincerely, gallantly. "No fucking way."

Readers also do a lot of work at the end of a narrative. A number of years ago I visited a class of ten-year-olds in New York. When I asked them about their stories, they all agreed that the hardest part was the ending—"Because you have to decide if the goodies or the baddies are going to win." I had never thought of endings like this before, but immediately it seemed right. At the end the writer decides who's going to win. As James Baldwin says, "The train stops here." Sometimes, as at the end of de Maupassant's "The Necklace," readers reconfigure an entire story. Sometimes the ending offers a more modest revelation. One way or another, readers place great stock in the ending. Aware of these expectations, writers struggle between being too meaningful and too subtle, writing with lyric passion and/or careful flatness. Sometimes the ending feels too abrupt, sometimes it feels drawn out, or overly meaningful, or as if there are several endings (and indeed in some of Alice Munro's wonderful stories there are). It's hard to make global suggestions about revising the ending, but writing past the ending—like writing outside the story—can help to discover a more satisfying conclusion. And of course, sometimes the reason the ending isn't working is because of something earlier in the story, not because of what's on the last page.

Beginnings and endings are also crucial on a smaller scale. The writer puts what she wants the reader to notice at the beginning or end of a section. These transitions, places where the story jumps in time, or mood, or point of view, are the signposts to the larger story, and it's especially important not to lose the reader. Later, when I'm editing, I scrutinize the first and last sentences of my paragraphs and often end up cutting the last sentence. The paragraph is already saying what I need but—worried that the reader hasn't quite understood—I repeat it one more time, to deadening effect.

Another useful revision task is to go back to your map and look at where you use narration or summary and where you expand into scene. Narration speeds up the action, scenes slow it down. Most stories need both, and most stories establish a rhythm between the two. Often in early drafts we make intuitive choices about when to go into scene. In revision we need to ask what justifies the length of a scene? What is at stake, and what are the key emotions? How does this scene advance the story? Later scenes ought to deepen the conflict; conflict is what reveals the inner lives of the characters.

Three other key revision tasks are making sure minor characters are earning their keep, scrutinizing memories and flashbacks, and thinking about shifts in psychic distance.

In early drafts my minor characters tend to be shadowy and vague; they aren't capable of putting pressure on the main character. In the first version of my story about Gilbert, his brother barely existed, even though Gilbert was living in his house. As soon as I began to pay attention to Patrick, Gilbert began to come into focus. The brothers acted as foils to each other.

Memories and flashbacks are among our main tools for conveying the inner lives of our characters. We go about our lives, we experience the world not just through our five senses but also through memory. The past claims us in unexpected ways. Seeing a crate of apples at the farmers' market, I picture my mother in Scotland meticulously peeling a Granny Smith at breakfast. As I reach into my purse, I recall the large bag of apples my friend Gail brought me from her trees in Vermont; it took me an hour to peel them. Then the woman selling the apples asks what I'd like, and I buy two pounds for five dollars. So too our characters inhabit the present moment in complicated ways.

Flashbacks, when a scene from the past is played out, occupy a different role. The narrative is taking time off from the present; we assume that the flashback is showing us something that will deepen our understanding of the characters. Too many flashbacks, too close together, can make the reader wonder why she's reading about the present rather than the past. One common but risky strategy is to interrupt a critical moment with a flashback. The pit bull is leaping towards Gertrude, she can see the dark pink of its throat and suddenly, rather than climbing the nearest tree, Gertrude is remembering her mother making raspberry jam. At its best this strategy deepens suspense and meaning; at its worst, it feels artificial and exasperating.

Almost all stories, whether told in the first or the third person, involve shifts in psychic distance. When I described buying apples, I first let you know my thoughts and feelings; then I showed you my exchange with the apple saleswoman from the outside. This sort of back-and-forth often happens, particularly in scenes. In revising and editing, I try to find a balance between interior and exterior.

Revision almost always takes several passes. New material does not fit smoothly alongside older material. A change in structure requires other, unforeseen changes. Moving the exposition means writing a new scene. Combining two minor characters changes the timing. Solving one set of problems reveals others that were previously hidden. At this stage I usually read the story aloud, and I look for new readers who aren't aware of the many changes I've made.

If Leah were to come and study me now, I would tell her about the different stages of writing fiction. If I were writing something new, she might observe me writing an awkward sentence followed by another awkward sentence and another. I hope she wouldn't catch me writing the first sentence over and over. If I were revising, she might find me making maps and indexes, poring over printouts, shuffling material around, moving a flashback from page 3 to page 10 and then back to page 7. If I were editing, there would be many keystrokes as I struggle to find the right adjective, the telling detail, a better place for a subordinate clause, a way to felicitously combine several lines of dialogue, cutting the words "thought" and "feel." Not until the fifteenth draft did Bishop change the second line of "One Art" from

> so many things seem really to be meant to be lost that their loss is no disaster

to

> so many things seem filled with the intent to be lost that their loss is no disaster.

We can't revise our lives. How fortunate we are to be able to revise our stories.

The Starting Line

STEVE YARBROUGH

One foggy morning, you find yourself poised at the starting line on a four-hundred-meter track. The fog is the thickest you've ever seen. There are spectators in the stands, of course, because this is a major event, but the fog has hidden them. Because you can't see them, you don't know if there are two hundred people up there, two thousand people, twenty thousand, fifty thousand. You assume that if you can't see them, they can't see you either, but the sun could come out at any moment and burn the fog away, and then you will be revealed. They'll see everything you do.

You know, because you've been to many tracks before, that at the end of this straightaway, there's a curve, followed by another straightaway, which in turn is followed by a second curve that leads to the homestretch. You can't see the curves, just as you can't see the other straightaway. But you accept, as a matter of faith, that they're there.

The thing is, there are no other runners. There's only you, alone in the middle of the track. Suddenly, as if from the heavens, a voice booms: *On Your Mark, Get Set.*

You're worried about those two curves that you can't see, as well as the other invisible straightaway. The homestretch, if you can ever find your way to it, doesn't scare you, though rationally you know it should, because that's precisely where most races are lost. They're lost because most runners are fading then, their energy spent. You've no sooner entertained this thought than another, truly paralyzing, worry comes to mind:

You have no idea what the length of this race is.

Is it one hundred meters? If so, you can just blaze out of the blocks and run as fast as possible all the way to the end. Is it two hundred meters? If it is, you will need to lean inward on the curve and relax as you come out of it, and you know that if you're already starting to tire, that kind of discipline is hard to come by. Is it four hundred? God forbid, are you going to need to run five thousand freaking meters? How in the world are you supposed to know how fast to run if you don't know how far you've got to go? So much seems to depend on that crucial piece of knowledge, and you don't have it.

Your position, in this moment, is roughly analogous to that of a novelist as she prepares to write her first sentence.

There is, it should go without saying, no one right way to begin a novel. Fiction writers, a sometimes fractious bunch, seem to agree all but unanimously about that. "When a writer figures out what it is that he does," John O'Hara once observed—offering advice that he did not adhere to himself—"he should quit immediately." Bernard MacLaverty recently told an *Irish Times* interviewer, who had apparently questioned why he had not published a novel for the past sixteen years, that "the story you just finished is no use whatsoever to the story you're about to start. It needs to be a unique event. To have a formula is not a good idea: each narrative, each story, is to be approached and told differently." Here, MacLaverty sounds conspicuously like Eudora Welty, who once remarked that every story or novel teaches you only how to write it. It doesn't teach you anything about how to write the next one.

What, then, can we learn from the experiences of others, if we can't even learn from our own experiences, and why I am writing this essay?

One thing we can learn from our experience of writing novels—and it never, ever loses its currency—is that we somehow managed to make it to the end of the last one we attempted, or the last two, or three or four or seven, and this comes in very handy when we reach that moment, as I have in each of the novels I've written, at which doubt sets in and the task we've undertaken seems insurmountable. This doubt, I should note, seldom comes at the very beginning. For me, it often comes between pages 60 and 90 and almost never after page 100. I've quit on a number of novels, but I've never gotten 100 pages in and bailed out. These days, when I quit, it's usually not because I have created technical problems that I don't know how to solve, though that was sometimes the case when I was younger. Now, it's nearly always because I've failed, for some reason, to become fascinated by the characters I'm writing about. I know absolutely nothing about why this happens in some instances but not in others. It remains as mysterious to me now as it was the day I wrote the first line of my first novel (which, by the way, I didn't even realize was going to be a novel). But I know that absent that fascination, even obsession, with the characters, continuing to write about them will not result in a book I want my name on. So I look elsewhere.

I can distill my advice about beginning a novel into a few sentences: In those opening pages, keep your foot on the brake, so that you don't reveal too much too soon. When you write the first page, try to envision the last. This vision will no doubt change—and if it doesn't, you might be in trouble—but at least it will give you what the late, great Cape Breton novelist and short-story writer Alistair MacLeod called "a lighthouse to which I journey." Think long and hard about the choices you're making with respect to point of view and narrative distance, setting and detail and, perhaps the hardest of these elements to discuss, tone. Remember that even as you teach yourself how to write this particular novel, you are also teaching nameless, faceless individuals how to read it.

The five-page chapter that opens *Embers*, a 1942 novel by Hungarian writer Sandor Marai, offers a magnificent display of authorial design. In the opening lines, we learn of the arrival of a letter at a remote castle where an old general lives. A few lines later we are told that for many years the general has not opened or read any letters, suggesting the degree to which he has removed himself from worldly concerns. That he recognizes the handwriting on this particular letter is made all the more significant and mysterious when we learn that he has not seen the unnamed correspondent for more than forty years. Before he has even finished reading the letter, he issues brisk instructions to his gamekeeper, telling him to get the carriage ready to go to the White Eagle Hotel, where he is to inform the staff that the carriage is ready for "the Captain," presumably the letter's author.

We learn of a meticulously arranged stack of notebooks of the type used by schoolchildren but not what might be in them or, for that matter, whom they belong to. We learn that July 2, 1899—"the day of the hunt"—is important to the general, but we don't know why and won't for a long time. Once he has read the letter—and again, we are not told what this missive conveyed—Marai writes that "he seemed calmer now," establishing a much more distant, authorial point of view, which is accessed again after the general, having spoken the words "So he's come back. Forty-one years and forty-three days later," suddenly seems exhausted. (Earlier, by the way, there was a quick shift to the gamekeeper's perspective, allowing us to see that the old general is "thickset" and "broad-shouldered.") The chapter concludes with his summoning a servant, who is instructed to "tell Nini to come up here, if she'd be so kind." We don't have the slightest idea who Nini is, since this is the first time we've heard the name. All we know is her gender.

This opening chapter, of a 210-page novel set on a single day, seems to me an absolute masterpiece in and of itself. Full of intrigue, rich with suggestion, it forces a reader to ask many questions but serves up no answers, beyond the most basic ones: *who* (an elderly general, disaffected from the world), *when* (forty-one years and forty-three days after July 2, 1899, or, in other words, August 14, 1940, a time when troops are massing on the Hungarian borders), *where* (a castle in the forest), *what* (the arrival of a letter from a man called "the Captain," whose connection to our main character seems momentous). Over the course of these few pages, the author has also been instructing us how to read this particular novel, letting us know that a certain degree of patience will be required and that no detail is too small or insignificant to merit notice.

Below are two excerpts from William Trevor's 1994 novel *Felicia's Journey*—the opening page of chapter 1 and, following that, the opening page of chapter 2. The novel concerns itself with a poor Irish girl named Felicia, who when we meet her is traveling to England in hopes of locating her boyfriend, who the reader correctly suspects has ditched her, though it will be a while before Felicia herself figures this out. In the meantime, she "falls in," as the jacket liner puts it, with a morbidly obese Englishman in his fifties named Mr. Hilditch.

> She keeps being sick. A woman in the washroom says:
>
> "You'd be better off in the fresh air. Wouldn't you go up on the deck?"
>
> It's cold on the deck and the wind hurts her ears. When she has been sick over the rail she feels better and goes downstairs again, to where she was sitting before she went to the washroom. The clothes she picked out for her journey are in two green carrier bags; the money is in her handbag. She had to pay for the carrier bags in Chawke's, fifty pence each. They have Chawke's name on them, and a Celtic pattern round the edge. At the *bureau de change* she has been given English notes for her Irish ones.
>
> Not many people are travelling. Shrieking and pretending to lose their balance, schoolchildren keep passing by where she is huddled. A family sits quietly in a corner, all of them with their eyes closed. Two elderly women and a priest are talking about English race-courses.

It is the evening ferry; she wasn't in time for the morning one. "That's Ireland's Eye," one of the children called out not long after the boat drew away from the quayside, and Felicia felt safe then. It seems a year ago since last night, when she crept with the carrier bags from the bedroom she shares with her great-grandmother to the backyard shed, to hide them behind a jumble of old floorboards her father intends to make a cold frame out of. In the morning, while the old woman was still sleeping, she waited in the shed until the light came on in the kitchen, an indication that her father was back from Heverin's with the *Irish Press*. Then she slipped out the back way to the Square, twenty-five minutes early for the 7:45 bus. All the time she was nervous in case her father or her brothers appeared, and when the bus started to move she squinted sideways out of the window, a hand held up to her face. She kept telling herself they couldn't know about the money yet, that they wouldn't even have found the note she'd left, but none of that was a help.

. . .

Although he does not know it, Mr. Hilditch weighs nineteen and a half stone, a total that has been steady for more than a dozen years, rarely increasing or decreasing by as much as a pound. Christened Joseph Ambrose fifty-four years ago, Mr. Hilditch wears spectacles that have a pebbly look, keeps his pigeon-coloured hair short, dresses always in a suit with a waistcoat, ties his striped tie into a tight little knot, polishes his shoes twice a day, and is given to smiling pleasantly. Regularly, the fat that bulges about his features is rolled back and well-kept teeth appear, while a twinkle livens the blurred pupils behind his spectacles. His voice is faintly high-pitched.

Mr. Hilditch's hands are small, seeming not to belong to the rest of him: deft, delicate fingers that can insert a battery into a watch or tidily truss a chicken, this latter a useful accomplishment, for of all things in the world Mr. Hilditch enjoys eating. Often considering that he has not consumed sufficient during the course of a meal, he treats himself to a Bounty bar or a Mars or a packet of biscuits. The appreciation of food, he calls it privately.

Once an invoice clerk, Mr. Hilditch is now, suitably, a catering

> manager. Fifteen years ago, when his predecessor in this position retired, he was summoned by the factory management and the notion of a change of occupation was put to him. As he well knew, the policy was that vacancies, where possible, should be filled from within, and his interest in meals and comestibles had not gone unnoticed; all that was necessary was that he should go on a brief catering course. For his part, he was aware that computers were increasingly taking their toll of office staff and when the offer was made he knew better than to hesitate: as a reward for long and satisfactory service, redundancy was being forestalled.

In the novel these two passages fall a mere five pages apart, as Trevor introduces the principals in this drama. When one reads these passages in immediate succession, it should become readily apparent that there has been a shift in tone and that radically different narrative techniques have been employed in the presentation of the young Irish girl and the middle-aged Englishman. Felicia is introduced first as "she," and the initial use of the pronoun always draws us much closer to the character than even a first name would. The middle-aged Englishman is not "he"—he isn't even Joseph. He is instead "Mr. Hilditch." The use of the honorific becomes a distancing factor and an indication that the author intends for us to observe this character from arm's length.

We learn of the physical sensations that Felicia experiences on the ferry crossing, and whereas we accede to the possibility of motion sickness, she is a young woman slipping away from home, in an Ireland far less enlightened than the one that in recent years legalized gay marriage and abortion, so we also must entertain the possibility that she might be pregnant and fleeing disgrace, which turns out to be the case. We are given immediate access to her fears and anxieties, and are told of the careful steps to which she has gone to avoid detection as she slips away from home. While Trevor eventually makes us privy to a couple of Mr. Hilditch's thoughts, such as the awareness that at his firm vacancies are normally filled from within and that computers have made many people in positions like his redundant, the first thing we are told about him is what he doesn't know about himself—namely, that he weighs nineteen and a half stone, or roughly 275 pounds.

If the overall impression created by Trevor's presentation of Felicia is one of vulnerability, it's fair to say that at the outset Mr. Hilditch comes across as vaguely sinister, an awareness that is enhanced on the second page of the chapter, when we are told "that the private life of Mr. Hilditch is on the one hand ordinary and expected, on the other secretive. To his colleagues at the factory he appears to be, in essence, as jovial and agreeable as his exterior intimates. His bulk suggests a man careless of his own longevity, his smiling presence indicates an extrovert philosophy. But Mr. Hilditch, in his lone moments, is often closer to other, darker aspects of the depths that lie within him. When a smile no longer matters he can be a melancholy man."

We know, because we understand how novels work, that the lives of these two characters, each of whom has been accorded a short chapter at the beginning of this book, must intersect, as indeed they do. When Mr. Hilditch begins to look for a new friend to go along with the five other girls on what he terms his "Memory Lane," we realize with horror that we are in the presence of a genial serial killer, and our fear that Felicia will become his next victim is the suspense that drives this novel. And at the risk of giving too much away, I will say that the seemingly innocuous detail about how Mr. Hilditch fastidiously ties his necktie into "a tight little knot" is by no means as trivial as it seems.

As the excerpts from the Trevor novel, with the readily apparent tonal shifts, would suggest, tone in most novels remains fluid, for the same reason that tone is fluid in symphonies: with larger works, a monotonal approach can become problematic, whereas it often isn't in a six-page story such as Raymond Carver's "Why Don't You Dance?" The best definition of tone I've been able to come up with is that it reflects the artist's attitude or stance toward the subject matter.

It might be useful, for a moment, to think about music. A guitarist approaching the Carter Family's classic tune "Wildwood Flower" could elect to play it in essentially the same fashion the group's seminal guitarist Maybelle Carter did, in a C position capoed up to F#, to produce an almost harp-like effect. On the other hand, he could transpose the melody to G, lower the thirds and fifths and let the open strings ring to create overtones, and turn the bucolic melody into a dissonant blues.

As a novelist, you can take any number of attitudes toward the story you're telling. Compare the opening page of Larry McMurtry's 1966 novel *The Last Picture Show* with the perfectly serviceable alternative version that follows it:

> Sometimes Sonny felt like he was the only human creature in the town. It was a bad feeling, and it usually came on him in the mornings early, when the streets were completely empty, the way they were one Satur-

day morning in late November. The night before Sonny had played his last game of football for Thalia High School, but it wasn't that that made him feel so strange and alone. It was just the look of the town.

There was only one car parked on the courthouse square—the night watchman's old white Nash. A cold norther was singing in off the plains, swirling long ribbons of dust down Main Street, the only street in Thalia with businesses on it. Sonny's pickup was a '41 Chevrolet, not at its best on cold mornings. In front of the picture show it coughed out and had to be choked for a while, but then it started again and jerked its way to the red light, blowing out spumes of white exhaust that the wind whipped away.

At the red light he started to turn south toward the all-night café, but when he looked north to see if anyone was coming he turned that way instead. No one at all was coming but he saw his young friend Billy, headed out. He had his broom and was sweeping right down the middle of the highway into the gusting wind. Billy lived at the poolhall with Sam the Lion, and sweeping was all he really knew how to do. The only trouble was that he overdid it. He swept out the poolhall in the mornings, the café in the afternoons, and the picture show at night, and always, unless someone specifically told him to stop, he just kept sweeping, down the sidewalk, on through the town, sometimes one way and sometimes another, sweeping happily on until someone noticed him and brought him back to the poolhall.

Sometimes Sonny felt like he was the only person in the town. It was a bad feeling, and it usually came on him in the mornings early, when the streets were deserted, the way they were one Saturday morning in late November. The night before Sonny had played his last game of football for Thalia High School, but it wasn't that that made him feel so strange and alone. It was just the look of the town.

There was only one car parked on the courthouse square—the night watchman's Nash. A norther was blowing dust down Main Street, the only street in Thalia with businesses on it. Sonny's pickup was a '41 Chevrolet, not functional on cold mornings. In front of the picture show it failed to start and had to be choked for a while, but then it started again and made its way to the red light, blowing out exhaust that the wind dispersed.

At the red light he started to turn south toward the all-night café, but when he looked north to see if anyone was coming he turned that way instead. No one at all was coming but he saw his young friend Billy, headed out. He had his broom and was sweeping the highway into the wind. Billy lived at the poolhall with Sam the Lion, and sweeping was all he really knew how to do. The only trouble was that he overdid it. He swept out the poolhall in the mornings, the café in the afternoons, and the picture show at night, and always, unless someone specifically told him to stop, he just kept sweeping, down the sidewalk, on through the town, until someone noticed him and brought him back to the poolhall.

The second version says essentially the same thing as the first, but much of McMurtry's attitude toward the material has been subsumed in this bland retelling. To say that Sonny—a seventeen-year-old high-school boy who lives with his best friend in a boarding house because his mother has been killed in a car wreck caused by a cattle truck and he's estranged from his father, who is addicted to pain medication—feels like the only person in town gets the job done. But to say, as the author does, that he feels like the "only human creature in the town" calls attention to his kinship with all the other creatures that inhabit the space, like stray dogs and coyotes. In a novel in which human beings frequently behave rapaciously and are often as mean as rattlesnakes, McMurtry's word choice makes all the difference in the world.

The magnificent film based on this novel was shot by Peter Bogdanovich in black and white, and this opening passage has a monochromatic quality: the old white Nash, spumes of white exhaust. About the only touch of color is that single red light. The landscape is depicted in harsh terms. The personification of the decrepit pickup, which resists Sonny's efforts to start it on this cold, blustery morning, suggests that even machines are among the forces he has to contend with, adding—along with the inhospitable climate—a naturalistic touch that is pervasive in the novel.

Obviously, a lot of time and attention is devoted here at the outset to the minor character Billy, a developmentally disabled boy who has been abandoned by his family. Why spend so much space detailing the manner in which he sweeps—"down the sidewalk, on through town, sometimes one way and sometimes another, sweeping happily on until someone noticed him and brought him back to the poolhall"? If you're familiar with either the novel or the more popular film, you know that eventually, when his protector Sam the Lion has died and Sonny is too caught up in his own loneliness and unhappiness to look out for him, Billy sweeps right through the intersection on another cold, windy morning, when dust has reduced visibility, making it hard for drivers to see that single red light we glimpsed back on page one, and wanders into the path of a cattle truck. Thus, at the end of the novel he dies in similar fashion to Sonny's mother. It is as if the author wants us to know that, if you live in this town long enough, you will eventually expire beneath the wheels of a vehicle loaded with cows and reeking of manure.

It's hard if not impossible to believe that the novelist, who, incidentally, was still in his twenties when he wrote the book, didn't have the ending in mind when he composed the first page. I'm not sure, by the way, that McMurtry would agree with those writers I quoted at the outset who claim that writing one novel tells you nothing about how to write the next. He is generally workmanlike in his approach to the opening of his novels. In nearly every one that I can think of—and I believe he's written thirty-two—the first chapter is one of the longest in the book, and it usually introduces most of the characters while covering only a day or a part of a day. Later on, the pace changes, and the narrative begins to move a lot faster. Just as a monotonal approach can become deadening over three hundred pages, so can a perfectly even pace.

As we near the finish line of this essay, let me say one more word about the proposition I advanced earlier: that one would do well to envision an ending before writing a novel's first words. Though Edna O'Brien's short 1960 novel *The Country Girls* could not possibly be written in a more straightforward style and might seem tame to a contemporary American reader, it occasioned widespread tumult when it appeared in Ireland, and caused the young author to be subjected to denunciations by the all-powerful Catholic Church, as well as male authors like Frank O'Connor and L. P. Hartley, who referred to her characters as "nymphomaniacs." Rereading it a few weeks ago for the first time in thirty years, I was reminded of the way my parents reacted just a few years later to the Beatles. The novel had the same kind of shattering effect on the Irish literary establishment. Below are two paragraphs from the book:

> I wakened quickly and sat up in bed abruptly. It is only when I am anxious that I waken easily and for a minute I did not know why my heart was

> beating faster than usual. Then I remembered. The old reason. He had not come home.
>
> . . .
>
> At half past seven I began to get anxious, because I knew that his plane went at half past eight and mine left shortly before nine o'clock. I sat on the edge of my suitcase and tried to look absorbed as the long-haired boys went in and out to play snooker. They were passing remarks about me. I began to count the flagstones on the lane nearby. I thought, He'll come now, while I'm counting, and I won't see the car drive up to the curb and he'll have to blow the hooter to call me. I knew the sound of the hooter. But I counted the flagstones three times and he hadn't come. It was nearing eight and there were pigeons and seagulls walking along the limestone wall that skirted the river Liffey.

In the text, these paragraphs are separated by two hundred pages. Reading them back to back, anyone who doesn't know the novel might conclude that the situation of the narrator at the end of the book is exactly what it was at the beginning: she is waiting for a man who doesn't come. In fact, a great many things have changed, though the key word "anxious" appears in both, and in both the cause of anxiety is the same: "*he* had not come." In the first case, though, the narrator is a middle-school girl in rural Ireland, and the man who did not come home the night before is her father, who, as is often the case, has been out on a bender that the narrator knows is going to cause yet more grief for her mother when he finally does return. In the latter excerpt, that narrator has become a grown woman, working as a shopgirl in Dublin, living in a boardinghouse and waiting to travel to Vienna with a rich man from the village where she grew up—a man who, I should note, is about the age of her father and is married. His failure to appear could be said to mark the end of her innocence.

When O'Brien wrote this novel, she was in her twenties. In a moving interview many years later with the *Paris Review*, she said,

> When I say I have written from the beginning, I mean that all real writers write from the beginning, that the vocation, the obsession, is already there, and that the obsession derives from an intensity of feeling which

> normal life cannot accommodate. I started writing snippets when I was eight or nine, but I wrote my first novel when I left Ireland and came to live in London. I had never been outside Ireland and it was November when I arrived in England. I found everything so different, so *alien*. Waterloo Station was full of people who were nameless, faceless. There were wreaths on the Cenotaph for Remembrance Sunday, and I felt bewildered and lost—an outsider. So in a sense *The Country Girls*, which I wrote in those first few weeks after my arrival, was my experience of Ireland and my farewell to it.

She goes on to say that, during these early days in England, something happened to change her writing style, which previously had been "flowery and overlyrical." The transformative event was attending a lecture by the American literary critic Arthur Mizener and hearing him read the opening paragraph of *A Farewell to Arms*, which she likens to "Saul of Tarsus on his horse!" What struck her so forcefully was that Hemingway's direct, pared-down, vivid prose had achieved the lyricism she had been straining for. "I can say," she tells the interviewer, "that the two things came together then: my being ready for the revelation and my urgency to write."

Matters of craft are certainly vital: most of us, whether we are aware of it or not, have spent years internalizing the architecture and mechanisms of the novels we admire before we are ever truly capable of writing one. But I believe that making it from the starting line to the finish line depends to a large extent on being ready for the revelation, on remaining open to the world around you and waking each morning with the understanding that today you might see something you have never seen before, or see something that's old in a slightly different way, and this might aid you in your endeavor. The task of writing a novel is both daunting and thrilling. One should always approach it with equal measures of humility and hope.

Unspeakable

Speech on Stage

DAN O'BRIEN

A lifetime ago I stood in a mansion beside an old poet as he sat in a chair like a throne. You know the place. We were waiting for the dinner gong; writers were drinking wine. He was a formidable, forbidding figure in most ways. We'd dined near each other along the interminable communal table many times that month, but I hadn't yet found the courage. Maybe it was the wine but I said, "You teach at this school. I went to this school. Do you happen to know this writer I know?" He fixed me in his sidelong squint: "Quit bugging me, man."

I was speechless. The Supreme Playwright might well have written "awkward pause," or even a Pinteresque "silence" in the script of our minuscule drama. The unspeakable yawning between us, I exited the mansion without dinner, pursued by my shame.

What makes a play play?

Other ways of writing tell stories of struggle and change like prose; are stirring and linguistically pleasurable like poetry. Ask any actor—ask Hamlet and he'll tell you: what makes a play playable is speaking the speech.

And not "a speech" necessarily (more of that soon) but words as they are spoken: fractured and failing yet almost always striving if not flailing toward the mouth's translation of the heart's tongue.

When we write speech we are really writing behavior. For what we say is arguably the most conspicuous thing we do. And what we do as playwrights is fashion words for a myopic medium. Film and television, theater's well-compensated cousins, communicate via close-ups on screens as big as houses, or discreet like decks of cards that we press into our faces in bed at night: every twitch and flicker of mind made transparent. Onstage even the most charismatic actor stands three hands high, or peanut-sized, depending on what we have paid for our seats. We see a play primarily with our ears.

To write a play is to write down literally what is said. Writing what-is-done is at best presumptuous and often in the worst cases cinematic. Acting notes are insulting; parenthetically describing characters' inner lives is uncouth if not verboten (entrances and exits, kissing and killing excepted). Stage directions should be written modestly and with regret.

I used to write stories. Maybe one day I'll try again. But at some point I grew tired of description—writing and, I confess, reading it. I wanted my stories to happen, and in the play I found a form that required—no, demanded—the barest essentials: where and when we are, how we got here, and how we will go.

When I'm writing I don't envision my plays so much as overhear them. I read the words on the page, but I try not to. I don't stage in my mind except vaguely, as if in shapes and motion. Because the theater is that most practical of magics, words must reach the back of the balcony where the face of the speaker has become a blur.

So we playwrights listen. It is a cliché of our craft: we imagine we are taking our characters' dictation. The better we know them then the clearer we hear them speak. We find ourselves by turns delighted and disturbed, that is, entertained, by what they say—what they have to say (and do, when they must do).

Conversation isn't dialogue, though. It is a beginning. It is a beginner's exercise to transcribe a meal with friends. Assuredly as performance it will bore. Even if your meal has been extraordinary—a breakup, say, or a seduction—enacting its transcription will produce a scene that is redundant and malformed, inchoate when not overelaborate.

By contrast, speech on stage is compressed and precise. Each line, sometimes each phrase or word, reveals something new, increments—or more—of plot or characterization or theme (in that order of efficacy, usually) conveyed without patronizing or outpacing the audience, while allowing for laughs and gasps and utterly airless points of apprehension, and all this without shattering the illusion of reality, if our style is naturalism, or the reality of the illusion if something else.

What is the audience apprehending exactly? It's hardly ever what's been said but the meaning: something true has transferred with the line—"on the line" is actors' lingo—but it is decidedly not the line. This unspeakable dimension of well-written speech is commonly and somewhat depressingly referred to as subtext.

I am trying to avoid jargon here, for not entirely aesthetic reasons. But yes, subtext—let's get this out of the way—consists of objectives and motivations and stakes. These words sound like actuarial terms to me, so I choose to speak rather of the inarticulate, the unspoken, even the unspeakable.

The unspeakable in life is easy—at least easy to recognize. We read it, or try to read it, in conversation all the time. Because who ever says what we mean? Who truly knows what we mean and how best to express it? Who can be sure what others mean when they're trying to speak to you? When your doctor tells you "fifty-fifty," he may mean survival rates are actually single digit. When your friend sees your play and says "congratulations," she may mean she has deeply despised it. We don't tend to trust people who speak in rehearsed, conclusive sentences and, God forbid, paragraphs: these are salespersons and politicians, clergy and TV news commentators. Most real conversation is composed of hints and guesses, feints and dodges, implication and inference. As playwrights we don't so much write speech-on-stage as improvise it, and then we must craft it.

For this reason almost every first draft (and third, and fifth) is overwritten. Sometimes too much is happening, but usually it's the talking that bloats and clogs. Now, too much of anything at the outset can be helpful; every tailor knows it's easier to cut cloth than to adhere it. But there is an art to cutting.

I spend a lot of time at my desk redacting. Because I am inveterately cautious I like to first bracket by hand, then strikethrough, then delete; and by decluttering my speech of the words that don't need to be spoken—that cannot be spoken—I find I am loosing, as it were, a living speech. Actors in rehearsal will often help a new play along with, "Can I cut this line and simply *do* it? If I step from Line A to Line C, or leap even to D or F, without these intermediate and preparatory words and phrases, will the speech make sense still? Will it make *more* sense? Will the speech—that is, will I, the actor—come alive?"

A living speech infused with the unspeakable will sound naturalistic. Neither expressive nor impressive, naturalism is the illusion of life and still the style of the popular, unpretentious play.

But even the most naturalistic of plays provides moments of clarity in which characters say exactly what they mean. If these words are earned—fomented in crisis and issued with surprise—then the audience will feel pierced by truth. If unearned, they will feel cheated; such speech sounds too perfect, that is, "on the nose"—like a punch on the nose, I suppose, its canniness offends.

What of speech without the unspeakable? Flesh without soul? Is it truly such a sin? Like lust it is tempting, and dangerous. In melodrama, and melodrama's happy shadow, farce, speech is too good to be true—yet satisfyingly so. A bargain has been struck: the audience has foregone intrigue for the spectacle of opera or slapstick. And yet a spectacle must beguile consistently, of course, or we will quickly grow tired of life lived against the flats.

Let us now look closely at the surface of the page:

Speech on stage is speakable. Actors call these lines "actable." The words just sound right because they feel right in the mouth and lungs (to say nothing of other body parts).

Creative spelling and compounding and capitalization for effect occurs. Italics are most common for emphasis, but overemphasizing *too* frequently looks amateurish if not domineering (some playwrights underline these words, perhaps in homage to something called a typewriter, and a few eccentrics have been known to **boldface**). Speech in ALL CAPS reads like a scream or shriek and is best reserved for wacky comedies and Grand Guignol.

The comma is special. We playwrights must forget what we've been taught, because speech is far from prose. Which is not to say commas in plays mean less but more: rhythm, rest, hesitation, breath. And what the breath reveals.

(Our liberal use of commas is one of many reasons why other kinds of writers look at us, and what we write, with some queasy mixture of admiration and distrust.)

Parentheticals in dialogue are unusual, but some playwrights use them anyway to suggest what a character is about to say or wants to say but can't, for one reason or another.

Semicolons seem literary; but, curiously, colons can be conversational: they seem to say, *Wait till you hear this!* Exclamation points should be used reasonably unless the speaker is feeling unreasonably.

Ellipses and em dashes are indispensable if sometimes too convenient. They're the wider cracks in speech where the light gets out (and in). Ellipses sink our speakers' words . . . inward; em dashes imply thought and speech casting out—reaching—racing toward. Em dashes, not to be confused with en dashes or hyphens, can suggest your *ums* and *ers* without the need to so crudely spell out these filled micro-pauses. Fragments for the most part play naturally. A slash in the line may indicate the point at which the next speaker begins to speak in overlapping dialogue. Columns are sometimes employed for extended simultaneous runs of speech for two or three or more characters.

A paragraph break in speech can denote a beat, which is of course not necessarily the same as paragraphing in prose, but most playwrights simply embed the stage direction "beat" or "pause" or "silence" like rivets in the fabric of the speech. A beat isn't always a pause—characters may sustain a shift in understanding or desire without taking the time to reflect. And an empty pause or silence is usually anything but: the discord will vibrate right through it.

Some poor souls like me like to write plays in verse. I haven't always done this, but I do so now—for selfish reasons mainly. For the clarity it affords me, the superstition of syllable, the compression and precision, the unspeakable ironies insinuated almost invisibly with the hitch of a line break. I don't care if an audience calls it poetry. Many playwrights set down their speech in a kind of free verse so that patterns on the page might inflect all kinds of intangibles like pace and style of playing, supple fluctuations of character and tone. There is no good reason other than difficulty why this kind of poetic (or "heightened" or "stylized") speech can't be actable.

Actors and directors and producers (and playwriting teachers) often look for "a lot of white" on the page, because short lines of dialogue consisting of words and fragments—toppling through blank negative space—promise to play quickly, often thrillingly, while speech packed into inky blocks is usually hard to perform, and even harder to sit through. And it's true that audiences typically like talk that plays like tennis—at least at first; volleys can grow vacuous, and occasionally a dense play is terrific. These rare "wordy" scripts may look impenetrable on the page, but in their playing their speech has become porous, riven with tantalizing gaps that allow actor and audience alike electrifying glimpses of the inarticulate.

There are tricks on the surface of the page, of course. Comedy has its catchphrases, for example. If you are new to playwriting you will find yourself acquiring an acquisitive ear; dining alone in restaurants, eavesdropping remorselessly, sifting conversation for the tics and tells that give us all away. The grosser of these verbal mannerisms captured on the page and reproduced onstage can elicit easy recognition—*Yes, I know who that is.* The man of a certain age who invariably responds, "That's right." The woman of a certain age fond of euphemistically "cutting the umbilical cord." (Many years ago while teaching I noticed how often I prefaced the explication of some element of craft with the phrase, "There's a way in which. . . ." Clearly I wanted to evade responsibility for what is, after all, just taste and bias.) These artifacts of speech may also help locate your characters in history, region, culture. I avoid writing in so-called "dialect," that is, speech rendered phonetically on the page, because I don't wish to reduce my characters to caricature or worse. I try to simply set down the precise words, correctly spelled, in their authentic order.

A few other practical suggestions: pronouns in speech are often best implied; try to make *wells* and *you knows* mean something; don't fake urgency by stating a character's name repeatedly; never echo a line or phrase at the end of a scene for dramatic effect.

I'll repeat that: Never echo a line or phrase at the end of a scene for dramatic effect.

There is of course something called "standard playwriting format," and while many like their plays to look a certain way, I find it too boring to describe here.

As for the problem of speeches, the secret about writing monologues is that there isn't a secret: monologue is simply dialogue when one character won't shut up. Can't shut up. But the listener is still very much present in the page. The listener interrupts, time and again, albeit wordlessly. The listener is an equal partner in the moment-to-moment story of the speech.

Some find it useful to classify monologues into three types: the conventional monologue, when a character speaks to another character (even if the listener resides in the audience's fourth wall, or the speaker's imagination); the soliloquy, when the listener happens to be also the speaker; and direct audience address, which is rather self-explanatory. Of course a vital play is multifarious. These categories, if they exist at all, comingle.

The conventional monologue is probably easiest—for the writer and the actor. These are the speeches actors prefer to audition with because they are comparatively clean and clear. The soliloquy is seldom seen and heard in modern plays because it's hardly naturalistic.

In direct address the speaker often narrates and, like voiceover in film, a little narration goes a long way. It may help the audience imprint, as it were, on the narrator as the protagonist, especially in a memory play. Longer, recurring speeches delivered to the audience will feel confiding if not confessional. This kind of monologue is prevalent these days, despite its usual lack of dramatic dimension and tension, and can impart a casual theatricality to an otherwise televisual play. Still, an exciting direct address is conflicted, however impersonally. Standup comedy, where the comic strives to "kill" without "dying" onstage, is a useful example of the nonspecific yet compelling dangers of talking to the audience.

Let us imagine I am reading this essay, performing it, as it were, in front of an audience. It must—I must—compel by the force of my ideas and my language and, yes, even my storytelling. Inject a bit of conflict though, between me and you, between these words and the listener, and things might get a bit more interesting. A heckler—an estranged and outraged relation—disrupts us. A medical emergency in the audience or on stage. Or say you happen to know—or I happen to let slip—that the success or failure of this performance could cost me my job. Maybe you've heard I need the money for an operation. Somebody of influence starts to snore, or clambers noisily for the exit. I veer off script and find myself improvising wildly. My words come alive.

Or perhaps without resorting to such cheap theatrics all I have to do to make speech more dangerous is to make it personal.

In the middle of writing this essay I underwent a procedure. It had been a year and a half since I finished treatment for a stage IV cancer, and two years since my wife finished treatment for her stage II cancer. In my paper gown and turquoise hospital socks, with the curtain rolled tight around me, I laid listening to the other patients in the lobby-like prep room behind their curtains conversing with the nurses. So many things said struck my ears vividly: "I'm from White Plains. No, above the Bronx. I used to take the BQE to White Castle. I liked jogging across the Washington Bridge." "My wife's Nadine. I told her, 'You go to a eatery [*note:* 'a eatery'; dialogue can be deliciously ungrammatical]. Don't wait here.'" "Hello, I'm Mr. Meeks. Gloria's just a friend. I don't have much family left here in Los Angeles." All I needed were the voices, really just the words, to imagine these people—not what they look like but who they truly are or may be. Perhaps these specks of speech dazzled me so brightly, just moments before receiving the blessed lethe of the Propofol syringe, because I was afraid and hopeful. As my characters are when they speak. As I am when I write.

And what I am most afraid of is silence. The best plays I've written, or the plays I've most enjoyed writing, have needed little or no cajoling. Their voices came unbidden, in whispers that grew insistently into a companionship of months or years.

Of course my reception is irregular. I transcribe in fits and spurts. I speak sometimes for my characters as a placeholder, often without realizing; I grow confused. How do I know I'm hearing their voices or my own? This is a personal question only to be answered in the gut. But do I like this talk or bit of it a lot? Does it impress me in some way? Is it, as they say, "well-written"? Then I must delete it. If a character says and keeps saying what I mean for him to say then I should probably disappear him from the play altogether. For some reason people still like to advise young writers to "find their voice"; for me the practice of playwriting has always involved doing everything I can to lose my voice.

My characters still sound like me, I know. I don't think this can be avoided. If not so obviously the way I speak, then the way I think and feel. But we contain multitudes, after all, even if they are kindred.

As a boy I was spooked by the story of the prophet Samuel. The seer. Though perhaps he should have been called a listener; for as a boy himself of eleven or twelve he heard God's small, still voice in the dark of the night calling his name. When he answered, "Here I am," his story could begin.

If you are regularly hearing voices then you're probably suffering from schizophrenia. But many of us have heard a voice or two in our time. While wide awake. My onetime mentor Charles Mee was a writer and editor of historical nonfiction when in middle age, sitting in the audience with his daughters at a theater as the house lights dimmed, he heard a voice behind him say: "This is the real world." He turned around to see who it was, and nobody was there. Considering that he had never heard voices before, he thought he should pay attention to this one, so he quit his job and started writing plays.

The voice I heard was both in my head and out. I was a few months free of college and anguishing alone in a narrow room in Cork City in Ireland, in a narrow apartment above the bloody-mouthed drunks and dirty gulls and black swans drifting along the emerald-churning River Lee. I was pining for my home in New York, for the young woman I'd eventually marry—even for the family that abused me—when I heard as clear as day: "Why do you ignore the doors?" The voice was male and female and neither. Ageless. I have tried to pass through every door since, especially when I don't know what I may find on the other side.

During my nine months of cancer treatment I did not, somewhat to my dismay, hear a voice. Perhaps I didn't need to. Or couldn't bear to.

But voices of a less psychotic variety have always defined my creativity. Early on I discovered I was a good mimic, at least on paper, like most playwrights. As several therapists over the years have asserted: I lack firm boundaries. Voices get under my skin.

The first voice was my mother's. Listening to nursery rhymes between her legs on the stairs, or in her rocking chair in the mornings when the rest of the family was busy elsewhere with school and work. Mother Goose. Humpty Dumpty, all the King's horses and lions and unicorns. Britannia, her fabled forebears. Poetry was inculcated here.

As I grew older I felt flattered by my mother's neediness. She seemed to consider me her equal if not her elder; her confidant, her lover; a boy she treated like a man and a man who could somehow save her. "You're very wise . . ." she liked to say, despite or because of my silence, but she would change the subject seamlessly as soon as she heard my father stirring elsewhere in the house.

My father, for what it's worth, didn't beat us. He bullied us. He shouted and punched walls and kicked our dogs, but most of the time he was just this silent, seething menace, ever-present because he was friendless and worked at home where, in actuality, he was acting out a pantomime of a career, as my mother's father was secretly propping us up, financially. My father was simple and resentful and essentially incoherent.

When did my mother's relentless talk first strike me as crazy? Long before I learned the word "logorrhea." Before I'd read Molly Bloom's soliloquy or seen Katherine Hepburn's spectral Mary Tyrone, I learned from my pathologically loquacious mother that talk obfuscates as often—more often—than it explicates or reveals, and that, when it comes, revelation is usually accidental. This knowledge has made me a dramatist for my pains—and a challenging one at that, or so I've been lucky enough to learn.

As a boy I found I could reproduce my mother's speech easily, if not in conversation then in my head. Hunkered in the bath I would argue with myself as if virtuosically, sustaining every dialogue in my mind's ear concerning anything really—phrases and words whirling in a seemingly inexhaustible vortex. Something like hearing voices. Though her voice was always most distinct. I still write my mother in the countless characters that derive from her, though I haven't heard her speak in more than a decade, and she is fading.

Her brother Bobby was twelve years old when he developed schizophrenia. Obeying the voices in his head, he set their mansion in Scarsdale, New York, on fire. Their father, a shirt manufacturer in Manhattan, had the resources to send him away—to be raised by a family of devout Christians in Calgary, near a doctor famous, and ultimately infamous, for claiming he could cure schizophrenics with massive doses of niacin. Needless to say, Bobby remained insane. My mother never saw her brother again.

Sometimes the phone would ring on my birthday, and if I answered an old woman would speak: "Danny? This is your Nana Ruth"—the grandmother I'd never met. She sounded like my mother, the same eerie, vacant chattiness. "You and I were both born on the same day! Did you know that? And *my* mother too!" Then she'd put Uncle Bobby on. She was visiting him in Calgary, something she did annually since her messy divorce from my grandfather in the sixties. "Hi," he'd say dopily like a kid; maybe he had been lobotomized? "Do you like baseball?" and I'd have to admit that yes I did like baseball, I hoped to one day play for the Mets but by then he would have hung up.

When I was young and feeling myself capable of poems like an oracle at Delphi or a young Dylan—Thomas or Bob, I loved them both—I'd wonder if these words came to me the way a voice might tell a schizophrenic to set his family's house on fire. My labile mind aflame, I felt elated, powerful; the gods speaking through my mortal mouth and telling me things I knew without knowing. The otherworld and the subconscious were synonymous, I understood then.

My mother must have been terrified: My hypochondria, just one manifestation of my undiagnosed (and therefore untreated) obsessive-compulsive disorder, often bordered on the delusional: I'd contracted AIDS by brushing against a stranger at the bookstore, I was certain; that stitch in my side was undeniably lung cancer. There are times I still wonder about my sanity, especially when I am writing well.

I have spent ten years writing about, and in a peculiar way with, the war reporter Paul Watson. I think of him now as a friend, in some complicated ways like family. As he stood amid an angry mob in the streets of Mogadishu in 1993, readying to photograph the desecrated remains of a US Army Ranger, he heard the voice of the dead man speak both in his head and out: "If you do this, I will own you forever." He snapped the shutter anyway, again and again, capturing a series of gruesome images that would win him the Pulitzer Prize and alter the course of American history for a generation to come. I too have felt haunted by this soldier; I never heard his voice, but I sometimes sensed his presence over my shoulder as I wrote at my desk, felt his gaze from the dark balcony at performances of my play about Paul. I don't know how the ghost, if he exists, feels about what I have written. He may be angry. But his voice is secondary; I took on Paul's voice when I took on Paul's story. As Paul is "owned" by the trauma he witnessed and suffered, so I am owned—that is, changed to some degree—by Paul's trauma.

Several years ago I went through a period of susceptibility to psychics. I was and remain as interested in their charlatanism and delusion as I am in the possibility of any supernatural reality. Spiritualists are at their very least theatrical, which I find to be true in the case of my self-professed Hollywood psychic, who actually lives in Burbank and claims to have been raised in bleakest Appalachia. He is flamboyant, his hair a frosty caramel, and his accent cornpone. I know it's a ready alibi, but I find him most sympathetic when he describes the voices he hears—voices of the dead, of angels, of his spirit guide Spencer—as imperfectly heard. He is better or worse at hearing these voices from day to day, from moment to moment. He needs rest, calm, focus. He must take care of his instrument. He is an artist.

For, make no mistake, there is a whiff of the occult about what we playwrights do. And believe it or not I resist it: that way lies not so much madness as solipsism. If you cede too much control to your voices, whoever or whatever they may be, they may lead you astray—that is, away from life. Like elemental spirits they are tricksters. But even those readers not spiritually inclined may find the psychological explanation convincing: emotion suppressed will find strange and startling voice.

As a boy I was fascinated by a few paragraphs in my family's *Encyclopædia Britannica* about the Fox Sisters of western New York, who one night in 1848 heard spectral knuckles knocking in the walls and along the bare boards of their shack of an unhappy home. Soon they were communicating as if telegraphically with the spirit of a murdered peddler buried in their cellar. It took me many years, and writing a play about them, to realize why the Fox girls' haunting was haunting me: their family has been dysfunctional like mine, and my writing, which I experienced often as a visitation, was a half-conscious attempt to channel my torment. A friend, himself also raised by abusive parents, is currently adapting this play as a low-budget horror film.

Perhaps every play I've written has been a kind of ghost story. Perhaps every play is. All theaters are haunted, after all, especially after hours. The ghost light burns like the lamp at Samuel's bedside. Late night in the theater's empty house we wait to hear our names called.

Since cancer, during this tentative recovery, I don't listen as closely for ghosts. I no longer wish to write about what's dead and gone. I would like to write my way, if I am able, into the present, even a future. I want to hear more life.

What I hear most clearly lately is my daughter's voice—who, I am astonished to realize as I write this, is almost five years old. I find myself longing to conserve, as it were, what she says and how she says it. Not only the sound but its meaning. What is unspeakably beautiful in her to me. Would that we could hear all voices in this way.

I'd like to conclude briefly with the unspeakable in its most profound sense.

I was twelve when my brother tried to kill himself by throwing himself out the window of our attic. I saw him stumbling around the side of the house in the snow in the moments after. I found his suicide note upstairs that read, "Dear Mom, looks like you'll get that playroom you've always wanted," and, regrettably, later that night I handed her the paper. She collapsed crying in my arms and whispered in my ear, "This is a secret we will take to our graves."

I knew in that moment she was wrong. In order to save myself—and her—I would have to betray her.

Every family is a culture. Ours was a tyranny in which we were not allowed to speak our minds, because our minds wanted desperately to protest our treatment at the hands of confused and cruel parents. No, protest wasn't our goal—love was. Understanding.

Displacing what I wanted to say, and what my subconscious needed to say, into the mouths of other, imagined people—this adaptation allowed me to thrive. At least for a while.

Of course I was afraid. The few times my parents read or saw my plays I worried: *Will they hear me in these voices? Will they hear themselves?* "You've always liked to make a scene," my father said after my first production, and that's all he said. I was safe—for the time being.

And he was right: I did like making scenes, because I had learned already that entertainment was a way to speak the unspeakable. When at the dinner table my father would bark something cruel about Blacks or Jews or women or gays, or his wife and children, I found I could undermine him with a joke. The closer I cut to his bone the better—and the funnier. I could make the whole table laugh, or titter at least. Even my father had to grin or chuckle sometimes, as if he hadn't understood that he was the butt of my joke; or if he had understood, he hadn't the wit for a comeback. I would play the fool to his thick-headed Lear.

Metaphor was another way to speak the unspeakable. My mother liked to sneak into my room and read my journal, ransacking me, then use this *kompromat* against me, claiming her insights came not from spying but from a motherly telepathy. So I wrote more difficult poems, more fictive fiction. I hid the truth in lies. Luckily, before I became a stranger to myself, I found the theater.

For the stage is a place that offers both displacement and transcendence, laughter and compassion, rage and forgiveness, disclosure behind the mask. With the actors as my surrogates and the page my public square, the play may become a wedding or an execution; the danger is real, but so is the reward of the audience's understanding. If I have been trying to do anything these past twenty years as a writer it has been to articulate the taboo, at first of mental illness, child abuse and suicide, then of war. I still feel compelled to tell the truth. To confront and to provoke with the truth. And to persuade. I am trying to do the same now with cancer.

Earlier I suggested that playwrights ought to lose their voice. But clearly a playwright has a kind of voice. We know it when we hear it, and we won't hear it in the speech. Our voice is the voices we hear and how we hear them.

So we listen for what's unspoken in our culture and our audience, and often it's not what they want to hear. And we use our art to make them hear it. They will disagree, of course. Because they see things differently. Because they don't yet know how they feel. Because they don't want to feel. This truthful play you write will make you allies and, if you're lucky, enemies. You will hobble your career by offending those who have risen in their ranks by institutional and commercial rather than artistic acumen.

We are living through unspeakable times. The poison in America has found its full flower. The retrograde are powerful and their cruelty reflexive, for kindness is weakness in their church of Mammon. True is false and the lie is king. Disparagement unto silence is only one strategy. They are working tirelessly to stifle and extinguish our smallest, stillest voices. We need plays now that shout in the square profanely. We need polemics. If ever an age deserved prophetic plays it is ours.

I have written about my friend the war reporter for many years now for many reasons: because his shell-shocked depression reminded me of my childhood turmoil; because like me he should have died but here we both still are. And all the while I have striven to emulate how, in Somalia or Afghanistan, South Africa or the High Arctic, he has listened to the voices of those without voices in the Western press. He identifies with the oppressed perhaps, he says, because he was born one-handed and his father died before memory. But he will protest fiercely that it's not altruism that drives him but empathy. If we are not too inured to injustice, the voices of those who suffer will—and should—haunt us.

It can seem that we are being told often these days that we should write only about ourselves. But who are we? This question is key. For the play that is alive with honesty and argument will be risky, and risky primarily for the playwright to write. The culture may be wrong, the audience too, but also the playwright. Plays that find ways to dramatize the unspeakable in the playwright will be personally political, and these are the plays that may transcend rhetoric and fashion. These plays may persuade.

Of course I am a hypocrite. There are so many things I cannot write about yet: unspeakable orphaning and widowing; unspeakable weakness and illness and need; unspeakable offense, prejudice, bargains, animosities, appetites. Hope and unspeakable gratitude.

And what of the virtues of keeping quiet? The necessity of privacy? Surely shame protects us. Even as a secret turns malignant it can confer self-possession and drive. All this is true. But I am romantic: were all our secrets exposed, how much more might we love and be loved?

Why did I begin with a memory of shame? When that aged, esteemed poet suggested I "quit bugging him," and I did so because I didn't matter, I was a youthful thirty and the wrong genre. I was just a bug bothering him. And I am still stung. Though with maturity I understand his annoyance: life can seem too brief for meaningless chatter with strangers. He was unwell—he died not long after. I respect him now for speaking his mind then.

But I wish in that moment I had spoken mine in return. Not to wound him but to answer his real speech with mine. For by speaking the unspeakable we may find ourselves conversing freely, creatively. We may listen.

Birds of America

Or, Tell Me a Story about Farming, Haunted Houses, and Poetry in Motion

MAURICE MANNING

Down on the Farm

One August a few years ago I was invited by my neighbor and friend Arthur Young to observe his farming operation. He raises sheep and cattle on about 250 acres of ridgetop land. Arthur is eighty-three, and farming has been his life. He and his wife, Martha, run the show. Arthur once followed the guidelines of the USDA and the University of Kentucky College of Agriculture, which recommend lots of chemicals to raise grain to feed his livestock. Somewhere along the way, Arthur had an epiphany. He saw that his land was not healthy and not productive. The various chemicals he'd been advised to use sterilized the soil. The chemicals, intended to kill certain bugs and unwanted plants, also killed microbes naturally present in the soil. These microbes actually feed the root systems of grass and other forage crops; healthy root systems keep the soil loose and aerated. Healthy root systems also hold soil in place and prevent erosion. The man-made and man-conceived chemical system, in short, was killing the natural system. And the chemicals were also costly—an annual cost Arthur figured he could eliminate. So he stopped using fertilizers and herbicides, and he stopped raising corn. His animals are ruminant creatures, intended to eat grass, not grain, so he set out to return his pastureland to its natural design and restore its health, beginning with the roots and the microscopic creatures living in the soil. Arthur's lifelong work has been grassroots all the way.

But I have just shared a bunch of information, and information alone does not explain this patch of farmland, nor does mere information explain Arthur's work and its successful operation. On this rather cool morning, Arthur and I walked out into his pastures. He said the first thing he does of a morning is walk the farm and observe. If one pasture has grown up and looks a little shaggy, it's time to bring in the animals to graze. His pastures are neatly fenced with gates between them. This way a pasture that has been thoroughly grazed will be left alone for a while in order for the grass to renew itself. The animals have aerated the ground by walking on it; they have also deposited fertile manure. Air and nutrients now reach the roots of the grass in the pasture. This process of rotating the animals from pasture to pasture is repeated in a geometric and orchestral fashion all year. Arthur *authors* this process. The big revelation for me that day was to realize Arthur's farm is in constant *motion*—it might be relatively slow motion, but the key features of his farm, from the pastures to his animals, from the creatures in the soil to the grass that grows out of it, are *moving*, always in an ancient dance with the weather. Standing in the field I realized I was not observing a static scene, but a living creation, filled with rhythm and breath. I also realized this: The *form* of Arthur's farm is not fixed. It is flexible. His pastures change shape and size; he runs new fences and removes others, and the whole arrangement changes from year to year. And thus the form is also in motion, and the form invites other kinds of necessary motion. This is a way to operate a good farm against the grain of modern convention and the bad ecological and economic and political powers behind that convention. It is also a way to think about poetry. And so we begin.

Roots in Romanticism

American poetry has an interesting connection to Samuel Taylor Coleridge and John Keats. In the early 1790s, Coleridge and his friend Robert Southey had their infamous "Pantisocracy" scheme, a utopian daydream in which they proposed leaving England to try their lot in the newly liberated United States, where they would live off the land and write poems. Their initial scheme was to settle in Kentucky, in the wilderness, on the frontier. The plan was a flop, of course. Keats's connection to America was more involved and direct. His younger brother, George, had sailed to America with his wife, Georgiana, in 1818 and soon settled in Louisville. George Keats eventually invested in a riverboat scheme with none other than John James Audubon, the famous painter of birds, of whom we shall hear more. The boat sank, and George Keats lost all of his investment. But while brother John was alive, he was sending some of his best-thought, task-of-the-artist letters to George and Georgiana, often also wondering about life in America. I have a pretty strong hunch that John Keats sent some of his best-known poems in letters to brother George in Louisville, well before the poems were published in England. One such poem I am certain about is "Ode to a Nightingale," a bird that is European and doesn't reside in North America.

I think it's worth noting these early inklings from two great English poets and to imagine their willingness to invest in American poetry, to imply its very possibility. Perhaps they imagined something *poetic* in America, in the very idea of such a country founded on ambitious principles. Something fruitful may have come from the mere long-distance process of imagination. Coleridge's poems—meditational, conversational, fantastic, psychological, supernatural—both utilized conventions of poetic form and also dispensed such conventions altogether to find new approaches to form. Coleridge, before any other poet, realized that form must be a flexible, variable, and often irregular feature of poetic composition. It depends on the poem and what the poem is up to. Form defines the space within which the poem exists, and if the poem is going to go into "caverns measureless to man," then the form of such a poem must be part of the downward plunge and provide the structure to enable the going down. And Keats, with his dependence on conventional poetic form and his neoclassical orientation, nevertheless applied the ancient conventions of form to new subjects, to the consciousness and anxieties of a mind we can easily recognize as modern, and therefore concerned with our own concerns.

But Coleridge and Keats uncovered something else. They noticed the surprising intimacy of a landscape, and they found a correspondence between landscape and the mind. This bond between the outer scene and the interior condition is interdependent—one realm clarifies the other, and deep understanding of one requires deep contemplation of the other. And poetry—or art in general—is the tool we have to go back and forth between these realms. Both Coleridge and Keats were easily seduced by the prospect of fusing together these two realms, but as their best-known poems admit, such a desire is impossible to fulfill. It's the going back and forth, between the *heard song* of the nightingale and how that song is received by the *mind*, that interests me, because the back and forth is *movement*. And that means "poetry in motion" is not the cliché we always thought it was.

What makes motion in a poem? There are the obvious multiplying and resonance-making features of the craft, such as imagery, simile, and metaphor, among many other figures of thought. To hear in the sound of the sea a female voice singing, or to hear in the sound of a female voice singing the sound of the sea, and, therefore to draw together into meaning qualities of *both* sounds, to allow a deeper contemplation of sound *itself*, is a movement between nature and the human that Wallace Stevens pinpoints in "The Idea of Order at Key West." And this drawing together, this sense of movement, is what permits Stevens to observe: "But it was more than that, / More even than her voice, and ours, among / The meaningless plungings of water and the wind, / Theatrical distances, bronze shadows heaped / On high horizons, mountainous atmospheres / Of sky and sea. / It was her voice that made / The sky acutest at its vanishing" (11. 28–35). This is metaphor blown wide open, not merely in the realm of description—which it certainly is—but more importantly in the realm of widening meaning. Metaphor, when thoughtfully applied, offers this kind of motion, a leap, a bound into another dimension, and also proof that such a leap is entirely plausible. *Metaphor* comes to us from the Greek and means to transfer, and to bear or carry. Built into the root of the word are both abstract and concrete connotations, a perfect foundation for how we use metaphor in literature. My point is to demonstrate that key terms and tools we associate with literary composition fundamentally resist stasis, and are in fact intended to keep things in motion.

But the idea of movement embodied by the poem is even more fundamental, woven into the terms we use to discuss poetic composition. Consider these familiar terms: foot, meter, and verse. If you go back to the earliest meanings of these words in English, more or less one thousand years ago, these words overlap, referring both to concepts and physical objects or action. Thus a *foot* in prosody originally referred to tapping one's foot to follow rhythm. A foot was a way to describe rhythm, but also length (a foot was considered the length of an actual human foot), and thus a poetic foot might be thought of as a step. A verse once referred to walking and then turning to resume the walk. Meter originally meant to measure, a physical action. The English language, at the level of vocabulary, was much more physical in its early stages, probably because people's lives were much more involved with the physical world—that is, with nature. So all of these features of prosody which we now grasp cognitively were originally bodily, and served the function of embodying the poetic line, and, the poem itself. One thesis I have is this: elements of a good poem are on the move, even when the poem appears to be sitting on the page. And the poems that really reach us do so because they have movement built in to their design. They are moving and we are moved. The purpose of human experience is not to bring grief into the world, nor to exult in whatever our personal grief may be. Grief will find us soon enough. Our human effort is to find some meaning and some expression that transcends and transforms inevitable grief, so that we may try to live with hope. To that noble end we have art and literature. Thus we have the Latin prefix *trans*, which means "across, to or on the farther side of, beyond, over," a notably poetic definition for a root associated with literal and metaphysical movement. Just as my neighbor Arthur Young assessed his farm beginning with the roots, we're now considering poetic roots, our humble green thought in a green shade.

How to Build a Haunted House

Motion of various kinds is inherent to the English language, and motion is also a feature of the original idea of the poetic line. The next degree of consideration then is poetic form. Are motion and movement built-in features of poetic form? Certainly. To see how conventional form moves, let's look briefly at two poems, Robert Frost's "The Need of Being Versed in Country Things" and Robert Penn Warren's "Boy Wandering in Simms' Valley." I have written about both poems before for various reasons, but find I come back to them. They are both haunting and haunted; both feature a haunted house, and both poems, in terms of form, *embody* a haunted house and make such house a living presence in the poem. I happen to live in a haunted house, which always provides curious imaginative and real encounters, and my personal experience of poetry itself has always had a haunted-house effect—perhaps that is why I continue to be drawn to these poems bound to an earlier murky time. They are simply familiar. But they are much more than that for the student of poetry, of which I am.

Both poems utilize the always serviceable quatrain, a stanza that apparently accommodates bare-bones narrative, which is the setup for the ambiguities probed by the much more involved lyricism of both poems. There's a story behind both poems; the stories are quite similar; the stories are also *over*, long over, so each poem is a partial retelling, by a narrator who had no direct involvement in the original story. What is it about these sketched-out stories that attracts a narrator? Both stories feature a farm where humans once lived. Both poems focus on the sudden end to a human presence in a place, and the place itself is on its way to diminishing the remnants of the human presence, returning to its original form. And yet the act of remembering at the heart of these poems is a kind of ceremony, a stately, decorous process enhanced by the presence of these stanzas—these *rooms* that define complicated space and provide the blueprint for a sufficiently haunted house.

What should we make of these stanzas, these poetic building blocks used to describe great *un*building? And in both poems the stanzas include rhyme, a little in the background, but for what possible purpose? In Frost's poem, the rhyme occurs only on the second and fourth lines, somewhat off-beat, and the sound of the rhyme is further obscured by Frost's characteristically eccentric syntax. With Warren's poem, the lines are so long, it's hard to hear the rhyme, but it's there. Warren's line is also so emphatically spondaic it's hard to know where it ends. Thus, both poets are hiding the music and the rhythm quietly playing in the background of thought and sketchy exposition. My question is why?

In many poems, particularly contemporary free-verse, nonmetrical poems, the stanza functions as a paragraph. In prose the paragraph typically marks linear thought, and follows a linear sense of development and progression. In these poems by Frost and Warren, however, linearity is not on the table. Narrative is at best a superficial feature of these poems. In both cases the real depth of the poem is lyrical, the underworld of the poem, and the undersong that quietly accompanies the journey into the deep dark below. The presence of rhyme, in fact, while it commonly plays into forward-moving narrative, also resists such forward motion. Upon the repetition of a rhyme, as much as we may move forward on one hand, we also jump back to the previous sound, to the original sound, and we are invited to wonder whether the relationship is merely sonic, or if it goes deeper. In both of these poems, the presence of rhyme asks the reader to hear rhyme as a means of going deeper. In both poems, the rhyme provides a backing-up, a stepping back in narrative time, which is indicated by "remembering" in musical time, a feature that runs counter to the surface-level forward motion of both poems. So, rhyme—as far as it is concerned in these two poems—invokes the emotional and metaphysical endeavor of *remembering*, and remembering, as an *imaginative* process, even if the effort is to remember what cannot be completely known, is what both of these poems are fully about. The music *has* a meaning; it is not a decoration or an ornament, though we cannot help but enjoy the fact that beauty is also a mesmerizing feature of these poems. This union of curiosity, compassion, grief, recognition, honesty, and hands-on craft adheres together to approach a serious description of art, as far as I encounter it.

Another feature of these two poems worth observing has to do with perspective. Frost's narrator is nonpersonal, and almost absent as a personality in the poem, other than to conclude that "one had to be versed in country things" to grasp the stark reality of the scene. "One" who encounters a lone chimney and the "awkward arm" of the water pump must be acquainted with such scenes and must stoically see nature going on, swallowing the human in its fold. Warren's narrator, on the other hand, is Warren himself recalling a moment in his childhood when he encountered the proof that a local legend was true. The bedpan high on the shelf is the proof, just as the pump arm is a proof for Frost. Whereas Frost's narrator brings knowledge to the plain scene of his poem to invest the poem with its meaning, Warren's narrator suddenly acquires knowledge from the more Gothic scene of his poem. We have more or less the same form working to serve different ends, proof to my thinking that form animates the otherwise static materials of the poem and sets them in dynamic motion.

A House Divided against Itself Cannot Stand

But I want to add a further observation about Warren's "Boy Wandering in Simms' Valley." The boy in the poem *encounters* knowledge, the sudden, life-forming recognition that love and despair are not far apart in the human world, and further recognition that nature continues always its process of life—which includes death, though death is quietly reclaimed by a larger Life. This is a stance the poet must accept, if he or she is to do the work of lasting poetry. This stance was clearly on Warren's mind in 1974 when he delivered his Jefferson Lecture in the Humanities, published as *Democracy and Poetry.* In that lecture—composed on the heels of the civil rights movement, the Vietnam War, and Watergate, not to mention the chaos and destruction that define the twentieth century more generally—Warren's thesis is to claim that the course of American literature has been to confront the "diminished self." He observes that the protagonist in many works of American literature is wounded and alone, an outsider to the mainstream, yet someone committed to restoring the integrity of the individual. The integrity of the individual, Warren claims in his lecture, has been diminished because the principles of our celebrated democracy have been eroded, by populism, by racism, by chicanery, by deceit, hypocrisy, Puritanism, and, above all, by mind-numbingly mindless violence and environmental desecration. Capitalism has been happy to profit from all of this, but the lowly individual has suffered, and only literature—meaningful, humane art—has a chance of offering both a response and a solution, or "the diagnosis and the antidote" as Warren puts it. I have studied and greatly appreciated Warren's Jefferson Lecture for twenty-five years. It is ultimately a message of hope, a belief that art—the humanities—always provides an alternative to violence, hatred, empty profit, fear-mongering, deception, isolation, and general meaninglessness. There is a point to being alive, Warren claims, and a good one, and we each must step up and get at it—and that's the point. I have paraphrased one hundred pages of Warren's dense thought, but even in this condensed form I find it inspiring.

Although violence and empty profit and environmental desecration proceed unabated, I still find hope in Warren's observations and carry it with me. What else is there to do? We have to live, and we have to live with integrity and individuality. And those of us inclined to poetry and the arts have to get on with the task. If we have a light leading us, so be it; if we are struggling in the dark, we must somehow go on. We may have to go beyond ourselves.

And knowing the self—however it may be composed or defined—and then going beyond it, beyond the composition and definition of *self* to find a reality that is greater and wholly human and yet connected to a greater reality—is Robert Penn Warren's most important discovery in his long poem, *Audubon: A Vision*. This sense of *self* beyond itself, this vision of connection that supersedes all things human, is what Warren claims is the aim of art. I wholly agree, though freely confess the challenges of coming to terms with such a claim.

Birds of America

Let us try to get hold of this poem. It is a poem about our country, foremost, about our flawed origin and where things stand today, and the artistic impulse to reconcile human experience to something else—we may call it wisdom or nature or the divine, or what Warren names it with a capital T, Time. John James Audubon ventured into the American frontier beginning in 1810 or so, and seriously commenced his life's work, to paint *Birds of America*, around 1818. This book was in process of publication from 1827 to 1838 and encountered various setbacks along the way. The final publication included 435 hand-colored, life-size prints of at least 497 bird species. Audubon's task was astounding and costly in all ways; that he achieved his desired outcome in his lifetime is miraculous, a feat not lost on Warren's poetic treatment of this chapter of American history. Audubon brought art and knowledge from the wilderness to civilization. And he used tedious, traditional methods to produce an entirely modern expression—the paintings are photographically realistic and intimate, they are dramatic and intensely alive. I believe Robert Penn Warren had such facts in mind as he commenced his poem, and I believe he must have been wondering, "What *are* the birds of America?" Clearly, Warren sees Audubon's project as a living metaphor.

Upon a first reading of Warren's confrontation with this national history, we find the poem has some of the structure of narrative—there is a tale to tell inside it, and parts of it indeed get told. But the standard features of narrative unravel as soon as they are presented. The "beginning" begins by *denying* John James Audubon's rumored beginning: he was *not* "the lost Dauphin," not at all the son of the "feckless" Louis XVI and Marie Antoinette. That myth sprung up soon after Audubon's death in 1851. In fact, as Warren provides in a headnote to the poem, Audubon was the child of a French slave trader and his mistress. We therefore begin with the negation of beginning, which we are invited to believe is more honestly American. And then, promptly, we are in the wilderness, the primal American wilderness, some years after the Revolution, when early European settlers are scrabbling to take root in a place that has no definition. And this place is presented as the first place of American civilization, our true national origin—raw, untamed, unvarnished, violent, ignorant, desperate—settled by people "Too sloven / That is, to even set axe to clean wood," by which the artful Audubon, in Warren's words means, these pioneers are living without talent or intelligence or practical skill, yet are nevertheless unleashed to found a nation. And Audubon is there, too—with his "passion." Warren imagines Audubon's blooming vision as he encounters *Ardea occidentalis*, the great white heron.

The tale within the tale now commences. In the long second section, "The Dream He Never Knew the End Of," we learn that Audubon has commenced pursuing his passion—painting the birds of America. The birds are majestic in their native place, wholly belonging to nature, to the primal wilderness and of it and singing of it. The birds live wholly integrated with Creation, untrammeled by human presence until recently, and Audubon is there to capture the purity of this art as it exists, though with the dark knowledge that this state of bliss will not last long. Everything is loaded, poised for irrevocable change. John James Audubon was there to see such a moment and live it—that is what Robert Penn Warren powerfully imagines in this poem. The poet has pinpointed a hinge in American history when, briefly, we believed we found ourselves in the Garden, and just as soon found ourselves cast out, yet forever yearning to return.

The scene in the rude cabin is proof of this. It is evening, and Audubon needs a place to sleep for the night. He hesitates knocking on the door of the smoky cabin, but he does. Inside he finds a large woman, older than her years, not particularly hospitable, unable to hide her cunning and the menace behind it. "Kin ye pay?" she asks. She informs Audubon she already has one lodger for the evening, an Indian, and adds in a line of Warren's pentameter: "And leastwise, ye don't stink like no Injun." Then Audubon notices the silent Indian who has a grotesquely injured eye, sitting by the fire. Audubon settles his dog—whose name was Plato, by the way (though this is not mentioned in the poem)—and his belongings, and commences to wind his pocket watch. The woman is drawn to the watch as a moth to flame. She is delighted with the watch and hangs it around her neck. A pitiful ray of innocence emerges from the woman, rousing Audubon's sympathy. But almost immediately it is clear the woman is plotting how to steal the watch, though, ironically, time doesn't matter to the woman—she is timeless, existing in a misery and ignominy time cannot measure. And she probably can't even tell time. The Indian, we are told, "Draws a finger, in delicious retardation, across his own throat." Soon her big brutish sons come through the door to eat, and the whole enterprise of this family comes into view. Travelers pay to stay with them for the night in their outpost, only to be robbed, or worse. Audubon lies down with his dog and his gun as mother and her benighted sons "slosh" a jug amongst themselves. He believes he has entered a story—a dark tale, a living nightmare, where all the world around is haunted and possessed by menacing spirits. As all of this unfolds, the reader is quietly invited to grasp one of Warren's larger points: this rude place is where we come from, and these rough people represent the roots of our national character, like it or not.

Just as Audubon expects the worst, however, three well-armed men burst into the cabin. They gag the mother and tie up the whole family, and somehow the night passes. These men, of course, do not represent law and order, or justice. They are simply better-armed, better-organized, and perhaps more intelligent, *competition*. This is the frontier economy, after all; there are no rules, no laws, and certainly no honor. The next morning the family is hustled outside to be hanged from a low branch of an oak tree. When the woman is offered the opportunity to pray, she bursts into mad laughter and says in another line of creepy pentameter, "If'n it's God made folks, then who's to pray to?" And in the next line she adds, "Or fer?" The point is to clarify her fundamental nihilism. What is the purpose of praying to a God who would make people like *us*, people driven by base appetite, greed, and violence, whose only ideology or creed is day-to-day mindless survival? This is a woman who has never known compassion or forgiveness or tenderness, and has therefore never been inclined to offer any of such virtues or expect them or to value them. Her life has occurred and now ended in a wholly amoral fog, surrounded by a wilderness that contains beauty and order, when properly observed, and is the first source of art. The wilderness is also the most obvious sign of Creation, to which the woman and her kind are indifferent. As Audubon studies the woman just before she is hanged, he observes some beauty in her, suggesting that, regardless of her mean existence and her low character, there is something redeeming or redeemable about her. Yet just as soon as he allows such a thought, he "becomes aware that he is in the manly state," the most disturbing and unexpected image in the poem.

The moment is intentionally shocking, and we must ask what Warren means by it. Surely adding such a detail has value beyond the shock of it. It makes the reader uncomfortable—this reader, at least—it tells us something we don't particularly want to know. And yet, I can concede that this disturbing moment merely allows Eros to become part of the mix Warren is stirring together. That mix includes more expected ingredients of the alchemy: the dark Garden of Eden setting, the flawed promise of America, violence, ignorance, greed, deceit, poverty, and mere appetite, commingled with a desire for order and an attraction to the force of pure beauty Audubon finds in his birds. This is the rudimentary and raw coagulation of art. Adding Eros to such a complicated mix further complicates Warren's vision and therefore makes it more natural, and more American. It also makes the vision more psychological, and thus gives this expansive vision an interior dimension. We are encountering, after all, an allegory, a literary mode and structure that operates like a pop-up children's book: the structure expands geometrically, in all dimensions at once, and a moral dimension is part of the consideration. Audubon's "manly state" before the hanging of the woman indicates the allegory is on the move—outward, downward, beyond. We see now that every feature of the poem is at once what it is, and also symbolic; the literal and the figurative are fusing together to become a single expansive expression, and the "vision" Warren claims in his title is one that penetrates the boundaries of conventional reality. I have in private moments thought of Robert Penn Warren as one of our most serious philosophical poets; that is, he viewed poetry as a philosophical endeavor, and this disturbing moment in *Audubon* I read as a step in Warren's combined poetic and philosophical process, a step that crosses one line in order to add another dimension to the thought the poem is plumbing.

Literature deals in intimacy, whether up close or broadly considered, and I think it's worth noting that violence, although we abhor it, may, perversely, bring with it a kind of intimacy. Think of the violence of a burning house in Frost's poem, and the intimacy of grief the poem implies. Think of old man Simms getting into bed with his shotgun beside his dead wife. But violence as intimacy is part of our national record; indeed, racial violence and violence toward nature are among our national original sins, and the consequences continue to unfold and expand. What does this moral nightmare, this jarring sense of intimacy, have to do with poetic form? A lot, is the short answer.

Audubon is organized like a grade-school outline for a paper, like an old-fashioned theme. Each section has a Roman numeral and a main title and is then divided into subsections indicated by letters. Some of the subsections feel complete, as if a paragraph, whereas others trickle off and feel more fragmentary. The recurring pentameter line is also notable throughout the poem, as if Warren doesn't want us to forget we are encountering a poem. What *kind* of poem? A poem whose purpose is *what?* What is this dense poem attempting to discover, or should we say, uncover?

After the narrative-heavy second section, Warren steps back. He imagines not only Audubon's artistic vision—the passion—but also Audubon's hands-on process, which required killing the birds he painted in order to pose them and make them look more "natural." This is an irony symbolic of a more general irony that any thinking human must encounter. It is, Warren observes, a reality we cannot escape, and one we had better acknowledge. Passion drives us through what seems to be moral contradiction, and yet to become a proper *self*, we must pass through this valley of the shadow. Coming to terms with the real truth is a human process and an artistic process, according to Warren; it is also the process through which the *self* is authenticated and revealed. In the fourth section, "The Sign Whereby He Knew," Warren claims the real *self* is found outside itself, and only such a *self* can make something meaningful from its passion:

> To wake in some dawn and see,
> As though down a rifle barrel, lined up
> Like sights, the self that was, and the self that is, and there,
> Far off but in range, completing that alignment, your fate.
>
> (IV, ll. 6–10)

It's not the warmest vision of how one transforms passion into wisdom and, therefore, art, but it feels rather honest. It certainly erases any illusions one may have about the process. Life and art occur in an environment. For Audubon that environment was the backcountry, nascent America in its wild place and human circumstances. Such an environment can inspire the artist's passion, but, as Warren reflects, the artist must remain somehow independent. Later in the fourth section Warren returns to Audubon's biographical record of his day-to-day work in the woods painting the birds of America. Warren notes, "After sunset / Alone, he played his flute in the forest" (IV, C., ll. 11–12). With such music, with such a call in the wilderness, Warren now sees Audubon's way of being himself a bird. The literal facts are now in the process of being transferred to the symbolic and the allegorical. This is very subtle motion; the mind of the poet is moving.

In section VI, "Love and Knowledge," Warren turns his thoughts to the actual birds Audubon painted, some of which are now extinct. I will quote this entire section because it is beautiful verse.

> Their footless dance
> Is of the beautiful liability of their nature.

Their eyes are round, boldly convex, bright as a jewel,
And merciless. They do not know
Compassion, and if they did,
We should not be worthy of it. They fly
In air that glitters like fluent crystal
And is hard as perfectly transparent iron, they cleave it
With no effort. They cry
In a tongue multitudinous, often like music.

He slew them, at surprising distances, with his gun.
Over a body held in his hand, his head was bowed low,
But not in grief.

He put them where they are, and there we see them:
In our imagination.

What is love?

One name for it is knowledge.

Now Warren has stepped farther back to imply the question: Just what are these birds of America? What do they mean, and what do they symbolize? And how do they capture the artist who would make art of them? A further implication Warren delivers is this reminder: the artist is not a different sort of self. She or he is always a human being, capable of the same heights that allow any human to seem transcendent, but thwarted by the same human tendencies that keep us on the ground. We love, we fail.

Let's go back to section V, "The Sound of That Wind." Here, Warren goes back to the last years of Audubon's life. He's finished his life's work, *Birds of America*. He's convinced wealthy patrons to finance his project; he's sold expensive volumes of his large-scale book of paintings and has come out on top. He's finally returned from the wilderness to his family life and toured Europe, where his primary audience resides. These folks were eager to have a glimpse of the New World. By the end of his life Audubon lived in material comfort, and in the comfort of stable civilization, following his extended stay in a realm that had little concern for civilization. And in this state of being, his passion exhausted and spent, yet given life, Audubon died, rather ingloriously, by Warren's rendering. And then, in this section, Warren returns his thoughts and his reader to the twentieth-century present:

> So he died in his bed, and
> Night leaned, and now leans,
> Off the Atlantic, and is on schedule.
> (V, B., ll. 1–3)

Now, perhaps suddenly, though perhaps not, Warren, from his present perspective, observes airplanes flying high above the original ground of his poem, "The Northwest Orient plane, New York to Seattle, has passed, winking westward" (V, B., l. 16). Here is another, a new bird of America, industrial, the vehicle of modern commerce, apparently immune to its more natural origins. But Warren wants his reader not to forget those roots. And what comes from those roots? A complicated story, an American story. And that is the title of the final section of Warren's poem, section VII, "Tell Me a Story." This is the one famous section of Warren's long poem about our nation that makes it into the anthologies. That's a shame, because the entire poem represents the real inquiry Warren has considered, as an artist, as a thinker, and as a human being. Warren begins this section of *Audubon,* a poem about the painter of the birds of America, by recalling his own young involvement with such creatures:

> Long ago, in Kentucky, I, a boy, stood
> By a dirt road, in first dark, and heard
> The great geese hoot northward.
>
> I could not see them, there being no moon
> And the stars sparse. I heard them.
>
> I did not know what was happening in my heart.
> (VII, A., ll. 1–6)

Here Warren acknowledges that the geese he heard on their way northward gave him knowledge. The heart's passion to give voice to that particular kind of knowledge—which sees all things in blessed unity—is the beginning of love, and for someone of Warren's inclination, the beginning of poetry, because it is the first intimation of *self*, the first sense of authentic and distinct identity.

Here are the final lines of the poem. Warren considers the value of this roots-feeding knowledge as it pertains to the forming *self*:

> Tell me a story.
>
> In this century, and moment, of mania,
> Tell me a story.
>
> Make it a story of great distances, and starlight.
>
> The name of the story will be Time,
> But you must not pronounce its name.
>
> Tell me a story of deep delight.
>
> (VII, B., ll. 1–7)

It's worth noting that the final image of the poem, a hooting V of geese flying north, is invisible, a subtle nod to the word *vision* in the poem's title. The sound of the geese is a kind of passion, and the boy's mind is invited to imagine the V, which is the geese in unison, rowing through the dark heavens.

Warren published *Audubon* in 1969. In August of that year an American spacecraft called the *Eagle* landed on the moon. Also at that time, military birds of America had been bombing North Vietnam, Laos, and Cambodia for a few years, and such bombing was secretly increased for several more. Five years after publishing *Audubon*, Warren delivered his Jefferson Lecture, *Democracy and Poetry*. Here is a section from that lecture:

> [I]n the colleges and universities there is a reaction against the arts and humanities as impractical and "elitist." But let us turn to a straw in the more general wind, a passage from the White House tapes. Here the former President and his closest adviser are discussing how the President's daughters should spend their time before the opening of the Republican Convention of 1972:

> *President:* For example—now the worse thing (unintelligible) is to go to anything that has to do with the Arts.
>
> *Haldeman:* Ya, see that—it was (unintelligible) Julie giving [given?] that time in the Museum in Jacksonville.
>
> *President:* The Arts you know—they're Jews, they're left wing—in other words, stay away.
>
> The passage is, clearly, the utterance of a paranoid, power-bit Philistine of no generosity of spirit, little imagination, and an education of the most limited technical sort—the blind striking out against whole dimensions of life which, because incomprehensible to him, seem to be, not only an affront to his vanity, but a sinister attack on his very being. (*Democracy and Poetry*, 35–36)

That sounds rather like our present moment of mania, which appears to be great. Perhaps the delight of telling stories, the knowledge and love and the skills required to make our passions live, will help us out of this mess. We have to be willing to try, and we have to do it with wisdom and good cheer. *Audubon* captures the poet's mind in motion, moving through time and contemplation, imagination and memory. The *form* of the poem, at once, isolates and unifies the graceful movements of the mind that made it, as if that mind were flying. And the form of this poem is the form of continuity, following nature, whose form is continuous, just as the form of time, and the form of love.

My connection to Robert Penn Warren, I should confess, has long been personal. I have been drawn to him more than any other American writer, for various reasons. And just when I think I can give my study of Warren's poetry a rest, it somehow comes looking for me. I realize my thoughts in this discussion have been years in gestation, and months now in an effort to find something useful to say. It so happens that, right in the middle of writing this essay, I was contacted by a relative who wanted to know details about my father's service in the Korean War. My father died two years ago, not long after our daughter was born. I had not had time to go through the old photos and papers Dad left behind. On finally going through these boxes I came upon a photograph of the ship my father was on, the *Missouri*, as it plunges into forbidding seas off the coast of North Korea, sometime in December 1950. I've learned a little history about this particular mission, but I think the note my father wrote on the back of the photograph will allow me to conclude my thoughts for the moment. Here is the photo of the *Missouri:*

And here is the caption my Dad wrote on the back of the photo:

HANGNUM

RESCUED 5 PILOTS

Five birds went down in that sea back in 1950, and the living pilots were miraculously saved, a moment of poetic grace in the midst of war and human desperation. Does such poetry have a form? Yes, I think Warren would say: We call it history, especially irony-saddled American history. It is raw and dark and sometimes beautiful. From it we learn our passion, and how to live in the world.

Haunted

JILL McCORKLE

Emily Dickinson—in a letter to her literary mentor and correspondent Thomas Higginson—wrote: "Nature is a Haunted House—but Art, a house that tries to be haunted." Her great appreciation for and curiosity about nature and the unending possibilities presented there needed to be captured and compressed in a way that mirrored those complexities. How could art simulate nature? There are time and texture / senses and emotions / the presence of that thing / the knowledge, the love, the meaning, just up ahead and around the corner. Claudia Emerson's beautiful collection *The Opposite House* references Dickinson's poem "There's been a death in the opposite house, as lately as today / I know it by the numb look, such houses have—alway—."

My key words in this essay are "Haunted" and "House"—as I make an attempt to explore the components of both in ways both literal and figurative. As writers, we often feel that we are on the outside looking in, much like Dickinson's narrator, and yet, I believe that we also are rarely divorced from that part within ourselves looking out on the world in search of answers and meaning. I think that every lecture I have ever given has included my belief that we will never be as smart as our subconscious, that try as we might, it will always be several steps ahead of us, working to make connections and find logic in places and ways that surprise us. The only real advice I have about writing is to seek the trust and patience that allow this to happen so that THEN you can really get down to work, structuring and then revising and rebuilding as you take that broadest sweep of nature and squeeze it into paragraphs.

House—a physical structure—something easily described.

Haunt—to remain, stay, linger, worry—an intangible element that fills a space.

Most of us have had that dream where we discover a whole new part of our house that we never knew was there. According to Jung, houses in dreams represent the self, and so such a dream means you are discovering something about yourself you didn't know before—different floors represent various levels of human consciousness. Some might say that the state of the house is representative of your current emotional state. You can read through the list of rooms outlined as dream symbols if you like from the attic of repressed thoughts and hidden memories to the confusing basement filled with things you need to sort through or discard. In *Mrs. Dalloway,* Virginia Woolf wrote: "There was an emptiness about the heart of life; an attic room."

On the page, just the movement from room to room—crossing a threshold—can create tension and suspense. There's the door that has never been opened—is it the Lady or the Tiger? Or if you're on *Let's Make a Deal,* a car or a basket of turnips? Choice / Decision / Surprise. In the old fairy tale "Bluebeard" the young wife is told never to open that door at the far end of the hall. There is nothing more intriguing than the forbidden. And of course she can't resist and opens the door to see all the other young wives before her strangled and hanging on the wall. The forbidden provides immediate suspense from Eve to Pandora / Lot's wife / Orpheus, the imaginary line your sibling drew down the middle of the back car seat, and so on.

In "A Rose for Emily," Faulkner wrote in the voice of the town: "Already, we knew that there was one room in that region above the stairs which no one had seen in forty years." We have already been introduced to Miss Emily's house "lifting its stubborn and coquettish decay above the cotton wagons and gasoline pumps—an eyesore among eyesores." And of course when that door is finally opened—the surprise awaits us. If you don't know this story, read it, for many reasons—the point of view as well as the lack of chronological order are worth the study.

This Gothic introduction might call to mind others—"We came to Miss Havisham's house which was of old brick, and dismal, and had a great many iron bars to it. Some of the windows had been walled up; of those that remained, all the lower were rustily barred." And in similar fashion, Carson McCullers in *The Ballad of the Sad Café:* "The building looks completely deserted. Nevertheless on the second floor there is one window which is not boarded; sometimes in the late afternoon when the heat is at its worst a hand will slowly open the shutter and a face will look down on the town. It is a face like the terrible dim faces known in dreams—sexless and white."

Haunted

I once had an argument with a friend while we were out on a walk. It was getting dark and we were walking through a neighborhood where many of the houses resembled one another—1960s split-levels and ranches, with matching window configurations and sidewalks leading up to their doors. But with darkness, they seemed to come to life in very different ways. Some remained dark with all curtains drawn, some were fully lit with no blinds at all, others clearly tracked the life within the light over the kitchen sink, another in what must be a bedroom upstairs.

Sometimes you might see someone in half dress run past, or a kid staring into the blue flickering glow of a television or bent over homework at the kitchen table. Sometimes you witnessed something that the person within assumed to be completely private—a tug at the crotch of his pants or a finger up the nose. This is where my friend said it was rude to look, a violation of their privacy. She said this when I commented on the child watching an episode of *Boy Meets World* and picking his nose with great abandonment, the kind of action that would have prompted my grandmother in my own childhood to ask if I needed a pail and a shovel. The memory of her voice coupled with the image of the child had made me laugh out loud, which started the whole debate in the first place. I said I thought it was more like theater—like a scene out of Hitchcock's *Rear Window*—if you don't wish to be seen, pull the shades, close the drapes.

Our stance as observer is an ongoing exploration of the objective or dramatic point of view. I hear snippets of voice and sound; I observe pantomimed gestures and embraces, animated hands that could be quick with fury and agitation or with exhilaration and excitement. The man, still in his suit jacket, has his back to the window and so I'm not sure. What I DO know though is that something has happened, something tangible in the physical world has taken place or some lightning bolt of a thought has entered his mind. The key to the information I need is in the recipient of this conversation, and it is hard not to wait to watch this person enter from the adjoining room, also lit but behind drapes. And then here she comes, moving quickly into the window scene (what was she doing in that room I can't see?), and she's laughing. Whew—It's a raise or a promotion! He sold his book! He won the lottery! The charges against him have been dropped! In that paragraph of a moment, they are happy—lucky. The darkness of the house next door reminds us that it won't always be that way.

Whatever is within my realm of seeing and hearing and witnessing as I pass through public streets is mine to observe. We observe something solid that can be described factually—a well-kept colonial or a ramshackle shed—a manicured lawn or a tangle of weeds—a dirt yard swept clean or a secret garden just behind the gate. Southern exposure, big oak tree, stack of newspapers at the end of the drive, tricycle visible in the open door of that cluttered garage. These facts are then easily washed through and over with all of the many possibilities of the stories there, both present and past. We are curious to know what is behind those doors and windows. Charlie Rich sang all about it—When we get behind closed doors—In that case "she makes him glad that he's a man" but of course we know that that isn't how that story would always turn out. There is always the other/opposite version. For instance, George Jones and Tammy Wynette sang about their "Two Story House"—He has his story and she has hers.

I have often told my students that, if you walk around with your eyes and ears open, you can't possibly live long enough to write all of the potential stories you will glimpse along the way.

I think when writing a story or a novel, it is always important—at least in revision—to think about the narrative stance. Are you on the outside looking in, or are you inside looking out. Are you inside waiting for the knock? Alarmed by the knock? Disappointed the knock never comes? Or are you walking the steps up to that strange dark door? That brightly lit door? That door you thought you would never darken again? That door you have dreamed about returning to for years? Certainly, there would be much to know about a person in either place and a whole lot of mystery and intrigue around what the future will bring.

Take the famous opening of Daphne Du Maurier's *Rebecca*—"Last night I dreamt I went to Manderley again," and then "there was Manderley, our Manderley, secretive and silent as it had always been, the grey stone shining in the moonlight of my dream, the mullioned windows reflecting the green lawns of the terrace. Time could not wreck the perfect symmetry of those walls," and "the house was a sepulcher, our fear and suffering lay buried in its ruins."

Or Bram Stoker's *Dracula:* "I am glad that it is old and big. I myself am of an old family, and to live in a new house would kill me. A house cannot be made habitable in a day; and after all, how few days go to make up a century. . . . I am no longer young and my heart through wearing years of mourning over the dead, is not attuned to mirth. Moreover, the walls of my castle are broken, the shadows are many, and the wind breathes cold through the broken battlements and casements. I love the shade and the shadow. . . ."

Or Steinbeck in *East of Eden:* "The house was clean, scrubbed and immaculate, curtains washed, windows polished, but all as a man does it—the ironed curtains did not hang quite straight, there were streaks on the windows and a square showed on the table where a book was moved."

Windows and doors are endlessly fascinating—the whole story completely changed by the point of view. Are you inside looking out or outside looking in? Think for instance what Joyce does at the end of "The Dead," Gabriel's vision within the room, the focus on his wife's singular expression of the grief that will always haunt her—and thus now will haunt him, shifting to the window where the snow is "falling faintly through the universe and faintly falling, like the descent of their last end, upon all the living and the dead."

Or Virginia Woolf: "With my cheek leant upon the window pane, I like to fancy that I am pressing as closely as can be upon the massive wall of time, which is forever lifting and pulling and letting fresh spaces of life in upon us."

Marsha Norman's play *'Night, Mother* is anchored by the visible bedroom door on stage. The daughter informs her mother very early on that in a couple of hours she is going to go into her room and kill herself. And then what had been witty banter between the two is suddenly weighted in suspense and dread. There are clocks visibly ticking. We see the threshold / the before and the after, and once we are aware of that threshold, nothing can be as it was.

I am someone drawn to houses. I like to look at floor plans, see how people decorate—color and fabric choice and furniture and picture placement—all somehow connected to who they are. You can walk into a house and within minutes might register how it makes you feel. Is it warm and comfortable or cold and unsettling? Could you curl up and take a nap, or do you feel the need to keep looking over your shoulder? If you're putting this house down on paper, all of those elements become important, details that reveal emotion or might suggest both past and future.

In my hometown, there is a house that my whole childhood we referred to as "the murder suicide house," and it's one I have used in fiction on more than one occasion. As a child, I was afraid to ride by it on my bicycle, and yet I also really needed to. It remained empty for a long time and, I as I rode by, I glanced quickly, just long enough to make sure there was no one within looking back at me. I could imagine that story from either side of the window.

I also knew that the beautiful mansion that housed the Methodist Youth Center had once been privately owned, and I loved to go there on Sunday nights—partly to sneak away from Baptist Training Union—a dismal organization with a depressing event called Snack and Yak where they served stale sandwiches and conducted Bible drills. There were several of us who, when the rear end of whatever parent's car had deposited us there disappeared, high-tailed it over to the Methodist Church just two blocks away and into that amazing mansion. This of course was very different from Snak and Yak, and we had heard that at the Episcopal Church they were dancing and playing spin the bottle, but it was too far to walk and get back in time to be waiting curbside at First Baptist for whatever parent was assigned to haul us home. So we dashed over to the old mansion that now was the Methodist Youth Center. The rooms looked like what you would find in a museum or courthouse and, if I ignored the black paint on the walls and the clunking of billiards from the enormous pool table, the jukebox playing CCR and Three Dog Night, and the smell of cigarette smoke wafting in from the terrace, I could imagine what this grand home once looked like—the curved wooden staircase and stained-glass window, the black and white tiles of the bathroom and kitchen, the huge old radiators that were dwarfed by the twenty-foot ceilings. There had also been a suicide years before in that house, or so I had been told, a young man who had leapt from an upstairs window, and I remember tracing windows to ground and wondering which one, wondering what the circumstances were that led him there. Had any neighbors witnessed the moment? So many stories, so much potential in the history of that one place, until the Methodist Church could no longer afford to heat it and it slowly deteriorated and then was razed. And yet, people still refer to where it once was, pointing as if it might suddenly rise up from the ground again.

My mother has dementia and, when she was still able to get out, and her cousin Vista—who also had dementia—was still alive, I would take them to get a hot dog and go for a ride. Every time they would ask me to ride by their homes, meaning of course the homes of their childhood; they would tell me my mother lived on the corner of Second and Chippewa. They had grown up just blocks from one another, neither house still standing. In fact, the corner where my mother had grown up had long been empty and then filled with a prefab building that had been a Laundromat and a grocery store and a storefront church that now is also closed and boarded up. Still, I rode up and down their street, both of them with their faces pressed to the glass, searching. "I know it's here somewhere," Vista kept saying. "Just go one more time and go real slow."

So many works of fiction begin in just this way—going home or leaving home—someone haunted by the memory of a particular place. I dreamed I went to Manderley—past and present—the juxtaposition of before and after is all we really need to provide tension and suspense. And so many houses! There's "The Fall of the House of Usher"—or *The Haunting of Hill House* or *The House of the Seven Gables, Bleak House,* Shirley Jackson's *We Have Always Lived in the Castle* or Marilynne Robinson's *Housekeeping. Wuthering Heights* and so on.

Perhaps—as in the dream world—what we are physically drawn to in structures reflects some part of ourselves. I am often drawn to those windows above businesses—the little bit of a curtain or a flower pot—I always imagine what might be happening up there—a hidden life—a nice comfortable dwelling easily camouflaged to all who pass by. It makes me think of the Elizabeth Bishop poem "Filling Station"—"oh but it is dirty! This little filling station. . . ." And then we learn that there is a dirty dog on a wicker sofa "quite comfy," there are comic books and a doily and a plant. In the final stanza, she begins: "Somebody embroidered the doily. Somebody waters the plant." And then the last line: "somebody loves us all." For me the use of "comfy" and "love" breathes life into the scene.

I am drawn to those tucked-away places because they do feel secretive and somehow removed from the rest of the world. Likewise, I love the tiny cottages of fairy tales—the rough stones and thatched roofs, the little wisps of smoke rising from their chimneys. They appear safe and comfortable, which of course is not always the case at all. A wolf might be trying to get in. There are evil stepmothers planning how to get rid of children, witches with an eye for baking and eating children, woodcutters who have been ordered to cut out a young girl's heart, and so on. And yet, before I can acknowledge the possibility of any horror, I have to work my way through a feeling of comfort. Is that me looking out from within? Is that me remembering without even knowing I am doing so the first times I saw those little cottages, the letters on the page all running together in total nonsense but the glossy color picture of a little cottage in the woods being my focus while what I probably really was focused on was the voice of the grown-up reading to me—the comfort of being able to either look at the little house or just close my eyes and listen, with a big strong arm holding me in place? Though I desired to know what all those words and letters meant, there was also a kind of comfort in trusting that I didn't have to know, that the person reading to me knew and I didn't have to worry about any of it, that I was not yet responsible for it. I think my attraction to those idyllic little cottages is just that. For me, they represent something simple and contained and comfortable and solid. A place where you know all that you need to know, no closets for something to jump out of. In the dream theory, this level of comfort would connect us to that very first home pre-birth.

My other fantasy house is the one in *It's a Wonderful Life*—that great big, rambling place in need of love and attention. I totally bought into the Frank Capra romance of how you can take what everyone else considers an eyesore and a ruin, and turn it into a home. Edward Hopper's painting *Railroad Crossing* does it for me and, in fact, there is a home near where I live that was long deserted and looked just like it, the tracks just a short distance from the front yard. I watched with great envy as the for-sale sign went away and then painters came and then there were curtains in the windows. A porch light turned on; there was a rocking chair facing the tracks. They were living my fantasy. And then they painted the window casings one color and the front door yet another color I felt was all wrong, and instead of one beautiful birdhouse, there were seven, some tilted and falling apart, and then a chain-link fence and a couple of goats and several old cars. It was all I could do not to run up and beg them to stop, to scream that they were ruining my dream.

I think if you are drawn to filling stations and seemingly vacant houses with an eye for windows and doors ajar, Hopper is an artist that immediately comes to mind. The more famous painting—*House by the Railroad*—is one the poet Mark Strand wrote about: "Standing apart, a relic of another time, the house is a piece of doomed architecture, a place with a history we cannot know. It has been passed by and the grandeur of its containment doubles as an image of refusal. . . . It defines with the simplest, most straight forward means, an attitude of resistance, of hierarchal disregard, and at the same time a dignified submission to the inevitable comfort in all the potential presented there." At the end of that book, Strand wrote: "It is as if we were spectators at an event we were unable to name; we feel the presence of what is hidden, of what surely exists but is not revealed." You could say we are haunted by their meaning. That these houses are haunted by their history—or in the case of the one I once coveted, a taste for decor and upkeep that doesn't mesh with my own.

The fantasy of salvaging an old house and bringing it back to life is probably not unlike that of the adolescent-girl missionary thing determined to tame and save that bad boyfriend and turn him around. Thanks to things like *This Old House* and Home Depot, and hopefully the wisdom that comes with age, the odds are much better in transforming and saving the house.

I think what attracts me to those houses by the tracks is that it does create the sensation of movement. Either you glimpse the structure as you pass it by OR you are somewhere behind one of the windows watching people pass, tracks extending in either direction as far as the eye can see. Sometimes you allow yourself to imagine both and the friction between the two. I've always been completely astonished to know that Ralph Waldo Emerson's grandfather and his family stood in their second-floor windows of the house known as the Old Manse in Concord, Massachusetts, and watched the Battle of Lexington taking place on that bridge well within their view—the beginning of the Revolutionary War. Talk about a reality show.

Writing a poem or story or novel is not unlike building or refurbishing a house; great attention must be applied to the physical structure. You want to gather the right materials—sifting through straw and sticks to find those bricks. You have to space the support so that it doesn't tip over or fall apart; you have to plumb and wire, sand and polish. Sound structure is key, but that is only half of it. Now there is the search for what haunts it. And so you think of what is invisible to the eye, the history behind this door or that staircase.

Perhaps when people say write what you know it is as much about locating a comfortable position for the telling and then mining all that can be found on that site. Location, location, location.

I teach at Bennington College twice a year and have done this off and on for over twenty years. The Music Department there, a big beautiful ivy-covered stone building called Jennings Hall, is one of those buildings you pass and feel that someone is watching you from an upper window. I felt this way even before I heard rumors that it was haunted and that Shirley Jackson had used it for her model for *The Haunting of Hill House*. "No live organism can continue for long to exist sanely under conditions of absolute reality. . . . Hill House, not sane, stood by itself against its hills, holding darkness within; it had stood so for eighty years and might stand for eighty more. Within, walls continued upright, bricks met neatly, floors were firm and doors were sensibly shut; silence lay steadily against the wood and stone of Hill House and whatever walked there, walked alone."

I've been in the house several times over the years, always perched between the awe of the beautiful structure and that kind of quiet observance that usually settles whenever anyone tells a good ghost story. About fifteen years ago, we had one of the faculty graduate dinners there. It was a beautiful late afternoon in June, and the whole large room was bathed in that kind of perfect light that always makes you feel like it's all too good to be true—it's like the light of a movie or a painting. In real time, you are aware of how fleeting this light will be.

I was at that dinner, and I was struck by an older visiting writer and his wife. It hit me that that was the truest most loyal and selfless love I had ever witnessed. Neither was posed—both so comfortable in their skin. I remember doing one of those notes to self—THIS is what it looks like. There's the golden marriage—that perfect capsule of love. And all around there were glasses clinking and toasts made and laughter, and then the glow had passed and the event ended. And yet, I went away feeling I had seen something really important and thought that, as crazy as it might sound, I was going to write him a letter and say what a joy to meet and hear him but more so to have observed this union. I remember thinking but what if I'm wrong—devil on left shoulder says: oh they are good—no marriage is that perfect, no person so selfless and loving, but the angel on the right kept saying: but I do believe—there are pure and golden examples out there and you did see it. I was going to write the letter. If it was all as I had imagined, they would be delighted and I might get a nice note in return. If I had totally missed the boat, then they might look at one another and have that come-to-Jesus moment: he might say: We can't go on fooling people the way we've been doing. It's not fair and if we have fooled someone as sharp and astute as her (my imagination said this of course), then we're fooling everyone and we should either feel enormous shame or quit our day jobs and hit Broadway.

I wrote my letter to them many times. When I was driving or walking or just as I was falling asleep but before I could put pen to paper, I heard that he had died. And so I thought I would write to her alone to tell about this moment, and I did the same thing, carrying all those words and sentences around in my pockets for several months and then heard the startling news that she had died as well. I had a moment and I missed it and so, all these years since, when I have passed by Jennings Hall, I have felt the eyes of the ghosts of the house that many have felt off and on for years, and I also feel the haunting of my own regret as well as the haunting of that beautiful perfect June evening where I glimpsed what I thought surely was the purest most balanced love I had ever seen, the kind we should all be seeking in life. Somehow over the years, that moment there in that dining room, green mountains outside the windows, golden light washing over us, has come to symbolize every letter I meant to write and didn't, every word I wanted to say but hadn't. I never pass by that building—and I do many times every year—without feeling haunted by my own failures. If I were to try and take that emotion and squeeze it into a short story, then obviously I would have to do more with my story—what was going on in my own life that I was so fixed on the couple in my presence, or perhaps I would explore their story—would I look for that human flaw that surely must have existed? I could ask the light to freeze and stay a little bit longer, time slowed and yet still providing the light and the sensation of movement.

As writers, such hauntings are what keep us in business as we work to build and rebuild our houses.

Why Literature Can Save Us

RICHARD BAUSCH

Of course I'll have to begin with the problem of our title. "Why Literature Can Save Us." The problem is one of definition. And the definitions, separately and in concert, can be the source of thousands of discussions and arguments, articles and, yes, books. In fact, the words have inspired just that down the generations.

So, what is literature and what constitutes salvation?

I'll begin with a brief surface definition of the terms. We all know that the word "literature" comes from the Latin plural, *litterae*, which means *letters*. But we also know that the meaning of salvation is almost as various as the kinds of people we may encounter, and might even vary from day to day in our own minds and hearts. The sense in which I mean it here will become evident as we proceed; but I should say at the beginning that I am not talking about salvation from near or present dangers, or threats to our safety. At least not directly. Emily Dickinson says

> Tell all the Truth but tell it slant—
> Success in Circuit lies
> Too bright for our infirm Delight
> The Truth's superb surprise
> As Lightning to the Children eased
> With explanation kind
> The Truth must dazzle gradually
> Or every man be blind—

So I will try to tell all the truth, but I must follow Ms. Dickinson's admonition.

I was thirteen or fourteen before I understood that parts of the Catholic Mass were taken from the Old Testament. Back then, the end of the world was always about to drop in our laps, and the monolithic communist conspiracy was in full swing; they were getting in everywhere (I remember associating the word *communism* with the phrase *communicative disease*).

As youthful members of the Roman Catholic Church, we were always being exposed to dire pictures of hell. I remember one depicting the souls tumbling into a fiery pit. They looked like a lot of very frightened people, most of them women. We heard their shrieks—I didn't think then about actors screaming—and we heard the roar of the flames. A murmuring dramatic recorded voice said, "Listen to the screams of the damned, as they fall into the torment of unquenchable fire." And a moment later, with the dull ding of bell, the machine made its small cranking sound, and the image was pushed aside for another: someone's idea of the glorious throne of God.

In important ways, it was a different church, then—the one that existed before John XXIII and Vatican II. We fasted from midnight on if we were going to go to communion in the morning. We did not eat meat on Fridays. We went to confession on Saturdays, and I was of course relatively new to the practice.

The only Old Testament that I knew was the Ten Commandments, which we were forced to recite in the religion classes we attended on weekends. Confraternity of Christian Doctrine, it was called, instruction for Catholic children who were forced by circumstances to attend public schools. We learned the Catechism, too, of course. *Who made you? God made me. Why did God make you? He made me to know, serve and love him with my whole heart and my whole mind and my whole body.*

But I don't remember much time spent on the commandments as such. We recited them. They were words. A lot of *Thou shalt* and *Thou shalt nots*. I loved my parents, and I was not likely to begin worshipping golden calves in the desert. At school there weren't many inducements to murder or slander. It was easy enough not to steal, since nobody had anything much to begin with.

Mostly, when the priests and nuns talked about sin, they were talking about sins of the flesh.

When, at that very tender and raw and innocently obsessive age, I discovered what all young boys discover about their bodies around that time of life, I was completely unprepared for it. In the first blush of the moment, I thought

I'd made the greatest find of the century, and wanted to tell everyone I knew. I didn't, though, of course. Since what I had uncovered was after all a privy act, and since the possibility had struck through me that I might in fact be the last person to stumble upon a thing everyone else already knew. Also, of course, I'd begun to wonder if it were not a sin.

So I consulted the family Bible, and looked again at those Ten Commandments. Since I did not know what *covet* meant, I fixed on the word *adultery*. I'd heard the word used in Sunday sermons about the sinful sex lives of certain Hollywood stars who flaunted their immorality before the public. This was 1958, when the Legion of Decency was rating motion pictures, and much of the world's greatest literature was proscribed.

Adultery. It was a mortal sin. I remembered with a sinking heart that this was what the priest had said, and now it seemed that the commandment must serve as a blanket for all sexual activity outside Holy Matrimony.

So I hurried to confession.

"Forgive me, Father, for I have sinned," I said. "My last confession was two weeks ago. I lied to my mother three times about the dishes. I said unkind things to my sisters four times. I hid my brother's baseball glove so he would have to play basketball with me. And—and I committed adultery fifty or sixty times, Father. I lost count."

The priest, a kindly man named Father McManus, gave forth what I thought was a cough. Argh—argh. Ah. Hah. Agh.

I waited. The cough lasted a very long time, it seemed. And then there was a breathing silence, which also went on, long enough to seem portentous: I was about to be told something big, something life-changing.

"And who," the priest began. Then coughed again. "did you—who did you—argh-hagh—uh—ah." More silence. A long slow breath, then: "Was there a—was there—who—did you do this with?"

"You mean you can do it with someone else?" I said, a little too loud. There was another coughing spell. A very long one, now. Followed by another lengthy, gathering silence, so that, quite tentatively, into the void of it, I said, "Father?" I was not astute enough to recognize any of these disruptions as caused by the laughter.

Finally he asked how old I was. And I told him.

"There—ah. Agh—argh. There was no one else involved, then."

"No, Father."

"Then—ah—that's—ah-hagh. That's not adultery."

"It's not a *sin?*" I couldn't keep the joyousness out of my voice.

"Oh, yes—Ah. It's a very big sin. The sin of self-abuse."

"Yes, Father," I said. Though I was thinking, *You're not doing it right, Father. It's really not abuse at all, because it feels really good. Are you sure we're talking about the same thing?*

He gave me penance, and I went out into the world the Bible had made, or that generations of people had made out of the Bible.

When I was twenty-two, and fancied myself a lyric folk poet, I traveled with four young women to Montgomery, Alabama. We were a rock 'n' roll band, and were booked for a week down there. The summer of 1967. We drove down in a light gold '62 Caddie with a trailer hitched to the back bumper, and at a gas station somewhere between the Mississippi line and Montgomery, I had a sort of blind fit over something I'll have to take some trouble to explain. Though I had grown up in Virginia, I had not been privy to the kind of systematic discrimination and racism then prevalent in the South. (I believe my very good parents, who then would have been called moderate southerners, or integrationist dissenters, depending on who was describing them, had kept me from this, Virginia being Virginia.) In any case, we had driven all night and after sunrise we stopped at this Standard Oil station, and everyone got out to use the restrooms. We had been talking about the Book of Job for miles.

We pulled into this gas station and piled out of the car, crossing the hot asphalt lot in the early morning sun, and I was the first to see that there were three bathrooms. The three bathrooms were designated, with painted black letters on two of them: MEN, WOMEN; above the door frame of the third bathroom was a gray plastic sign made of letters: COLORED. Below the letters was an open, dirty doorway.

I stopped. They looked at me: four young women, the Luv'd Ones, led by Char Vinnedge, to whom I was engaged—and you can look her up on YouTube and Wikipedia and several other sites, because that band, the Luv'd Ones, has gathered a cult following, and is listed under garage bands of the sixties. They were way ahead of their time: an all-girl band at a time when that was not considered something marketable. Char Vinnedge was the driving force of it all—lead guitarist, singer-songwriter, designer, ad manager, arranger; she would later do session work with Jimi Hendrix, and then a separate album with Hendrix's bass player, Billy Cox, an album called *Nitro Function* that made money in Europe.

The Luv'd Ones' only album, *Truth Gotta Stand*, was released from demos and studio tracks in 1999, a year after Char Vinnedge's death, and the last song on it is a song I wrote, called "Please Get Up."

So. Four women, and me—combination roadie and sometime singer (a novelty bit where I'd do Bob Dylan's "Like A Rolling Stone," and I could do Dylan's voice and it drove crowds to a frenzy, too, since Dylan was still in seclusion after his motorcycle accident). Anyway, I had known them for a period of years. Had traveled with them and spent many long hours in cars and restaurants and motel rooms. They ranged in age from twenty-four to eighteen. I was twenty-two. They were my dear friends. Beloved friends, and we were idealistic and hopeful about the future (after all, there were so many like us, surely we would transform the face of the world). Looking at the gas-station emblem—Standard Oil, the headquarters of which I knew to be in New Jersey—I had an image of this company in the North cynically agreeing to build a gas station with three restrooms, and something drifted loose inside me. It may have been that I had this friendly audience, though I don't think so: I wasn't likely to impress them, or change anything about their feeling for me. It may have been the grogginess of being on the road all night; it also may have been simple indignation, though I don't think it was that alone. It felt like a kind of fit, a spasm of the purest frustration. I went to the open doorway, jumped up and hung on the plastic sign, and bent it down far enough to stand and pull on it until it came loose—it did so with a cracking noise that echoed—and then I sailed it off into the farm field beyond that end of the lot. Char and the others approved. We stood there. We might've been people waiting for some indication of life in a ghost town. There wasn't even any traffic.

"Justice," our drummer said, smiling at me. Her name was Faith Orem. "We're prob'ly in someone's sights right now. Either there's nobody here, or any second we're gonna hear the shots."

Char went out into the field and brought the sign back. "I'm keeping this," she said, opening the trunk of the car and throwing it in with the harmonicas and the dirty clothes and the bags of books.

A moment later, the proprietor walked out from the side of the building and asked in a normal tone of voice if he could help us. He was evidently not aware of what had just happened.

"No," Char Vinnedge said. "But we do wonder why you wouldn't build *four* bathrooms if you really wanted things to be separate but equal."

"I never built no bathrooms."

"No, of course not. But does it seem a bit odd to you?"

The man was wiry, blond, not much older than we were. He looked at us, then at the license plate on the front of the gold Caddie. "Y'all fixin' to cause trouble down here?"

"No," Charlotte's sister, Christine, the eighteen-year-old, said. "But it isn't equal, like you all say. Is it."

"I never said nothing about nothing like that. Separate *or* equal. Y'all want some gas? A cold Coke?"

"Don't you think it's unfair?" the rhythm guitarist, Mary, said. She stood there with her hands in the back pockets of her jeans and waited for him to answer.

"Well, you know," he said, shifting a little to one side, "I'll be honest, this seg or de-seg stuff, I never give hit much thought." He looked off toward the field. Then he spit a little and wiped his mouth. "Don't really know what's fair. *Or* equal neither. Y'all want gas or not?"

"You don't own this place," I said.

He smiled. "Whad d'yew think?"

"If you did, you'd—you wouldn't—" I couldn't finish the thought.

He was our age. He was of us, if that makes any sense; I knew he listened to the same music, and watched much of the same television and saw the same movies, and maybe he had even read some of the things we'd read. In any case, I felt the need to hear from him that he was not part of the system he was in. He shook his head a little. "I ain't got all day, folks."

"But you don't really believe in segregation," I said. People used the word casually and often, then. It was a word as loaded as the term "pro-life" is now.

He seemed to pull into himself. "Well, hit's, um, in the Bible. I heard hit read on Sundee."

We got back into the car, and rode away with his sign. He was a boy who went to church each week, who no doubt possessed all the virtues valued most in the place where he lived: he was hard-working, independent-minded, industrious, loyal to his family and friends, helpful, serious, good-natured, kind, generous.

Bigoted.

In the beginning was the word. And the word was with God. And the word was God.

I believe that if that young man had been given literature in its fullness, say, more than the smattering he might've had in high school, if he had been given the gift of having people around him who valued literature, and on whom it was not lost or wasted, if he had been opened to its vast power to evince and to expand the imagination, he might have seen the injustice all around him in his native country.

I'm past seventy now. The question of salvation is still unanswered, of course, and like Job I have stood in winds and demanded answers that I did not get. I'm only mildly facetious in asserting this. I've taught young adults who are completely ignorant of the Bible, and of all the literature that is out there for the taking. Riches. And though every day they swim in intellectual and spiritual and cultural waters that spring from literature, they are suspicious of it and feel that it is trivial. Or, as a certain vice-presidential candidate called it in an interview, "frivolous." And how strangely secular this time is—even in the midst of so much public religious fervor—just nineteen years past the brink of the new millennium and whatever *that* will hold: some unifying struggle, perhaps, undreamed-of catastrophes, deliverance. Recently I looked at the film of Dwight David Eisenhower's last speech in office, the famous "Military Industrial Complex" speech. I saw a president whose party had just lost an election. Eisenhower looks into the camera and says, "We have a new president, and I wish him God speed." And it struck me how far we have come in our sound-bite invective culture from that civility, how deeply we have fallen from the habit of thinking about the country and its people first, and party and politics second. It seems to me that gains in the social fabric are being eroded, and that there is a new separatism afoot in the land; a fragmentation, groups clamoring to embrace abstractions about each other and about all the other groups. And so, for me, the *stories* which connect us—perhaps now more than ever in our history—have a much deeper worldly and spiritual significance. Therefore, if you have any talent at all for it, there can never be anything in your working life so important as the writing of stories. Stories, those explorations of the lonely self, are more important in our time than they ever were. Poor old suffering

Job, that man who played out his drama with his lord and demanded an answer from him, an answer that sounds in fact like a piece of petty belligerence: "Can you call Leviathan out of the deep?" That story speaks down through the ages because it is the story of one man's struggle with his God. And then there is Gerard Manley Hopkins's great poem about despair, the last line of which is "That night of now done darkness when I, wretch, lay wrestling with (my God!) my God."

If you really look at it, every great story or poem seeks grace, and partakes of sanctity. *He who has ears to hear, let him hear.*

Moreover, I believe that there is a form of imaginative genius present in every act of mercy, in every act of understanding, in every act of the affirmation of individual dignity. I believe if the person who has the power to destroy another life can be given the ability, the gift, of seeing the reality of that life beyond abstraction—of making the leap of imagination that gives forth a sense of the other in completeness, free of concept—then the carnage, physical and intellectual, can stop, and a real transformation can begin. I know that I'm not the first to say that violence steals not only the life of the victim, but the life and being of the person committing the violence as well. Yet violence is more than the violent act itself; that is only a result, and paradoxically, like beauty, it belongs to the world of effect. Violence is more than the moment of its eruption; it exists like a fog through which we strive to see each other, in the air and in the breathing and dreaming and speech we are born and raised in, and it has its impact on us long before it becomes the actions we see in the world.

For me, the greatest hedge against that evil has always been the power to imagine the other. To enter into the reality of the other. And literature is, isn't it, an exploration of and confrontation *with* the other. My father had a thing he used to say to us when we were growing up, and it is so simple: "Everybody, one at a time." He explained that the idea was not to make any assumptions about the people we would come into contact with in our lives—not to believe or be influenced by the stereotypes and prejudices of life in the world, not to see a single person as part of some monolith of a culture or religion or race or country, but to see each person first as an individual someone: Everybody, one at a time.

I think this is the basis for all literature, no matter who produces it.

I believe the thing which connects every writer who is interested in the truth, every writer who is determined to tell truly not just what is in his own heart, but what he sees in the heart of experience, is that the emotional truth and felt life that he finds in the writing of a good story *breaks down the walls between people,* obliterates the assumptions and falsity in how we see the other. It flattens the barriers of culture, and closes the divide between young and old. He knows that if the story is good, it will have this effect. And though he can never know whether or not it will find its way into the general mind, if you will, he hopes it is good enough *always* to have this effect for whoever may come upon it, wherever they may be, and, truly, *when*ever they may be. In any case, trying to be clear, and to be truthful, partakes of the great miracle that defines all of us as human.

All other mammals care for their young, and seek warmth and surcease from pain or suffering. Many animals sign, and transmit elementary kinds of knowledge; but you will never see two elephants or chimps, or even porpoises, gathering to exchange stories about a third elephant or chimp or porpoise who is not there. We alone are the creature that can seek comfort from the long record of our journey in the world, through this defining miracle—and it is something so common to our experience that we scarcely notice it. But it *is* a miracle. The linguists call it a triadic event. The simplest human transaction: two minds communicating about a third thing. We see it every single day, everywhere around us, as gossip, anecdotes, news, speeches, debates, jokes, or simply entertainment. But think where it leads, where it has led. It has given us literature. Here is an example: Greece, 700 BC. Chapman University in Southern California, where I teach, in the early spring of 2019. That constitutes two parts of the triad: Homer in Greece, and me in California. And the third thing—the thing between our two minds, one of which has been dust since seven hundred years before Christ walked the earth—that third thing is the fictional hero, Hector, tragic Hector, in Homer's beautiful epic poem, translated here by Richmond Lattimore. It is the scene of Hector before he must fight Achilles; he is with his wife and baby son, and his wife, Andromache, has just expressed concern for his life:

> "Lady . . . I too am concerned," said glorious Hector "But if like a coward
> I hid from the fighting, I would be shamed before all the Trojans
> And their wives in their trailing robes. Nor is it my nature, since I have
> Striven ever to excel always in the front line of the battle, seeking to

Win glory for my father and myself. And deep in my heart I know the
Day is coming when sacred Ilium will fall, Priam, and his people of the
Ashen spear. But the thought of the sad fate to come, not even
Hecabe's or Priam's, nor my many noble brothers' who will die
At the hands of their enemies, not even that sorrow
Moves me as does the thought of your grief when some bronze-clad
Greek drags you away weeping . . . Perhaps in Argos you'll toil at the
Loom at some other woman's whim, or bear water all unwillingly
From some spring . . . bowed down by the yoke of necessity.
Seeing your tears, they will say: 'There goes the wife of Hector,
Foremost of all the horse-taming Trojans, when the battle raged at
Troy.' And you will sorrow afresh at those words, lacking a man like
Me to save you from bondage. May I be dead, and the earth piled
Above me, before I hear your cries as they drag you away."
With this, glorious Hector held out his arms to take his son,
But the child, alarmed at sight of his father, shrank back with a cry
On his fair nurse's breast, fearing the helmet's bronze and the
horsehair crest nodding darkly at him . . . and glorious Hector at once
removed the shining helmet from his head and laid
It on the ground. Then he kissed his beloved son,
Dandled him in his arms, and prayed aloud: "Zeus, and all you gods,
Grant that this boy like me may be foremost among the Trojans, as
Mighty in strength, and a powerful leader of Ilium. And some day may
They say of him, as he returns from war, 'He's a better man than his
Father,' and may he bear home the blood-stained armour of those he
Has vanquished, so his mother's heart may rejoice." With this he
Placed the child in his dear wife's arms, and she took him to her
Fragrant breast, smiling through her tears.

When we read this, we are moved by it. We are moved every time we read it. Because as the fine poet and critic Mark Van Doren puts it, mortality still stings. Yet the moment, as described, is at least 2,700 years old. A father, a mother, and a son. Their reality. And we respond to it out of our own reality, millennia and countries away. Across time and past epochs and lost empires and the chasm of death itself. That is the miracle of literature. We know that it is out of the abstractions, and in the name of them, that we judge, and turn our backs, and even kill. Yet the words "love," "mercy," "hope"—these are all abstract words. And I am aware that in stating all this, I have been using abstractions. But that is why I would never use anything of the kind in anything where I am striving, as all writers in some way do, to make something that might last. To tell a story that has the possibility, no matter how small, of meaning something to someone far away, in whatever distance, because it partakes of that kind of truth. The truth that stays true, is always true. One hopes to see through and around and beyond abstractions, to achieve real being, real imagining. For me, that's the whole point of all of it.

Inside "Out, Out—"

ANDREW HUDGINS

'Out, Out—'

The buzz saw snarled and rattled in the yard
And made dust and dropped stove-length sticks of wood,
Sweet-scented stuff when the breeze drew across it.
And from there those that lifted eyes could count
Five mountain ranges one behind the other
Under the sunset far into Vermont.
And the saw snarled and rattled, snarled and rattled,
As it ran light, or had to bear a load.
And nothing happened: day was all but done.
Call it a day, I wish they might have said
To please the boy by giving him the half hour
That a boy counts so much when saved from work.
His sister stood beside him in her apron
To tell them 'Supper.' At the word, the saw, As if
to prove saws knew what supper meant, Leaped
out at the boy's hand, or seemed to leap—He
must have given the hand. However it was,
Neither refused the meeting. But the hand!
The boy's first outcry was a rueful laugh,
As he swung toward them holding up the hand
Half in appeal, but half as if to keep
The life from spilling. Then the boy saw all—

Since he was old enough to know, big boy
Doing a man's work, though a child at heart—
He saw all spoiled. 'Don't let him cut my hand off—
The doctor, when he comes. Don't let him, sister!'
So. But the hand was gone already.
The doctor put him in the dark of ether.
He lay and puffed his lips out with his breath.
And then—the watcher at his pulse took fright.
No one believed. They listened at his heart.
Little—less—nothing!—and that ended it.
No more to build on there. And they, since they
Were not the one dead, turned to their affairs.

—ROBERT FROST,
Collected Poems, Prose, and Plays, 1995

Fifteen, bored to near desperation in tenth grade, I flipped through my literature textbook, searching for something, anything, that might interest me. Back in the last half-inch of the book, in the part the class never got to, I discovered Robert Frost's "'Out, Out—,'" a poem that reached out, snagged my attention, and changed forever my ideas about what poetry could be. Though the art of Frost's poem was invisible to me, I was riveted by the poet's depiction of a boy leaving boyhood behind for manhood, which meant becoming a worker alongside men—something I'd already begun to contemplate fearfully.

I was thrilled, disturbed, and at some aesthetic and philosophical level relieved to read about a boy my age, doing work similar to work I'd done, and dying because of it—and after he dies the rest of the world goes about its business as if his death had not affected them in any essential way. I was thrilled and relieved because Frost was saying something I had noticed but that no one I knew had ever admitted. The dead, even those grieved deeply, are soon forgotten.

Though I was first drawn to the poem by what it said, the way it said it is what has made me return to it for the next half-century, pondering the sources of its power in the author's choice of words, details, and structuring.

One means of understanding an author's decisions is to change them and observe how the alterations affect the poem. We can find a warrant for this approach in *Structuralist Poetics* by Jonathan Culler (1978, rev. 2002). Drawing on the work of the Russian formalist critic Viktor Shklovsky, as well as Roland Barthes, Culler writes:

> Shklovsky seems to have realized that the analysis of plot structure ought to be a study of the structuring process by which plots take shape, and he knew that one of the best ways of discovering what norms are at work was to alter the text and consider how its effect is changed. The analyst of narrative, Barthes has observed, must be able to imagine "counter-texts," possible aberrations in the text, whatever would be scandalous in the narration ("L'analyse structurale du recit," p. 23). This would help him identify the functional norms. (223–24)

Frost himself made something of the same point when he said in a 1960 interview with the *Paris Review:* "The whole thing is performance and prowess and feats of association. Why don't critics talk about those things—what a feat it was to that that way, and what a feat it was to remember that, to be reminded of this by that" (*Collected Poems, Prose and Plays,* 1995, 892).

One useful way to see what feats Frost performed in "'Out, Out—'" is to cut the poem to pure narrative, slashing it almost in half, from 310 words over 34 lines to 164 words in 18 lines.

> The buzz saw snarled and rattled in the yard
> As it ran light, or had to bear a load.
> His sister stood beside them in her apron To tell
> them "Supper." At the word, the saw Leaped out
> at the boy's hand, or seemed to leap. The boy's
> first outcry was a rueful laugh,
> As he swung toward them holding up the hand
> Half in appeal, but half as if to keep
> The life from spilling. Then the boy saw all—
> He saw all was spoiled. "Don't let him cut my hand off—
> The doctor, when he comes. Don't let him, sister!"
> So. But the hand was gone already.
> The doctor put him in the dark of ether.
> He lay and puffed his lips out with his breath.

And then—the watcher at his pulse took fright.
No one believed. They listened to his heart.
Little—less—nothing! And they, since they
Were not the one dead, turned to their affairs.

"Harsh" is a word that occurs with some frequency in the criticism of "'Out, Out—,'" but our truncated version is harsher yet, revealing the ameliorations Frost worked into the poem. We miss the concerned speaker's voice, the voice that says things like:

Call it a day, I wish they might have said
To please the boy by giving him the half hour
That a boy counts so much when saved from work.

Or:

. . . the saw,
As if it meant to prove saws knew what supper meant,
Leaped out at the boy's hand, or seemed to leap—
He must have given the hand. However it was,
Neither refused the meeting.

Or:

Then the boy saw all—
Since he was old enough to know, big boy
Doing a man's work, though a child at heart—.

The narrator's three major emotional intrusions into the story are all isolated in the middle of the poem, and the emotions are weakly arrayed against the force of the terrible accident they first intimate, then depict, and finally respond to. The first and third tilt toward the sentimental—"the half hour / That a boy counts *so much* when saved from work" and "big boy . . . though *a child at heart*"—while the description of the amputation is almost dithery in its refusal to describe what happens. The suggestion of the boy's complicity with the saw is, in context, a similarly weak and failed, but psychologically accurate, attempt to assign meaning where there is no meaning. In other words, it's supposed to sound as unconvincing as it does, the human voice useless against the inexorable recounting of the boy's meaningless death.

In the shortened version of the poem, we also lose almost all sense of a larger community at work beside and around the boy, as well as the most lyrical poetry in the poem, the five lines sandwiched between the first and second appearance of the buzz saw:

> The buzz saw snarled and rattled in the yard
> *And made dust and dropped stove-length sticks of wood,*
> *Sweet-scented stuff when the breeze drew across it.*
> *And from there those that lifted eyes could count*
> *Five mountain ranges one behind the other*
> *Under the sunset far into Vermont.*
> And the saw snarled and rattled, snarled and rattled[.]

The passage is only five lines, but in a thirty-four-line poem that's about 15 percent of the whole and most of the opening. Without this passage, the poem forgoes any sense of the pleasing sights and smells of the natural world. With their lyricism and their vision of a lovely distance, these lines create a bit of Eden between the fierce and threatening appearances of the buzz saw. Though the saw wins this round, there is, inside the irony, a tantalizing suggestion of a better world beyond the world these characters are in at this unhappy moment.

What happens if we liberate this lyrical looking off into nature from the saw's snarls and rattles, and use it as the conclusion of the poem, a time-honored and dishonored trope of closure? In *Structural Poetics*, Culler, leading up to the section we've already looked at, turns a skeptical eye on such an "illusory ending": "But there is also what Shklovsky calls the 'illusory ending'—an extreme case which nicely illustrates the power of readers' formal expectations and the ingenuity that will be used to produce a sense of completion. 'Usually it is descriptions of nature or of the weather that furnish material for these illusory endings. . . . This new motif is inscribed as a parallel to the preceding story, thanks to which the tale seems completed'" (176–77).

A description of the weather can provide a satisfactory conclusion because the reader gives it a metaphoric or synecdochic interpretation and then reads this thematic statement against the actions themselves. By way of example, Shklovsky cites a brief passage from *Le Diable boiteux* in which a passerby, stopping to help a man mortally wounded in a fight, is himself arrested: "I ask the reader to invent even a description of the night in Seville or of the indifferent sky and to add it on" (177). And certainly he is right; such a description would give the story a satisfactory structure because the indifferent sky presents a thematic image which can be read as identifying and confirming the role of the preceding event in the story. By confirming the irony of the story, it isolates, as the dominant structure of the plot, the ironic movement of the action (223).

But resorting to nature for closure and the facile assurance it implies are exactly the expectations that Frost wants to challenge. Here's how such an ending might look in "'Out, Out—'":

They listened to his heart.
Little—less—nothing! And they, since they
Were not the one dead, *turned back to the door,*
And from there those that lifted eyes could count
Five mountain ranges one behind the other
Under the sunset far into Vermont.

This ending was depressingly easy to attach to Frost's poem; I simply removed its head and stapled it to its butt. I'm exhilarated, though, to observe just how exemplary it is in its awfulness. The change drains the tough intelligence from the poem and replaces it with a gauzy promise that somehow nature, a gesture toward God, and the loveliness of language itself will assuage all loss. Here, outside the three, hard, crashing repetitions of "snarled and rattled," the three prepositional phrases that end the sentence, the final line, and now the poem are, after the death of the boy, completely inadequate to the moment: "Five mountain ranges one *behind* the other / *Under* the sunset far *into* Vermont." Juxtaposed to the saw, working in tension with them, the lines are hopeful, rueful, and ironic with a rich amplifying of the poem's intelligence among the tones. But at the end, bearing the weight of the entire poem on a triad of prepositions, the lines' irony and rue fall away, leaving only a mawkish and untenable hope that is echoed in the attenuated dying fall of the syntax.

While we are altering the poem, let's consider some word choices and see what happens if we change them. As early as the second line of the poem, the somewhat limp-seeming verb "made" draws my attention. It's exactly the sort of word that in workshops student writers always want to replace with a "vivid verb," and since I'm a fan of vivid verbs, I'm going to slap some in that place to see why Frost turned a deaf ear to the advice of our hypothetical workshop. What vivid verb should we employ? If we stay close to Frost's choice, the thesaurus antes up a slew of problematic options—*rendered, created, produced, yielded,* and *caused. Rendered* and *created* are troublesomely biblical. *Produced* and *yielded* sound both agricultural and industrial with the suggestion that sawdust is the goal of the sawing, while *caused,* a bad fit for describing what a buzz saw does, also brings in the issue of causality that the poem is challenging. What about something more visual? *Spray* comes to mind, and another visit to the thesaurus turns up *spurted, spouted, gushed*—all too tidily anticipatory of the boy's amputated hand. *Cast* and *raised* evoke Jesus casting out demons or raising the dead, neither helpful associations, and *slung, flung, threw,* and certainly *spat* are too cartoonishly vivid for what occurs later in the poem.

What happens if we substitute *sprayed* for *made?* Sonically the only change is the introduction of the slight sibilance from the *sp* in *sprayed.* But the sibilance in the lines is already near a tipping point:

> The buzz saw snarled and rattled in the yard
> And made dust and dropped stove-length sticks of wood,
> Sweet-scented stuff when the breeze drew across it.

An amusing, anonymous 1905 article in the *Journal of Education,* "Tennyson's Geese: A Study in Euphonics" (vol. 37: 711), draws from a couple of widely separated observations about blank verse recounted in Hallam Tennyson's memoir of his father. Tennyson told his son that one key to blank verse, which of course "'Out, Out—'" is, is "kicking the geese out of the boat":

> There are many other things besides, for instance, . . . the kicking of the geese out of the boat (*i.e.,* doing away with sibilations), that help to make the greatness of blank verse. I never, if possible, put two *s s* together in any verse of mine. My line is not, as first misprinted and often misquoted,

"And freedom broadens slowly down"

but,

"And freedom slowly broadens down."

The well-known first line of Alexander Pope's "The Rape of the Lock"—"What dire offense from amorous causes springs"—drew Tennyson's derision: "'Amrus causiz springs'—horrible! I would sooner die than write such a line!"

Though the first three lines of Frost's poem have only one pair of esses set head to toe and adding *sprayed* to the line would not make another pair, raising the sibilant sum from Frost's twelve to thirteen is probably not a good idea. If goose number thirteen doesn't sink the skiff, it certainly makes it ride dangerously low in the water. As a vivid verb, though, *sprayed* has some advantages. We get a stronger, more insistent sense of the violence the saw is capable of, and as anyone who has worked with a circular saw, a radial arm saw, or a table saw can attest, sawdust *is* sprayed all over the eyes, hair, face, clothes, and shoes of the sawyer. Frost is not interested in that much or that kind of vividness. Consider what is left out of the narrative after the boy loses his hand. The poem was written in 1915–16. People, especially farmers, would know to leap on the boy and clamp the wound with their hands, while another man whipped off his belt and cinched it around the boy's forearm. Blood would have been everywhere. But the poet does not tell us about it. He is not interested in moving the poem beyond realism to the ugly and sometimes cynical realm of naturalism.

Perhaps I'm being fanciful if I also suggest that Frost uses the verb *made* because he wants to keep those five lines of pastoral possibility, hope, or delusion untouched by the violence of the saw. The language is mild throughout the passage, even to the blandness of "Sweet-scented stuff." Until I thought my way into it more deeply, I disliked the phrase for its deliberate evocation of pastoral banality. "Sweet-scented" is firmed up by the bluff word *stuff*, which according to the *Oxford English Dictionary* has been used since the sixteenth century to mean "The general designation for solid, liquid, or (rarely) gaseous matter of any kind: used indefinitely instead of the specific designation, or where no specific designation exists." So far, so obvious: *stuff* has a long history of being used vaguely. But moving further into the definitions and closer to Robert Frost in time, we see that the older definition of "garden stuff," meaning "Plants grown in a garden; vegetables for the table," had generalized by 1813 to mean "Cultivated produce of a garden or farm; natural produce of land." That natural produce of the land might well, to a farmer's eye, include firewood, as well as the livestock, driftwood, and poultry specifically cited by the *OED*. Venturing even further into the *OED*, we find this one-word definition of *stuff*, dating back to the fifteenth-century: "Dust."

Perhaps, then, in *made dust* we hear, very lightly, an inverted echo of Genesis. There, God takes dust and makes life, but now, the saw, the machine in the garden, takes life and makes dust.

What about adjectives then? In poetry, one detail or two must do the work of many, so the heavily freighted detail is often halfway to symbol before the poet can stop it—and adjectives only push them further down that path. For instance, if we take the sister's apron and try to make it more vivid with an adjective, all sorts of monkeys start jumping out of the barrel. If the sister's apron is besmirched in any way, it starts to pick up sexual overtones almost as clearly as Caddy Compson's muddy underwear does in Faulkner's *The Sound and the Fury*.

"His sister stood beside him in her *dirty/stained/splattered/torn* apron." If Frost employed one of those adjectives, the Freudians would have a field day with the poem, and rightly so. If the apron were clean, spotless, or unblemished, we'd wonder just how much help the sister had been in preparing supper, but, more importantly, we'd wonder why the poem was emphasizing her purity. And if the apron were *worn, tattered, faded,* or *old,* a Marxist case for the poem being a critique of rural poverty would be strengthened. For Frost's purposes, it's better to leave the apron unmodified. It's simply a garment that connects the sister with the message she is bearing, "Supper."

One of the cruxes of the poem, one to which puzzled critics have returned repeatedly, is the absence of the parents. Where are Mom and Dad? Let's put them in and see what happens. The first appearance of a mother is easy to effect: "His mother stood beside him in her apron." Immediately we are aware the boy is diminished. The fact that his mother has come to fetch him makes him more like a child. And the mother's standing by helplessly as her son dies is both sensational and a grating convention of sentimental literature.

The second time we transmogrify *Sister* to *Mother*, the aesthetic problems metastasize. Would a rural boy in the early twentieth century, say, ""Don't let him cut my hand off— / The doctor, when he comes. Don't let him, *Mother!*" Not likely. It's too tony, too upper-class, too literary, too studied for the extremity of his situation. *Mom* is too modern. The boy would have said *Ma* or *Mama*, and the moment we consider the choices is the moment we know why Frost does not use them: "Don't let him cut my hand off— / The doctor, when he comes. Don't let him, *Ma!*" I cringe to read it. The gooey sentimentality completely overwhelms the seriousness of the poem. The line is now so bad it's funny.

But the parents' absences not only avoid inflicting an injury; they also provide an aesthetic benefit to the poem. As several critics have pointed out, isolating a brother and sister in a rural landscape is reminiscent of a low mimetic fairy tale, especially "Hansel and Gretel," which is about the children of a woodcutter. In the Aarne-Thompson Classification System, "Hansel and Gretel" is type 327A and 327B—"The Children with the Witch" and "The Small Boy Defeats the Ogre." But in Frost's inverted fairy tale, Hansel dies, maimed by the heavily personified, snarling buzz saw, which fills the role of an ogre or cannibalistic witch.

With the word *So* beginning line 27, the poem changes. The long, indulgent *so much* of "the half hour / That a boy counts *so much* when saved from work," is replaced by a short, emphatic *So*. It is the *So* of acceptance. It is the *So* that says, "I must put aside my earlier hopes, sorrows, and attempts to understand what happened and accept it." It is also the *So* of logic, of *thus* and *ergo*. The logical voice must accept illogic as the way of the world, and from here on the poem is brisk and almost utterly narrative.

For a time, the final word of the poem, *affairs*, like *made* before it, troubled me with its blandness: "And they, since they / Were not the one dead, turned to their affairs." Trying to find a better word convinced me of its understated precision. Any alternative I can think of is bad. *Next chores* trivializes the boy's death. *Business* tips the poem toward social and political critique. *Families* sentimentalizes and limits the scope of the ending. And any mention of prayers, even with any negating adjectives (*fierce, false, inept, stunned, angry*, and so forth) denies the whole movement and tone of the poem up till now. *Affairs* suggests everything that Frost wants suggested—business affairs, personal affairs, public affairs, private affairs—without limiting him to any one, and it lets the poem end on a minor key that is completely appropriate to the poem's meaning.

In that same low-key way, the last sentence of the poem evokes and answers the end of the most famous elegy in English, "Lycidas," a pastoral elegy for another "hapless youth." In Milton's poem "the uncouth Swain,"—*swain* simply means "a country lad"—consoled by his own song, considers a view west into the hills, just as Frost's narrator does early in "'Out, Out—,'" before turning away from his grief to his traditionally poetic affairs:

> Thus sang the uncouth Swain to th'Okes and rills,
> While the still morn went out with Sandals gray,
> He touch'd the tender stops of various Quills,
> With eager thought warbling his Dorick lay:
> And now the Sun had stretch'd out all the hills,
> And now was dropt into the Western bay;
> At last he rose, and twitch'd his Mantle blew:
> To morrow to fresh Woods, and Pastures new.

Frost's country people, unlike Milton's, live in a smaller and more realistic world, and they turn to pastures and work that are the same as they were before the boy's death.

The very first explication of "'Out, Out—'" was half a sentence by Robert Penn Warren and Cleanth Brooks in the 1938 edition of their influential textbook *Understanding Poetry.* They observe that the poem is about "the pathos and horror of the unreasonable and unpredictable end that at any moment may come to life" (31–32). Nothing I've pondered in this essay challenges that first interpretation. But taking Frost at his word and looking at the poem as a performance, considering the choices he made and the choices he didn't make, we can more clearly begin to appreciate the complex intellectual and emotional richness of it, despite the "meaning" to which it can be reduced.

Technique Makes Imagination Matter More

ALLEN WIER

Eudora Welty, in *On Writing* (a little book that looms large for me), declares: "Looking at short stories as readers and writers together should be a companionable thing." That sparks to life in my memory a remark by novelist Wright Morris, whose fiction and critical writings instruct and inspire me. (I echo his notions a time or two in this essay.) In his book *About Fiction,* Morris says: "The writer learns to write, the reader learns to read." This *mystique*—the singular and mysterious *craft* required by the practice and passion of writing *and* of reading, especially of "reading as a writer reads"—is what I want to ponder.

I preface my comments by telling you that for a class in the form and craft of fiction I include on the syllabus this advice from Carl Sandburg: "Beware of advice. Even this."

It's hard to talk about craft without sounding pontifical, but nothing I say is intended to be prescriptive, as I speak out of my personal experience only. For me, *Craft* is not Imagination's handmaiden. Craft—or technique—is the shapeshifter imagination couples with. We use almost interchangeably with *craft* the words *style* and *technique. Craft* is from the Old English *creft* for "physical strength or power." *Stile* is from the Latin *stilus* for "stake, writing instrument, or manner of writing." *Technique,* from Greek *tekhne* for "art, skill, craft in work," was first used in the nineteenth century in criticism of art and music. *Style,* in use a century earlier, suggests an individual artist's fingerprint, the unique use of learned and developed *craft.* When we read critically, as writers read, we observe the *technique* used to achieve art. There's a story behind every word. Language is how the literary artist *fabricates* the actual out of the imaginary—the verb *fabricates* includes the duality of fiction: constructs and counterfeits, makes and fakes, creates and contrives. Another story behind the word *craft* is about *witch-craft, magic,* from the Greek *mag-ike*—with *tekhne* "art," so we're back to *technique. Mag-ike* means the "art of influencing events and producing marvels using hidden natural forces." I'll take that as a description of fiction writing.

I believe in the spiritual power of the imagination. I believe all literature is *inspired*—the *seat* of inspiration is usually in one's chair in front of the page. For me, the creation of a story or a novel is a mystical, but not necessarily religious, experience. That the Bible contains so many "poems" and "stories" diminishes its power for those readers who require holy sanction to give literature authority. For me, a compelling voice earns its own authority. When His disciples fail to understand the figurative meaning of a metaphor that Christ uses for hypocrisy, He reacts as a frustrated professor might: "Having eyes, see ye not? and having ears, hear ye not?" Or, as my Southern Baptist mother told me years ago after she took me to Roman Catholic mass, and I said I didn't understand the Latin: "You're not listening hard enough."

Having eyes, and *having ears,* and *listening harder* I equate with *learning how to read,* and *learning how to read* I equate with *learning how to write.*

Wanting to write good fiction, I listen hard to narrative voices. I read with one eye on point of view, the other looking for structure. I delight in rhetoric. I've learned to read as a writer reads. For me that's included the discovery of some of the techniques of fiction. Literary critics share the writer's interest in technique, but (as teachers of literature can affirm) the techniques of fiction are of less interest to many other readers. I've been told by less interested readers that focusing on technique is "picking a story apart." I point out that critical analysis is not a destructive act, since we are going to put the story back together.

Analyzing a poem, story, or novel is neither mechanical nor cold-hearted. As a child, I took apart an alarm clock, my lever-action Daisy BB gun, and thousand-piece picture puzzles to better understand how they worked and to see if I could reassemble them. If something *moves us,* we want to understand how *it moves.* When a writer transforms ideas into a dramatic situation in which I share the consciousness of a character, I'm in a realm where I've never been before. The fully realized, fictional world comes from a person—it's not from God—but it seems as if it must be from God. It moves as a living creature moves. Samuel Taylor Coleridge uses the image of a snake to describe Shakespeare's imaginative process: "Shakespeare goes on creating and evolving, B out of A, and C out of B, and so on, just as a serpent moves, which makes a fulcrum out of its own body and seems forever twisting and untwisting in its own strength."

Coleridge describes the imagination as "a synthetic and magical power" that "fuses . . . the idea with the image." He uses the figure of a snake again in a letter to Joseph Cottle in 1815: "The common end of all narrative, nay, of all Poems is to convert a series into a Whole: to make those events, which in real or imagined History move on in a strait Line, assume to our Understandings, a circular motion—the snake with its Tail in its Mouth." The transforming power of the imagination unites disparate parts into a whole, turns base metal into gold.

In my memory, Margaret Schlegel's thoughts resonate, from E. M. Forster's novel *Howard's End:* "Only connect! That was the whole of her sermon. Only connect the prose and the passion. . . ."

Prose and passion—form and content—truly are inseparable in any work of art. We experience both at once. I can't separate my perception of a subject from my perception of the technique that renders and reveals a subject and its nuances.

As I've learned to read as a writer reads, I've come to appreciate various techniques of fiction, but my narrative lust has not diminished. My experience as a reader has been amplified. The expression *reading for pleasure* assumes a *guilty* pleasure, as if one is reading something slick or trashy, for subject matter alone. The implication is that we don't read literary works for pleasure, but as an assignment. Literary fiction—we've been told—is good for us. For pleasure, we want stories full of sugar and fat. But once you develop a taste for literary fiction, the sugary stuff no longer satisfies.

I once suggested to a writer in a graduate fiction-writing workshop that he read Caroline Gordon's short story "The Last Day in the Field." Aleck, the story's first-person narrator, seems to me somewhat rare in modern literature: an almost wholly decent man, and I hoped the writer in my workshop might more fully realize the narrator of a story he was writing if he saw Caroline Gordon's technique. Next day, he came by my office to say he'd not finished reading the story because it wasn't interesting. I asked: "What interests you?" I made it clear that I was not encouraging subjectivity. I meant that *language* is at least part of what every story is about, and what writer thinks language is uninteresting?

"I'm not into hunting," said the writer who wanted to skip Caroline Gordon's story only because its subject is hunting, and he didn't like hunting. I read aloud to him from novelist and critic Mark Shorer's classic essay—first delivered as a craft lecture at the Utah Writers' Conference in 1947—"Technique as Discovery": ". . . to speak of content as such is not to speak of art at all, but of experience. . . . it is only when we speak of the *achieved* content, the form, the work of art as a work of art, that we speak as critics. The difference between content, or experience, and achieved content, or art, is technique." Hunting is the experience or subject or raw material that Caroline Gordon transforms through the alchemy of her imagination into art. Gordon's technique and talent turn a day of hunting into a visceral yet lyrical experience of human mortality.

Talent, Thomas Mann writes, is "permanent dissatisfaction." If we want to make connections between the personal and the public, we develop our talent. Every one of our lives contains secrets, vivid imaginings, and each of us has a vision of the world around us, but to write well is not just to report the facts of our experience, our subject. Our concern is with the ways whereby we can create an experience that really happens in our reader's imagination. In "Technique as Discovery," Mark Schorer goes on to say: ". . . everything is technique which is not the lump of experience itself, and one cannot properly say that a writer has no technique, or that he eschews technique. . . . We can speak of good or bad technique, of adequate and inadequate, of technique which serves the novel's purpose or disserves."

Alive in my memory, this cartoon needs no caption: *Viewed from the doorway, on the far side of a room a man, paintbrush in hand, squats in the white, yet unpainted, corner of the floor he has painted black.* Inventing a way to hover there and finish painting the floor and then to float over the wet paint out of the room without leaving any prints, that's technique.

Technique can be the difference between anecdote and story, between fact and fictional truth. As I've come to read as a writer reads, my pleasure in reading has become multilayered. I am deeply moved by story *and* by artistry that I recognize in myriad manifestations. A writer's *technique*—not just his or her *story*—knots my throat.

"What I should like to do is to write a book about nothing," says Flaubert, "a book which would have hardly any subject—there are neither good nor bad subjects—from the point of view of pure art, there are none at all, style being itself alone an absolute way of looking at things."

It's easy to poke fun at writing rules, yet rules may be generally helpful, so long as we remember the first rule, that there are no hard and fast rules for fiction writing, and the second rule, that any rule may be effectively broken—if you're a good enough writer. You have to understand a rule before you can effectively break it. Before he painted cubist portraits, Picasso mastered naturalistic representation. Picasso says, "Learn the rules like a pro, so you can break them like an artist." Advice that has proven to be true for most writers most of the time, may still be imaginatively questioned, and such a question may lead to a kind of inverse validation of the advice. I discover a story as I'm writing it, and the story may make me see ways to alter or transform rules of craft. If I do that, I'm not abandoning or breaking a rule so much as I'm exploring all of its implications. One usually effective rule is to use dialogue to interrupt narrative when you want the drama of a "scene" to draw your reader close. But, *what if* the story were all dialogue except for one, brief narrative passage? Or, *what if* the story were all narration except for one half-scene—would that effectively call special attention to the story's sole dramatic moment? Out of "what if" we often get "oh no," but the occasional "my god" is worth the speculation. I think that kind of openness to possibilities is what poet Mary Oliver is talking about when she says, "Sometimes breaking the rules is just *extending* the rules."

When a reader tells me that a particular story "defies analysis," I consider what such a comment reveals about a particular reader. That's not sufficient critical response if one is being paid by a university to get between a reader and a story, so I merge my emotional and intellectual responses in an effort to articulate something helpful, maybe even meaningful. (Meaningful doesn't necessarily mean *true.* As I consider what I've read and been told over the years about the techniques of fiction, even bad advice has often turned out to be meaningful.)

I recall telling writers in a workshop that dialogue is not like actual conversation, that it's a conjured illusion. By rote, I recited one of the golden rules for writing good dialogue: "avoid the use of dialogue for exposition." This advice I got for the first time in an undergraduate Southern Literature class when the professor made fun of Thomas Wolfe's rhetoric. Immediately after repeating that generally revered advice, I passed out copies of "Aren't You Happy for Me?" a story in which the author, Richard Bausch, makes dialogue accomplish several different things *at once,* not the least of which is some overt exposition. "Notice," I said, "how this writer effectively breaks that so-called rule I just gave you about dialogue and exposition."

It seems to me dialogue seldom works as Questions followed by Answers.

I think of dialogue as more like bumper cars. In dialogue, words are irregular, sporadic, and their rhythms and collisions, their tone and connotations may be as important as their meanings. We've all interrupted a conversation with the question, "How'd we get into a discussion of the Ferris Wheel?" And tracked the dialogue backwards, Ferris Wheel to rooftop views to the uncle with an elevator in his house to Rapunzel letting down her golden locks to the long-haired mostly Collie dog rescued from the pound. In a game called Gossip, a group of people sits in a circle, and the starter whispers a word to the person next to her. He whispers it to the next person, and so on. The word that eventually reaches the last person in the circle is almost always a different word than the one with which the game was started.

Exercises may help turn good advice into muscle memory, as when a runner trains with ankle weights that she removes for a race. Because I want them to work the exclamatory *tone* into a sentence *before* the reader gets to the end, I ask writers in my workshops to figuratively remove the exclamation point from their keyboards. An exclamation point reminds me of an "i" dotted with a heart. It's like a smiley face, a choirboy singing "Oh!" at the end of a sentence. I know there are good stories that contain exclamation points. Still, I agree with Mark Twain when he says using an exclamation point is like laughing at your own joke. Here's Number 5 of crime novelist Elmore Leonard's "Ten Rules for Good Writing": "*Keep your exclamation points under control.*" All of Leonard's rules are good ones, but his annotations are even better. He qualifies the exclamation-point rule: "*You are allowed no more than two or three per 100,000 words of prose. If you have the knack of playing with exclaimers the way Tom Wolfe does, you can throw them in by the handful.*" Most of us, Leonard advises, should avoid exclamation points, but if you can "make them new," use as many as you like.

Advice I've heard all my life is to "write only about what you know." I'd call this advice *incomplete.* There's a great deal we don't realize we know—things we've experienced only in our imagination. We've all heard that a writer must first "experience life." I'm glad Emily Dickinson didn't take that advice and leave the bedroom in the family house in Amherst where she wrote most of her poems. Flannery O'Connor says that "Anybody who has survived his childhood has enough information about life to last him the rest of his days." Saul Bellow says: "By refusing to write about anything with which he is not thoroughly familiar, the writer confesses the powerlessness of the imagination and accepts its relegation to an inferior place."

Like bad advice, a bad professor may be meaningful. My Southern Lit professor—and a couple of others—*inspired* me to become a teacher. Surely, I thought, I can do a better job of it than this guy. He told my class that no poet writing in English may rhyme *breath* with *death*. I did not forget his advice. Years later, after the death of my father, I wrote a story called "Things About to Disappear" in which I use these lines: ". . . the name of the man who had left me, the man I was leaving behind, his name I could not speak. And the name that rhymed with breath and was forever." The same professor advised us that *no one* writing a Civil War novel may include as characters brothers who fight on opposite sides. When I wrote a novel, *Tehano,* set in the nineteenth century, that absolute rule inspired two unanticipated characters, identical twin brothers who fight on opposite sides of the Civil War. This is the "put-this-in-your-pipe-and-smoke-it" school of writing.

If I could go back in time, I'd tell my professor Thomas Wolfe's rhetoric *is* good—not *in spite of,* but *because of,* its excessiveness. My professor's critical aperture stop was set for a short depth of field, and that distorts the image. A writer reading switches to "wide-angle" in order to clearly see a larger scene, or to appreciate a verbal painting that uses bigger brush strokes. As you learn to read as a writer reads, you learn to open up the aperture of appreciation to let more light shine on the images, and your vision becomes more inclusive.

Much of my own vision has been framed by a car window, especially when I was younger. For one period of seven years I spent almost the same amount of time driving as I spent sleeping. Looking ahead, down the road, I gazed behind me, too. Where I was headed was before me in the windshield. Where I had been was before me in the rearview mirror. Both my future and my past shared the same moment, the past eternally before me, the mirror presenting the past to the future. Framed in that mirror, what had been behind me often overtook me and receded into the future, appearing in the mirror only to disappear beyond me in the windshield. I used the rearview mirror not to see where I'd been, but to get me where I was going. The rearview put the timeless past right there in the active present, where I could see past, present, and future without moving. The rearview mirror alters and restructures space and time in ways similar to fiction's manipulation of time. In fiction, time is not chronological—in fiction nothing is any kind of logical. Time does not pass in the pages of a novel—time passes in the consciousness of a reader. Fiction frames past and present and can freeze time as a mirror or a photograph can.

Stories remain frozen in time yet alive in our emotions because all literature is born in human emotion. I'm an only child, and my mother's death only a few years ago fused with the *memory* of my daddy's death over forty years earlier. I no longer had a superior officer to turn to. When my mother died, my hand was on her back, gently rubbing. She was not responsive, but I was talking to her in the hope that hearing really is the last sense we lose. When Mother stopped breathing, the room—in which I stood beside the bed that held her body—faded away, and I was at a kitchen sink where I'd bathed my infant son two decades earlier. I laved warm suds over his hands that moved through water like small starfish. His spine made a tiny mountain range that bumped the bar of soap I ran down his back.

And then, as if I were a character in a story's flashback, I was transported backwards in time a dozen years, to *before my son was born.* Beside me in a familiar blue denim skirt, arms bruised from lifting my father, Mother asked me to give him a bath. I had asked how I could help. I'd had in mind the miraculous: procuring healing powder from the bark of a remote Mexican tree, a cure that had eluded modern medicine. I feared seeing my father's naked, cancer-ravaged body, but worldly embarrassment fell away with his robe. Warm, sudsy water—respite for the bedridden—rinsed away my self-consciousness. I bumped the soap down my daddy's back, and my fingertips felt the vulnerability of flesh and bone. At the moment of my mother's death, my hand was on *her* back, *and then* my hand was on my son's back, *and then* on my father's. The remarkable *and then* of memory and of fiction mesmerizes and transports both reader and writer. Canadian storywriter Clark Blaise says *Then* means to the reader, "I am ready. The moment of change is at hand, the story shifts gears and for the first time, plot intrudes on poetry." In the moment of my mother's dying, memory wedded past to present, made an arc of connections as a story's beginning anticipates or contains its ending as it passes through its middle. A story's plot, like memory and dream, moves characters and readers not through *all* time but through time's meaningful moments.

Each time I begin a new story, I begin as an ignoramus. Let me repeat that: Each time I begin a new story, I begin as an ignoramus. I trust in the alchemy of the imagination and in discoveries I'll make through technique. In the *process* of writing, I learn how to write. Maybe one has to complete a story or a novel to realize that doing so will not much help one write another story or novel, because every tale is new. I apply technique, and then mystery comes along.

Wallace Stevens says it this way, in "Notes Toward a Supreme Fiction": "You must become an ignorant man again / And see the sun again with an ignorant eye / And see it clearly in the idea of it."

Functional, lyrical, comical, incantatory, words are stories in and of themselves. Since the first storytellers moved their hands in front of people clothed in animal hides and sitting around a fire, writers have named the things of our world. What we care about, we name, and the names merge with our lives. No one calls a child Hamlet or Hester or Tristan or Tess or Huck or Emma or Ichabod or Scarlet without being mindful of literature.

We have personal and local allusions, too. After World War II, my daddy had a short-lived job as a ribbon seller. He loaded the back of a '46 Jeep Willys station wagon with florist's ribbon samples, and he and my mom and I—I stood between them on the front seat—hit all forty-eight states. In California, I toddled into traffic at the touristy intersection of Hollywood and Vine. My dad caught my collar with his left hand and swung his right hand hard to spank my bottom and swat me up out of harm's way. In the urgency of the moment, Daddy forgot that I collected rocks that I packed tight in my hip pockets. He burst two blood vessels, and from that day on his affectionate name for me was Hot Rock. Not long after my son was born, I swooped him from the cradle and, *without premeditation*, the name came out: "Hey, Hot Rock."

Is there any nonsense poetry better than family euphemisms for body parts and bodily functions? I recently learned that the word my mother used for my rock-stuffed rear-end, "Tokus," is from the Yiddish *tokhes*, "buttocks," from the Hebrew for "beneath."

I try to be receptive to the fictions of ordinary life, the found poems and stories that come my way, regardless of whether they lead to anything beyond their own humor or mystery. A guy I went to high school with sends out occasional group emails to and about our graduating class. Increasingly, the emails are death notices. Last month, this message appeared: "We learned this morning of the death of our classmate Benny Baker. We know of no cause. There is no obituary. His wife survives. survives."

Benny Baker and I were on the school's track and cross-country teams. His legs were so white the coach called him Benny Blue Legs. Attached to the email announcing his death is a yearbook photo: Benny in a plaid sport coat, a thin black tie. In my peripheral vision, his skinny, blue-white legs sashay beside me on the red-cindered track. Half-a-century ago, I thought that Benny had old-man legs, hairless and pale. Reading the email, I thought *the rest of him has caught up to his legs*—an old man who died of no cause and with no obituary but with a wife who survives. survives. A. E. Housman writes that when he shaves he has to "keep watch over my thoughts—if a line of poetry strays into my memory, my skin bristles so that the razor ceases to act." The words that tell the stories of ordinary life surprise me daily and take me places I've never been.

William Gass says, "I don't write stories, I write words." The Russian nesting dolls of literature: inside the book, pages; inside the page, paragraphs; inside the paragraph, sentences; inside the sentence, words. Truman Capote: "To me, the greatest pleasure of writing is not what it's about, but the music the words make." Elizabeth Bowen compares the work and tools of the writer with those of the painter: "Often when I write I am trying to make words do the work of line and color. I have the painter's sensitivity to light. Much . . . of my writing is verbal painting." Paintings rely primarily on the visual, but writers use words in an effort to stimulate *all* of the reader's senses. Among the many writers who've compared fiction to other art forms is Croatian American writer Josip Novakovich, who points out that most medieval paintings depict holy figures and lack depth or space—they have no landscapes. Later paintings include setting. Novakovich advises writers to fully paint-in setting in order to create territory for character action.

For any writer, words exist outside of their meaning. Partly, I'm alluding to a word's denotative and connotative meanings, to the associations we have with words—some universal, some personal, some private. I'm also thinking of our sensory perception of words. Researchers say we have at least twenty-one senses, counting not just "taste" but five different taste receptors, and they subdivide "touch" into the ability to feel *temperature, pressure, itching,* and *pain.* Researchers separate from *taste* and *smell* our sense of *hunger.* I can name stories and novels that make me hungry. Understanding the numerous cell groups that respond to specific phenomena may add to a writer's descriptive arsenal, but it seems sufficient to appeal to the original five senses with the look and sound of words, the texture and, even, the taste and smell of words.

When scratch-and-sniff ads—mostly for cologne—began appearing in magazines some years ago, I had the whimsical notion of a scratch-and-sniff novel—olfactory descriptions rubbed with a dime and released. One drawback, they couldn't be reread with the same gusto, as the scents would be evaporated. Then I discovered Patrick Süskind's novel *Perfume* about a Parisian with an extraordinary sense of smell who sets out "to possess everything the world could offer in the way of odors." Süskind fully realizes odors through catalogs of sensory words and olfactory metaphors. When his main character, Jean-Baptiste Grenouille, smells a scent altogether *new* he thinks: "This scent had a freshness, but not the freshness of limes or pomegranates, not the freshness of myrrh or cinnamon bark or curly mint or birch or camphor or pine needles, not that of a May rain or a frosty wind or of well water . . . and at the same time it had warmth, but not as bergamot, cypress, or musk has, or jasmine or daffodils, not as rosewood has or iris. . . . This scent was a blend of both, of evanescence and substance." Süskind's specific, sensory words conclude with abstractions—evanescence and substance—recalling some often cited, and usually sound, writing advice, Ezra Pound's dictum: "Go in fear of abstractions."

Katherine Anne Porter's stories are chock full of *earned* abstractions (as well as healthy doses of exposition, generalization, and symbolism). This is from her story "Flowering Judas": "[Laura] is . . . determined not to surrender her will to such expedient logic. But she cannot help feeling that she had been betrayed irreparably by the disunion between her way of living and her feeling of what life should be, and at times she is almost contented to rest in this sense of grievance as a private store of consolation." These elements—symbolism and abstraction especially—are usually in the service of theme, which may make their use heavy-handed. But the achievement of this story is the revelation of Laura's inner life, the dramatization of her consciousness. "Flowering Judas" succeeds emotionally and does so primarily through Porter's *style* that extends so many writing rules.

Theodore Dreiser—not, I'd say, a great stylist—calls words "little audible links, chaining together great inaudible feelings and purposes." When I ride south of New Orleans in Eudora Welty's story "No Place for You, My Love," with the woman from Ohio and the man from Syracuse, I give myself over entirely to words, the little audible links that chain together moments during the journey. Hurtling forward in the oppressive heat of the story, I feel much the way I feel on certain moonless nights when I stare up at trillions of stars with a wonder surely similar to the wonder that's filled the chest of every stargazer who's ever drawn breath. Words that describe my celestial awe are these: "an intellectual and emotional complex in an instant of time," the definition of *image* given to us by Ezra Pound.

Pound, the word's sound, strikes me with force, a fist, a musical instrument, a fusillade. God and I collaborate to take away the ground beneath my feet as I gaze up into dark oblivion so pierced through with points of light that I fill up with possibility, terrified and hopeful at once. Eudora Welty and I collaborate to take away my chair and lamp as I look down at the threadbare canvas top of the faded-red Ford that will take me south of south. Miss Welty says that fiction is more full-of-mystery than she knows how to say. "The mystery lies in the use of language to express human life. In writing, do we try to solve this mystery? No, I think we take hold of the other end of the stick. . . . we rediscover the mystery."

Each of our personal histories is a collection of stories. Each of our lives contains a whole library of stories. It doesn't bother me, much, that so few others value literature as much as writers and teachers of writing and those with the habit of reading do. I am sorry that everyone doesn't know its myriad delights. Literature may be useless in the world of events, yet we know of no societies that did not tell stories. Aren't we blessed, those of us who are readers, that we have *eyes to see* and *ears to hear* poems and stories and that we *listen hard* to know their palpable and everlasting pleasures.

Metaphor

The Fundament of Imaginative Writing

SIDNEY WADE

Metaphor is omnipresent in literature. From the simplest image or figure of speech, to the larger form, found sometimes in character and narrative, metaphors are far more than decorative elements to our work. In fact, according to I. A. Richards, "Metaphor is the omnipresent principle of language—we cannot get through three sentences of ordinary fluid discourse without it." In the broadest sense, metaphor can determine our basic structures of language, thought, and perception. I'd like to share with you some of the more remarkable instances of metaphor-making and metaphor-consciousness I'm aware of, in order to encourage you to pay close attention to the metaphorical turn, the metaphorical image, the metaphorical power in your own work.

In his beautiful book *An Elemental Thing,* Eliot Weinberger includes a chapter? prose poem? poetic essay? collage? (it's very much its own thing), which he calls "The Stars." He collates the myths and beliefs about the stars from cultures around the world and presents them to us in short sentences and clauses over six pages of text. What are myths, fundamentally, if not extended metaphors we use to explain to ourselves the inexplicable? I've selected several sections from "The Stars" and have structured the following essay around them. I hope the strange beauties of the many diverse metaphors represented in this piece will serve as a sustained harmonic note, an ostinato, if you will, to the music of what follows.

The Stars: what are they?   They are chunks of ice
reflecting the sun;   they are lights afloat on the

waters beyond the transparent dome;   they are nails
nailed to the sky;   they are holes in the great curtain
between us and the sea of light;   they are holes in
the hard shell that protects us from the inferno beyond;

Metaphor is the queen of tropes. Metaphor is the secret weapon in every writer's backpack. Metaphor is the giver of life, metaphor is the magic wand that can make a brave new world spring out of a handful of words.

In Greek, "metaphor" means "to carry over." Willis Barnstone, an all-around linguistic genius who is at home in about twelve different languages, opens his wonderful extended meditation on translation, entitled *The Poetics of Translation*, with a striking visual—motor vans, all across Athens and beyond driving around with the word "Metaphor" printed on their sides. Can you guess what they are? They are moving vans. They carry physical objects from one environment to another, much as we do with ideas, images, themes, and/or emotions when we create a literary metaphor.

they are birds whose feathers are on fire;   they
impregnate the mothers of great men;   they are the
shining concentrations of spirit-breath, made from the
residues left over from the creation of the sun and moon;
they portend war, death, famine, plague, good and bad
harvests, the birth of kings;   they regulate the prices
of salt and fish;

Of course we use many different kinds of metaphor in different situations. "Common," as distinct from "literary," metaphor is an ever-present element of our everyday speech and communication, and always has been. When, for example, we indicate that we understand something by saying "I see," we are using one of the oldest and most widespread metaphors in common usage throughout the entire Indo-European language group.

Some researchers suggest that metaphor-making may be hardwired into our neural pathways, by way of a fundamental kind of synesthesia. Let's do a little experiment here: "Bouba or Kiki?"

Which one of these images is a Bouba, and which one is a Kiki? It turns out

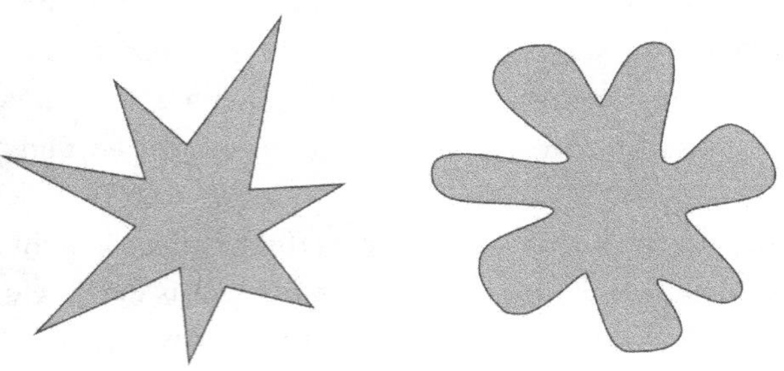

98 percent of everyone who considers the question, including children as young as two and a half, confidently associate the spiky blot with the *sharp-sounding* name of Kiki, the rounded blot with the *softer-sounding* Bouba (James Geary, *I Is an Other: The Secret Life of Metaphor and How It Shapes the Way We See the World*). According to some experts, the visual and auditory pathways in the brain are located reasonably close to one another. They often fire in unison, when subjects are presented with a single stimulant. For example, some musician friends of mine claim they see colors when hearing certain musical chords. I remember one acquaintance of mine describing the C Sharp Major chord as brilliant yellow. In associating the spikiness of the sound of the name "Kiki" with the visual spikiness of the blot, we are transposing one sense onto another, using synesthesia, or the blending of sense impressions.

they are the seeds of all the
creatures on earth;   they are the flock of the moon,
scattered across the sky like sheep in a meadow, and she
leads them to pasture;   they are spheres of crystal and
their movement creates a music in the sky;   they are fixed
and we are moving;   we are fixed and they are moving;

Geary has this to say about metaphor: "Synesthesia creates the experience of one sense in the context of another. Metaphorical thinking creates a kind of conceptual synesthesia, in which one concept is understood in the context of another. The abstract is understood in the context of the concrete, the metaphysical in the context of the physical, the emotional in the context of the biological. *Through metaphor, body and mind are inextricably intertwined*" (emphasis mine).

According to Albert Einstein, productive thought is what he called "combinatory play," where one entertains two concepts at the same time and together they create a third concept. The processes of "combinatory play" mirror exactly the processes of metaphor-making and enlarge our understanding of the concrete world in front of us and our understanding of the way the world works in general. The workings of scientific creativity are not that far removed from those of literary creativity after all.

One of the cardinal points I insist on, in teaching any level of student, is to always remember that poetry is a physical art. It began, we assume, millennia ago, with the physical repetition of verbal patterns. In song. In prayer. In incantation. Where does the fundamental English-language poetic foot, the iamb, come from, do you imagine? It mimics the heartbeat. For those of you not familiar with the iamb, it is a two-syllable vocal unit with one stress. Words like "create," "pursue," "protect" come to mind. The stress is on the second syllable—ba BUM, ba- BUM ba- BUM. It's a perfect imitation of a physical, voiced-by-the-body expression. It makes use of the similarities of the basic sonic units of life in order to illuminate and enrich the experience of the poem. In my opinion, the best poetry privileges physical rhythm, voiced pattern, fundamental sound.

the Emperor Mu Wang
and his charioteer Tsao Fu, who went in search of the
peaches of the Western Paradise, are there;   the beautiful
Callisto, doomed by Juno's jealousy, and the goddess
Marichi who drives her chariot led by wild boars through the
sky;

If poetry is fundamentally based in the body, it follows that you can enlist the help of your own body in refining your work. For example, when composing your poems, you must always read them aloud to yourself and/or others. Any stumbling over a word is likely your body telling you there's something wrong with that line or word. It's an unconscious, perhaps subconscious operation that the tongue itself manages to communicate to your consciousness. Robert Graves tells us that when he hears a great poem the hairs on the back of his neck begin to rise. When I hear a great poem, the hairs on my arms begin to rise. When Emily Dickinson is in the presence of true poetry, she tells us, she feels as if the top of her head were being blown off. When we attend a poetry reading, and the poet reads something to us that we feel is powerful, or exciting, new, moving—what do we do? We respond physically. We murmur something like "hmmm" in unison. It feels involuntary. I can confidently tell you this is one of the most satisfying moments in a poet's life—to hear an audience give up that physical respect in admiration for your words. These are deeply physical reactions to art. Since metaphor-making is based in the physical and is one of the most fundamental ways of understanding our world and may even be hardwired into us, making good use of metaphor seems to me one of the very best ways to lend power and depth to a poem or, for that matter, any manner of creative writing.

Let's look at some examples from a poem written by one of the greatest metaphor-makers of the twentieth century, Sylvia Plath. From "A Winter Ship":

> The pier pilings seem about to collapse
>
> And with them that rickety edifice
> Of warehouses, derricks, smokestacks and bridges
> In the distance. All around us the water slips
> And gossips in its loose vernacular,
> Ferrying the smells of cod and tar.
>
> Farther out, the waves will be mouthing icecakes—
> A poor month for park-sleepers and lovers.

This poem always takes my breath away (notice the metaphor!). Aside from its incredible formal dexterity, the metaphors here are as fresh and illuminating as they come: the water "slips and gossips," like human chatterers, the alliteration of the esses hissing like snakes and adding to the power of the metaphor; "the waves will be mouthing ice-cakes"—(one of my favorite metaphors here)—you can physically feel the chill of the ice-cakes in the mouth. You notice how every one of the metaphors in the poem involves physical sensation—it's what gives them their extraordinary power. Elsewhere she says "Even our shadows are blue with cold." Even though the poem itself could be said on one of many levels to be a metaphor for the malevolent power of nature, and even though the poem ends on a rather threatening note, the brilliance of the images, the liveliness of the action all around, even, I would say, the decidedly cheerful notes in the poem, written into the metaphors, wrestle and clash with the cold undercurrents to create a vividly whole, living scene. "They are unloading three barrels of little crabs." The scrabbling of these lively creatures adds a sprightly, quietly humorous touch. This is a poem that, thanks to its sparkling metaphors, lives in and tugs at the body. In my opinion, it's "awful but cheerful," to quote another fine metaphor-maker, Elizabeth Bishop.

Here is another poet who is exceptionally handy with the metaphor, Les Murray, as shown in his poem "Shoal."

> Eye-and-eye eye an eye
> each. What blinks is I,
> unison of the whole shoal. Thinks:
> a dark idea circling by—
> again the eyes' I winks.
> Eye-and-eye near no eye
> is no I. . . .

This poem is, body and soul, itself a metaphor for what it must feel like to be present in the swirl of consciousnesses that makes up a shoal of fish, or the shoal as the soul of the compound being. The homophones, the uniform vocalizations in the first half of the poem, mimic the mirroring of the physical action here, the eye-to-eye connections. "What blinks is I, / unison of the whole shoal." Every element of these metaphors is sensorial in nature—"tasting, each being a tongue," or the "vague umbrations of chemical: / this way thrilling, that way Wrong." The poem is in constant, twitchy, swirling motion, echoing the visuals of the whole shoal; it privileges sound, but not at the expense of texture. The reader can feel the almost sonic explosion of "the bird-dive boom" and resonate to the doom-laden tolling of the "redfin's gaped gong."

> they are the eyes of Thjasse flung into the sky by
> Thor;   they are the white ants in the anthill built around
> the motionless Dhurva, who meditates for eternity deep in
> the forest;   they are a kind of celestial cheese churned
> into light;

Another poem whose whole body, it seems to me, functions overall as does the metaphor, is section viii ("Lightenings") from a long series called "Squarings," which appeared in Seamus Heaney's remarkable book *Seeing Things* and which itself, as the book title suggests, is a strongly metaphorical attempt to help us know, to understand, some of the greater mysteries of this human world.

> The annals say: when the monks of Clonmacnoise
> Were all at prayers inside the oratory
> A ship appeared above them in the air.
>
> The anchor dragged along behind so deep
> It hooked itself into the altar rails
> And then, as the big hull rocked to a standstill,
>
> A crewman shinned and grappled down the rope
> And struggled to release it. But in vain.
> 'This man can't bear our life here and will drown,'
>
> The abbot said, 'unless we help him.' So
> They did, the freed ship sailed, and the man climbed back
> Out of the marvellous as he had known it.

In one of Heaney's Oxford lectures, he said that implicit in this poem was something he wanted to affirm in the lecture series: that "within our individual selves we can reconcile *two orders of knowledge which we might call the practical and the poetic,*"—here we have an explicit description of the superimposition of one pattern on another and the blending of patterns that is essential to the operation of metaphor.

> they are the ostrich
> hunters, out all night, and at dawn they huddle near the
> sun to get warm, which is why you cannot see them;

When I was thirty, I suffered through a shattering divorce, which ended up being one of the best things that ever happened to me, but at that point it certainly didn't feel like it. During this difficult time, somewhere, I stumbled across a tiny powerhouse of a poem of Denise Levertov's which ends on this sentence:

Someone
entered the dark woods.

The poem is about mortality, about journey, about illumination, but mostly, to me at that difficult moment in my life, it was a metaphor for threshold. The speaker of the poem is standing on the metaphorical threshold that the leaver of the prints, the "someone," who begins the poem, has already passed over. The poem makes beautiful literary use of the very commonplace metaphor—*Life as a Journey*. Crossing the field, entering the dark woods—does this journey end in death? or in a strange and new difficulty? could it represent a raw beginning after a trying period? It employs the Dantean metaphor of the dark woods, the *selva oscura*, which represents a certain disorientation in the traveler—whether spiritual, physical, psychological, or moral, we can't be sure.

Since we endlessly repeat these metaphorical expressions, it would seem our minds are conditioned to understand the world in the comparative terms of metaphor. Intensify your use of metaphors. They will enrich everything.

up
there the daughter of the wind, mourning for her husband
lost at sea;   the Strong River is there, and the Palace of
the Five Emperors, the Kennel of the Barking Dogs.

Paul Violi was one of the most formally inventive poets I've ever read. He would take the most outlandish and "unpoetic" of forms, and turn them into extraordinary poems. He has created poems out of, for example, an errata sheet, a police blotter, a fireworks catalog, boat names in a marina, a letter of submission to a poetry editor, an excuse to a policeman writing up a speeding ticket, and, as we see in the following poem, an insincere apology. The poem is formally classical in most respects, including the title, the sonnet form, the fourteen lines, the beginning octet and following sestet, and it delivers a delicious reversal of perspective, much as Heaney does at the end of his "Lightenings" poem.

In his poem, "On an Acura Integra," the speaker is jotting down what should be "the usual information"—contact number, insurance company, name, and so forth—on the fender of a car whose bumper has been damaged by the careless driving of the speaker, but what is really the poem itself. The poems ends on the true *raison d'être* of the poem: "So that these onlookers who saw me bash / In your fender will think I'm jotting down / The usual information and go away." He clearly has a specific audience in mind—he assumes the reader of the poem will primarily be the injured party, the owner of the wounded car, but he also assumes this person is a reader of poetry, one who depends upon language to fulfill his or her longings, one who understands the experience of being drenched in "several levels of meaning at once," which is the basic operation of metaphor, as it is, centrally, of poetry. The language is wonderfully elevated, classically formal, except for the fabulous phrase, which lives at the very heart of the poem, "who saw me bash / In your fender." The fact that "bash" ends the line gives it weight and substance and heightens the humor implicit in the contrast of levels of diction.

there are the Sea Goat, the Danish Elephant, the
Long Blue Cloud-Eating Shark, and the White-Bone-
Snake;   up there is Theodosius turned into a star and
the head of John the Baptist turned into a star and Li Po's
breath, a star his poems make brighter;

there is the Thirsty Camel, the Camel Striving to Get to
Pasture, and the Camel Pasturing Freely;

One can't properly discuss metaphor in contemporary poetry without, at some point, bringing in Anne Carson, another of the twentieth and twenty-first centuries' preeminent masters of metaphor. This may be because, if we can characterize her extensive body of work in broad strokes, she is constantly examining the question of *how we know.* She is a classicist by training and inclination, but her literary experiments encompass a great many other historical and cultural moments. She writes about, explores, and learns from diverse sources, including St. Augustine, Emily Brontë, Gertrude Stein, Antonin Artaud, Simone Weil, and the film director Antonioni, to name just a few. Her remarkable long poem, "Book of Isaiah," is a retelling of that particular Biblical source. She does extraordinary things to the biblical original, which is a complex series, written, it is believed, by several hands over several centuries. It is understood to be the first of the books in the Bible to assert the monotheistic model of Judaism. In addition to the themes of holiness, righteousness, and God's plan for Israel,

Carson develops a feminist motif and imagines that the wisdom Isaiah gathers along his path as prophet might be similar to the wisdom gathered by Tiresias, in that both prophets at some point in their lives experienced the physical realities of living in both male and female bodies. Here is a section from part IV of that poem:

> Isaiah withdrew to the Branch.
> It was a blue winter evening, the cold bit like a wire.
> Isaiah laid his forehead on the ground.
> God arrived.
> Why do the righteous suffer? said Isaiah.
> Bellings of cold washed down the Branch.
> Notice whenever God addresses Isaiah in a feminine singular verb
> something dazzling is
> about to happen.
> Isaiah what do you know about women? asked God.
> Down Isaiah's nostrils bounced woman words:
> Blush. Stink. Wife. Fig. Sorceress—
> God nodded.
> Isaiah go home and get some sleep, said God.
> Isaiah went home, slept, woke again.
> Isaiah felt sensation below the neck, it was a silk and bitter sensation.
> Isaiah looked down.
> It was milk forcing the nipples open.
> Isaiah was more than whole.
> I am not with you I am *in* you, said the muffled white voice of God.

Poetry, like metaphor, gives us double vision, as two things unite to become a third, and yet at the same time remain themselves. The metaphors in "Book of Isaiah," and indeed throughout all of Carson's remarkable work, allow us to envision completely new ideas, which may or may not be erroneous, but which are almost always thrilling. "I am not with you I am *in you*, said the muffled white voice of God."

up there
is the broken circle that is a chipped dish, or a boomerang,

or the opening of the cave where the Great Bear sleeps;
up there the two donkeys whose braying made such a racket
they frightened away the giants and were rewarded with a
place in the sky;
there is the Star of a Thousand
Colors, the Hand of Justice, the Plain and Even Way;
there is the Double Double; there the Roadside
Inn; there the State Umbrella; there the Shepherd's
Hut there the Vulture; look: the Winnowing Fan;
there the Growing Small; there the Court of God;
there the Quail's Fire; there St. Peter's Ship and the
Star of the Sea; there: look: up there; the stars.

The Directing Sentence

CHRISTINE SCHUTT

Three words are all it takes for Mona Simpson to check off the requisite features to a story, a form, unlike the novel, which prizes economy. Her title "Lawns" provides setting, and "I steal," as the opening sentence, delivers character, conflict, point of view, and tone. It points to the middle of the story, if not to its end: sometime, in the future, the narrator must stop stealing. She has already begun to tire of getting away with it. "No one notices," she says, which is to say, no one ever gets caught.

Pronouncements made in opening paragraphs must be overturned and returned to; the recursive gesture makes for profounder meaning. All too often for a writer learning the craft, the utterance that puts a fiction in motion is forgotten, and the writer, lost, forges ahead by addition—new action, new character, new scenery—when it is subtraction that shapes stories. A writer would do well to look back at what she has written and consider the ways in which the directing sentence has been recalled and rewritten. Reconfiguration of the most lighthearted proposition darkens it.

Flannery O'Connor's stories, with their traditional architecture, are a good place to start in defending this theory of the story contained, and forecast, in the opening paragraph. "A Good Man Is Hard to Find" serves as example of an efficiently constructed beginning with the central character, the grandmother, badgering her only son, Bailey, to reconsider the family trip's destination. She wants to go to Tennessee, not Florida, and tries to persuade him with the news that an escaped criminal, "The Misfit," is even now on his way to Florida. The grandmother will not even repeat what this criminal has done to others but asserts, "I wouldn't take my children in any direction with a criminal like that aloose in it."

The simple sentence *I wouldn't take my children in any direction with a criminal like that aloose in it* directs the story. By the time O'Connor's fiction ends, the old lady has led her children to the Misfit himself. "'I recognized you at once!'" she says and immediately begins to appeal to his better nature that he might spare them. In this way, the old lady and the Misfit are alike. Their faith in Jesus is faint-of-heart. Because the Misfit wasn't there to see Jesus raise the dead, he cannot wholly believe in the promise of life after death, and the old lady's frantic fear in the face of death suggests she does not entirely believe in that promise either. Then in the last moments, the old lady's recognition of the Misfit goes well beyond his face, and she ceases to plead for her life, recognizing her connection to him. "You're one of my own children!" she says, and these, the old lady's last words, are offered up on another, loving note, open-armed and full of grace. She has traveled from nettling her only boy, Bailey, about the threat of the Misfit to embracing her son's killer as one of her own children. She touches his shoulder, and the Misfit recoils on the instant and shoots her.

A sometimes profitable game for starting a story is to see how much of the essential information can be conveyed in as few words as possible. In his well-known story "A&P," John Updike fits in all that is needed in eleven words, including the acronym for the Great Atlantic and Pacific Tea Company. The A&P, the supermarket chain, in business for 156 years, was the largest US retailer of any kind in 1965. ("A&P" was published in 1961.) I used to think "A&P" as a title was a cheater 's way to concision, using the title to establish setting, but I have come to appreciate it: "A&P," a deceptively shrunk term for the universe that it was in mid-twentieth-century America.

Updike's trick is to fit in all that is needed in the first utterance, eleven words, counting the title, and point of view follows in the second sentence.

A&P

In walk these three girls in nothing but bathing suits. I'm in the third check-out slot, with my back to the door, so I don't see them until they're over by the bread.

In walk these three girls in nothing but bathing suits. Eleven words, counting the title, deliver characters, problem, and enlargement of setting: It's summer and warm enough for bathing suits. Water must be nearby. And the problem? They are not wearing shoes or cover-ups, so will the three girls be suffered to stay? Point of view follows in the first word of the second sentence. First-person then, which reinforces the casual tone of the speaker; moreover, the speaker's clarifying that he didn't see the girls enter the store establishes the retrospective quality of the story. The narrator is recalling an event significant to him however brief the encounter. Writing retrospectively means the narrator has more room in which to analyze and elaborate on events.

Restrictive setting, short time frame with the ambition to deliver a wider world: Updike makes the decision never to go beyond the parking lot of the supermarket, and then only briefly. Most of the world is calculated in the store itself. Updike gets outside of the supermarket in the narrator's imagination, which is sparked by the words one of the girls uses, *herring snacks*. From the term he conjures a social event of men in seersucker and bow ties, women in sandals, toothpicked snacks; by comparison, his own parents serve beer in hokey glasses at their fancier events. Updike touches on class disparities, especially as they are experienced in a community with summer people living on the waterside, and fulltime residents inland, working and often serving these same short-term residents. Despite their privilege, the three girls are confronted by the manager of the A&P, who scolds them for their attire and makes them blush. The lead girl, in a two-piece bathing suit, defends herself and leaves with her friends, but not before the narrator, in a foolish gesture to stick up for them and play their hero, says, "I quit." With this confrontation the opening sentence is profoundly rewritten. *In walk these three girls . . .* now applies to the narrator in the checkout slot, who goes through with an action he knows he will regret even as he removes his apron. He quits work he needs and leaves the A&P, makes a clean exit into the dumb summer dazzle of the parking lot where he sees—and we see—the mother behind the son and what the job represents. Of course, his grand exit has gone unnoticed. Only he is there to take in the scene as he looks back at the A&P windows and sees the manager has replaced him in the checkout. *In walk these three girls in nothing but bathing suits:* out walks this boy, no longer costumed for work, vulnerable.

Consider the Stanley Elkin story, "A Poetics for Bullies"; consider its title. "Ways to Be a Bully" or "How to Be a Bully" or simply "Bullies" might have served, but the literary term *poetics* indicates the bullies under consideration overmaster others with linguistic techniques; those shovers and punchers are shabby practitioners; real powerhouse bullies employ language artfully. The title anticipates highwire prose, and Push, as the instructor delivers as much in the opening lines: "I'm Push the bully, and what I hate are new kids and sissies, dumb kids and smart, rich kids, poor kids, kids who wear glasses, talk funny, show off, patrol boys and wise guys and kids who pass pencils and water the plants—and cripples, *especially* cripples. I love nobody loved." The first sentence *is* a bullying sentence. Catalog sentences overwhelm with their length and density; here, a long list of dislikes concludes with the repeat of cripples in italics. Elkin ends on a bully's characteristic aggressive, impolitic, offensive speech: who would say such a thing and repeat it? A bully.

The last sentence of the opening paragraph to a "Poetics for Bullies" is a compressed rewriting of the first. *I love nobody loved* sounds almost epigrammatic with the poet's trick of using the same word as a different part of speech. Pithy sentences can powerfully reveal character. Iago's similar construction sums up his approach to bullying: "I am not what I am." Push's short utterance forecasts a confrontation: will Push love a beloved figure? The story will test his assertion.

Enter a tall boy new to town with the socially impeccable name of John Williams. Push describes his expensive clothes and imagines the sleek, rich world he comes from in a catalog of the privileged life, a long sentence with breathless interruptions and qualifications that add to the line's urgency. Faced with John Williams's manipulation of Push's harried gang, Push considers the limitations of what he, as a bully, can do: he can duplicate a kid's physical flaws. What Push can't do is enchant; he cannot imitate the new boy's formal, dreamy locutions. So for a time, Push listens to John Williams tell stories of adventure in foreign lands with strange beasts. He is a most persuasive storyteller; he enthralls, whereas Push threatens. The magic Push practices as a bully is no more than a kid's trick, wordplay, clever and cruel, hardly narratives on a level to compete with stories that feature elephants and tigers.

Push seeks out this newly arrived prince to find a flaw, something he might exploit. Their meeting occurs in the middle of the story. Push is overexcited. He wants to know all about John Williams. He wants to know if the new boy's story was true, but John Williams deflects his questions with repeated, incantatory requests to be quiet. His short responses convey other mysteries: "'There's a woman who's ill. A boy who must study. There's a man with bad bones.'" With such music John Williams thwarts Push. He uses a bully's best trick: seductive language. Push, as a lesser practitioner—his puns and conundrums are a "sleight of mouth"—cannot persuade, whereas John Williams's can move his listeners with utterances that hint at truths. Push, however failed, understands the bullying use of language, and he calls out the princely newcomer. "You're the bully!" Push says, and as he watches John Williams ascend the stairs to his apartment, he whispers the word *Lover.* The word, in italics in the middle of the story in the middle of the page, recalls Push's assertion in the opening: *I love nobody loved.* Whether Push genuinely loves or not, the remark is a reversal of his opening declaration. Push follows this whispered endearment with a challenge as to which of them will prevail: the bully Push or the hero-bully John Williams?

Early in the story, Push says that to be a bully requires bravery. Cowards will not succeed. Here the story goes beyond recording cruel locutions to comment on what is required in the production of literature. The writing profession is not for the timid. A writer may be shy at the party, stay indoors or abed, but on the page she will be best served going down steep roads, finding out places that put her at risk, braving the subject she promised never to broach with language that does not allow for obfuscation. Write bravely. Dismiss the trivial topic, the easy, the known; take on what is not understood. Such subjects, when seriously engaged by the writer, will lead her to truths about the essentials: sex and death and nature and god.

"A Poetics for Bullies" may be read as a poetics for fiction writers: the writer as bully or the writer as seducer. The writer draws in the reader by subject, sound, difference.

Helen Vendler has written that we "perceive poetic shape through oddness." The same is true of a directing sentence in a short story: it stands apart for its subject, its declaration, its syntax, its diction. The reader need not know which sentence, but the writer must know as the ensuing action—the story itself—revolves around this remark. Such sentences alter the tone. They are most often abstractly and formally composed as in the opening of Leonard Michaels's "Murderers."

In the middle of a long paragraph on the first-person narrator's resistance to a narrow, cowardly life that ends in a contemptible death, he asserts, "I wanted proximity to darkness, strangeness."

The title may entice, but the life the narrator takes up after the death of his

Uncle Moe is foremost. The narrator doesn't intend to wait for death at home but strikes out for the subway and the new places it takes him. The directing sentence, the abstract expression of his ambition to see everything, is buried in a paragraph of underground experience. The *darkness* he means to know is literal until one afternoon he runs into friends who tell him the rabbi is home. They have spied on the rabbi before and quickly agree to go to their spot with its view of the rabbi's apartment.

If the opening paragraph starts underground, it ends with the narrator and friends running for this lookout on a bright, tin roof with the view of the rabbi's apartment window, blinds up, curtains pulled, brilliant in the sun. From Uncle Moe's death to life as witnessed in the rabbi and his wife, coupling. As brightly lit as this primal scene might be, the sentence giving the story its direction still applies. Sex is dark and strange to the young; the roof, some distance from the human figures and their imperfections, is proximity enough.

The second paragraph dwells on light as they experience it on the tin roof. The narrator describes how they sit "like angels . . . derealized in brilliance." Their perch is precarious; they have risked their lives for this view. They have not waited timorously at home. The rabbi's wife—today a blonde—has other wigs, other colors, other styles; she is every woman in her dance with the rabbi. The scene is full of light and music. Every gesture, action, sight in these next few paragraphs rise humorously. The rabbi is described with "his balls afling." There is joy to be had in watching the rabbi, or as the narrator calls him, "Mr. Life." Several of the boys engage in masturbating when, in two short sentences that go by so quickly a first-time reader sometimes misses the action, the youngest of the boys slips and slides down the roof: his ring hooks a nailhead, and all that remains of him is the ring and ring finger. The word *death* does not appear in the sentences.

Darkness in "Murderers" is first the exterior, literal dark of subway travel; then the interior with witness of sexual congress; then with witness of death; and last, with experience of existential terror. Out of the mouth of the bearded rabbi issues condemnation. "Murderers!" he shouts and damns the "angels derealized in brilliance." At the end of the story, darkness for the narrator is a sound "blooming" inside him "like a mouth." The potent terms used in the last sentence, *darkness, blooming,* and *mouth,* are in response to the sentence that put the story in motion.

The Directing Sentence

The directing sentence serves as a compass, the needle of which twitches ever farther away toward an ending that is a reimagined version of itself. It is the essential recursive gesture in the making of a short story. The writer's work involves knowing that sentence and all the ways in which it might mean.

Rationed Compassion

Philip Larkin and Richard Wilbur

WYATT PRUNTY

"Why should I let the toad *work* / Squat on my life?" Philip Larkin asks at the opening of "Toads." And "Give me your arm, old toad; / Help me down Cemetery Road," he says at the end of "Toads Revisited." "High Windows" begins:

> When I see a couple of kids
> And guess he's fucking her and she's
> Taking pills or wearing a diaphragm,
> I know this is paradise.

Larkin is our genius of complaint. The best he has to say of youth is that it is not age. And the "paradise" he has in mind shares a duplex with oblivion. "High Windows" ends:

> Rather than words comes the thought of high windows:
> The sun-comprehending glass,
> And beyond it, the deep blue air, that shows
> Nothing, and is nowhere, and is endless.

The oblivion "High Windows" described in 1967 is the "nothing" described in "The Snow Man" by Wallace Stevens (1921), reminding us that Philip Larkin is a late modern, even as much of his project has been to recapture romantic ground. One means for Larkin's doing this has been his tough-guy poesie, his cynical-sounding stance against false hope. At the same time, while shadows grow long in Larkin's poetry, he hints at something brighter. He despairs over the lack of meaning, yet he frames that lack in figures worthy of a symbolist—the windows and their height, the light, the ineffable blue beyond. The windows open on high artistic aspiration, yet they are institutional too, so they belong to all of us—a library, church, classroom, government building. By teetering between aspiration and emptiness, architectural balance and utilitarian limit, Larkin buys credibility among readers.

Symbol sleuths might associate "High Windows" with Mallarmé or Baudelaire. Allusion sleuths might turn to Milton, Herbert. That Larkin was in conversation with the tradition is clear, but he argued his own time's questions. The strength of "High Windows" is its predicament. A generation's having pushed taboos aside, their liberation exposes a new limitation. Speaker for this, Larkin's character refuses to go beyond "the thought" of new restriction. And that thought is of "high windows" viewed from inside a space where the enclosed speaker looks skyward into the blue, such as Mallarmé's (*l'azur*), and doing so sees oblivion rather than correspondences on the order of Baudelaire. Why flirt with romantic understanding only to reject it? For the same reason Howard Nemerov's poem "Larkin" speaks of "Larkin of the anastrophic mind." What was desired had to be broken of expectation to save it from sentiment.

By another view from another window, Richard Wilbur's "Love Calls Us to the Things of This World" begins with "a cry of pulleys," as "spirited from sleep, the astounded soul" described here "Hangs . . . bodiless and simple / As false dawn." The person waking sees laundry on a line being pulled in a circle as more laundry is attached. During readings Wilbur often paused to explain what the literal situation was, someone in a time before clothes driers existed waking early to the sight of fresh laundry being pinned on a line. Wilbur's persona sees laundry and fuzzily thinks "The morning air is all awash with angels." (Wilbur defuses the situation with a pun.) After a moment the person waking realizes all that's seen is laundry, "bed-sheets," "blouses," and "smocks." Human limit is restored to the confusion of another day, with Wilbur adding, "Let there be clean linen for the backs of thieves; / Let lovers go fresh and sweet to be undone, / And the heaviest nuns walk in a pure floating / Of dark habits." Larkin associates "high windows" with "oblivion." Wilbur's view outside is very human.

But Wilbur did have his doubts. Answering a question during an interview with Peter Dale, Wilbur said his imaginative territory was a "Marchlands." He added that his experience during World War II and after left him with the "shaken sense of meaning and purpose" that "in France" led "to existentialist philosophy." It left him, he said, writing "to have objects speak," to free "the devout intransitive eye." Another close reader of Wilbur, John B. Hougen, has said Wilbur's project occurred in liminality, and that his goal was "not to rationalize the irrational" but to assert "that in ecstasy what has been separated may be reconciled."

The vampires in Wilbur's poem "The Undead" are extreme in their version of a "marchland." They are "possessed" by "one wish, their thirst for mere survival." Gradually, however, the reader's understanding of them increases to the point that Wilbur can say, "vampires, / Colorful though they are" endure a "pain" that "is real, / And requires our pity." They are trapped—thirsting for but unable to drink the "scorned elixir, / The salt quotidian blood." The ordinary life they in their self-obsession reject has passed them by, leaving them like pockets of seawater trapped in "rock hollows" at low tide along a New England coast. Salt, the sea, the action of tides and waves—these are the elements of an inclusive sea. While the mirror, the dawn, the cross, and stake are terrors for vampires, what they cannot understand is that their real fear stems from their "one wish" for "mere survival." Self-preservation isolates them from the sea (the *mer* of "survival" for translator Wilbur) ordinary life, leaving them neither living nor dead, the "Undead."

And then there is Wilbur's poem "Tywater," which describes a cowboy who shares some traits with baseball legend Ty Cobb. Tywater's name represents the will's defeat: no one can lasso and tie up water. Wilbur calls Tywater "Sir Nihil," on the one hand seeing him as a nihilist, and on the other hand in terms of *nihil obstat*. The choices here are between philosophical meaninglessness and theological confirmation. Tywater is a complicated instance of an un-Christian knight; at the same time he is a rejoinder to E. E. Cummings's poem "Buffalo Bill's / defunct." When Tywater dies, "his body turns / To clumsy dirt," as Buffalo Bill's did. But the nature of Tywater's death raises a question that Buffalo Bill's did not. Cummings ends, "how do you like your blueeyed boy / Mister Death," while Wilbur ends asking, "And what to say of him, God knows." For Wilbur, the expression "God knows" is at once idiomatically expressive of a riddle *and* theologically freighted.

In another poem, "Potato," Wilbur describes his subject as "An underground grower," a "common brown" that has "a misshapen look." But he adds, "What has not lost its savor shall hold us up." Our need is part of that. The potato, with a "stench" like "a strangely refreshing tomb," is an "earth-apple," a reminder of the *felix culpa*, even as it also has its history as a last defense against starvation. The potato, Wilbur tells us, is "beautiful only to hunger." Wilbur often pairs lack with the discovery of plenty. He is fond of the words "save" and "savor." His response to scarcity is opposite to Larkin's. Imagine Larkin praising an "underground grower . . . with a misshapen look," let alone a tomb-like "stench." Larkin's answer is "the wind's incomplete unrest" ("Talking in Bed"). "I lock my door. / The gas-fire breathes. The wind outside / Ushers in evening rain. . . . solitude" ("Best Society"). "All the spare time . . . flown / Straight into nothingness" ("Vers de Société").

Wilbur acknowledges the doubt upon which Larkin ruminates so memorably, but Wilbur's impulse is to turn such questioning inside out. His "Misshapen" potatoes derive their beauty from hunger the way his "Mayflies" swarm up in sunlight to become "The weavers of some cloth of gold." For Wilbur, limit (hunger with the potato, mortality with the flies) causes metamorphosis in those perceiving them. The potato suffices physical need, and by their beauty the flies suffice metaphysical need. "Mayflies" begins, "In somber forest, when the sun was low," then describes "a mist of flies" rising "In their quadrillions," forming "no muddled swarm" but "a manifold / And figured scene." The poem ends:

> Watching those lifelong dancers of a day
> As night closed in, I felt myself alone
> In a life too much my own,
> More mortal in my separateness than they—
> Unless, I thought, I had been called to be
> Not fly or star
> But one whose task is joyfully to see
> How fair the fiats of the caller are.

Mortality represented by "lifelong dancers of a day"? An orderly world ruled by "the fiats of [a] caller"? Such ideas are opposite to the Larkin who begins, "They fuck you up, your mum and dad." Larkin's "Aubade" starts with "soundless dark," then becomes a shaded world in which "the curtain-edges will grow light." Wilbur's "Mayflies" also has its shadows. But it describes the end rather than the beginning of the day. Wilbur says the hour is late, the sun "low," the "forest" grown "somber," with *somber* a derivative of *umbra,* "shade." Writing of himself in his eighties, Richard Wilbur sees the shades of Hades lengthening his way. The scene he describes echoes Keats in "To Autumn," with a "maturing sun" and "bees" instead of flies. Wilbur's flies are bright and active, but "night" is "clos[ing] in," leaving the speaker, as Wilbur says, "mortal" in his "separateness." At the same time, Wilbur is careful to say the flies are "no muddled swarm." They may rise from "unseen pools" into "a manifold," but they make a "figured scene." What Wilbur sees is something made intentionally by "weavers." It is "fair," implying something just, or something "fair" in the sense of light, bright, or with no blemish. Larkin studies up through institutional windows and, in a way that speaks for many today, sees nothing beyond the glass.

Wilbur may have spoken of his living with a "marchlands" and "liminality," but in "Mayflies" he is the one "whose task is joyfully to see." And what he sees is a "manifold / And figured scene" of forest, sun, mayflies. To the speaker who beholds all this the flies are beautiful, a "great round-dance showing clear." The speaker is separated from all this but part of it too, by his response to beauty. Wilbur compares the "round-dance" of the flies to stars as they appear at night through "gap[s] in black and driven cloud." They are part of an order larger than the speaker's individual interest, except perhaps for Wilbur's "task," which, as he says, "is joyfully to see / How fair the fiats of the caller are."

Meanwhile, were Wilbur's "caller" to dial up Philip Larkin, the other end might not answer. Equally important, Larkin's "The Whitsun Weddings" makes generous answer. There Larkin describes a series of weddings observed by a passenger taking a train to London, who as he goes through towns notices young couples boarding at every stop. The educational and material limitations are evident here, but there are moments of happiness and hope as well. The young couples are launching their lives as they board the train for their honeymoons. In this, Larkin the fellow traveler becomes sympathetic participant as well as shrewd observer. The reader trusts his account. Approaching the end of the train trip the passengers are thrown forward by the complicating detail of the train's brakes catching and slowing them to their destination—which is the anonymity of London's sheer number of others in its "postal districts . . . packed like squares of wheat." The newlyweds arrive like a crop ready to be harvested. Also, Larkin adds, with the brakes throwing them forward, they are an "arrow-shower / sent out of sight," that is, beyond volition, "somewhere becoming rain" as Cupid's English longbow releases their hope into new life.

Describing the way he first noticed the weddings, Larkin adds, "Struck, I leant / More promptly out next time, more curiously," as at this point he has seen "it all again in different terms." Yet in the moment Larkin goes about rationing he does so while he lists all the human detail he has noticed: "parodies of fashion," as in "the nylon gloves and jewellery-substitutes," or "fathers with broad belts under their suits . . . mothers loud and fat; / An uncle shouting smut." Contrary to reputation, Larkin is a wonderfully humane poet—as "The Whitsun Weddings," "To the Sea," "Wedding Wind," and "An Arundel Tomb" demonstrate. But he also tends his customary bog, much as Richard Wilbur does his "marchlands." In fact Larkin is the master of bog.

In "Church Going" he is the one who visits a church only "once" he's certain there is "nothing going on . . . inside." And then there is Larkin's "Vers de Société," in which receiving an invitation he first rejects, then rethinks, then accepts: "*Care to join us?* The speaker reads and repeats. *Dear Warlock Williams: I'm afraid* he composes in response. Then thinks again and replies, *Dear Warlock Williams why of course.*"

Couples on their honeymoons sent like an "arrow-shower" out of "sight" "somewhere becoming rain?" How different this sounds, coming from the man who also wrote, "*My wife and I have asked a crowd of craps / To come and waste their time and ours,*" and "Man hands on misery to man. / It deepens like a coastal shelf. Get out as early as you can, / And don't have any kids yourself." Or so it would seem. Larkin rations his compassion by a wryness that sustains that in the face of an otherwise skeptical view of a wisely qualified world.

It is with rationing in mind that Larkin's "Wedding Wind" balances a bride's happiness with a damaging storm from the night before. Her husband has departed to survey the effects of the weather, and this leaves her alone to contemplate her doubly changed world. "Wedding Wind" is an early poem by Larkin. Later he inoculated his work with the wit and comedy of his hard-boiled style. But the public toughness of the older Larkin only enriches a sensitivity present beneath from the beginning. Larkin's tough-guy poesie, seemingly so antithetical to romantic expression, is in fact the means by which we are convinced that his longing is a reliable feature of our own lives. The focused detail of "To the Sea" exemplifies this.

In "To the Sea" Larkin's thin-lipped observations build to muted hope for the families he describes. And Larkin gives broad context to this hope. People milling over the sand and a ship on the horizon. Larkin catalogs the "Steep beach" with "towels, red bathing caps," and "the small hushed waves' repeated fresh collapse." The adults in this scene teach their children "by a sort / Of clowning." And the children, as they are led by their parents, raise one free hand "grasping at enormous air." "The rigid old" are present too, rolled "along for them to feel / Final summer." This is the little world of "transistors," childhood pleasures, and the stalled distractions of the old. It is a world framed by the "low horizon" that stretches over "cheap cigars, / The chocolate-papers, tea-leaves, and, between / The rocks, the rusting soup-tins," all of these documenting the limits of our little lives while at the same time demonstrating the dearness of such lives. That is Larkin's installment of rationed compassion. Thus by the end of the day "the first / Few families start the trek back to the cars. / The white steamer has gone. Like breathed-on glass / The sunlight has turned milky," and Larkin is able to say of this, "If the worst / Of flawless weather is our falling short, / It may be that through habit these do best."

Where Larkin sees "habit" leading to the good, Richard Wilbur sees something more interactive. Even in a poem entitled "Lying," Wilbur is capable of observing "Out of what cognate splendor all things came." In "The Beautiful Changes" Wilbur says,

> Your hands hold roses always in a way that says
> They are not only yours; the beautiful changes
> In such kind ways,
> Wishing ever to sunder
> Things and things' selves for a second finding, to lose
> For a moment all that it touches back to wonder.

For Wilbur "hunger," "scattering," and "wonder" are answered by plentitude, order, and assurance. Addressing our role by considering both extremes, Wilbur's early poem "Praise in Summer" asks "why this mad *instead* / Perverts our praise to uncreation, why / Such savor's in this wrenching things awry?" His answer is given in various ways, with wit in this poem but by description and transition in other poems. Wilbur's "Year's End" catalogs "frozen-over lakes," "late leaves" frozen in ice, "Great mammoths" frozen in ice, "The little dog" of Pompeii preserved in ash. The poem opens, "Now winter downs the dying of the year, / And night is all a settlement of snow." Using these details as evidence of his path, Wilbur reaches the end of the poem only to find reversal. The "late leaves," "Great mammoths," "the little dog" are replaced by "The New-Year bells . . . wrangling with the snow." The "night" that was "a settlement of snow" has now been stirred to start another year.

Larkin also contemplates transitions, but he is skeptical about anything suggestive of comfortable illusion. For him there is always "the dread / Of dying," as he says in "Aubade," and any distraction from this is delusional. One delusion is "Religion," what Larkin calls "That vast moth-eaten musical brocade / Created to pretend we never die." Larkin prefers doubt to disappointment. In pursuit of this he uses a tough-guy poesie as an astringent applied to facts to earn our trust. The "kind ways" Richard Wilbur alludes to in "The Beautiful Changes," for instance, are matched by what Larkin, in "An Arundel Tomb," describes as time's "Untruth." Even saying that, however, Larkin there turns to end, "What will survive of us is love." Larkin turns often. Time's oblivion is the minus by which Larkin magnifies his positive. And by this kind of exchange Richard Wilbur operates similarly. Wilbur's "Tywater," "The Undead," "Cottage Street, 1953," and "The Writer" stand on one side of things, while on the other are the assurances found in poems such as "Loves of the Puppets," "Love Calls Us to the Things of This World," "My Father Paints the Summer," and "The Beautiful Changes." "Cottage Street, 1953," describes an attempt by Wilbur's mother-in-law, Edna Ward, to balance the despair of Sylvia Plath. It is Edna Ward, Wilbur tells us near the end of the poem, whose "thin hand reaching out" accompanied her "last word *love*." Wilbur has said he did not mean to be critical of Plath when writing "Cottage Street, 1953," but he did conclude by mentioning what he called Plath's "brilliant negative," her "poems" that were "free and helpless and unjust."

Opposite to Plath in "Cottage Street, 1953," there is Edna Ward. And between Plath and Ward there is Richard Wilbur finding himself of two minds. As he says of his being introduced to Plath his role was "to exemplify / The published poet in his happiness, / Thus cheering Sylvia, who has wished to die." Wilbur continues, he was a "stupid life-guard," one "impotent to bless." In contrast, Wilbur's poem "The Writer" ends differently. Considering his daughter's hard work at her typewriter, Wilbur uses first one comparison and then another. Imagining the "great cargo" of her life, he wishes her "a lucky passage." But she in her upstairs room keeps working so that Wilbur turns to a second figure to wish her well. What follows is an account of a bird trapped once in the same room the daughter is in until father and daughter engineered escape. The two opened a window in the room then waited to watch through a door ajar until the bird having hit closed windows repeatedly finally found the one opened. This limited solution caused the bird to bloody its head before it found the right way out, "clearing the sill of the world," as Wilbur puts it. The compassion here is rationed much the way Larkin would choose. Limiting help, opening only one window, creates the drama of the poem. The "room at the prow of the house" has many windows. Limiting opportunity to only one guarantees the drama of the poem. Richard Wilbur was kinder than that. But this is art. Withholding choices makes the bird's one chance more meaningful. And the same applies to the young writer struggling upstairs, in fact applies to all of us. Wilbur wishes his daughter what he wished her "before," he says, now only he wishes "harder." Most who read Wilbur's poetry come away with the understanding that he wished so generally. Making meaning out of hope, not doubt, was much of Richard Wilbur's achievement. The age in which he wrote supplied the doubt.

Compared to Richard Wilbur's opening one window so as "not to affright the bird," some of Philip Larkin's accounts can seem rough. But Larkin had his sympathies. To return to "An Arundel Tomb," Larkin says of visitors to the Fitzalan Chapel in Arundel, West Sussex, "How soon succeeding eyes begin / To look, not read." "Identity" has become a "scrap of history." Then having said that Larkin turns again, assuring some survival through "love."

Larkin's "Aubade" expresses his more familiar tone. The poem's speaker says, "I work all day, and get half-drunk at night / Waking at four to soundless dark." As the speaker waits, "Slowly light strengthens, and the room takes shape" and, as he says, "all the uncaring / Intricate rented world begins to rouse." Larkin's "Faith Healing" continues his debate between "love" and "uncaring." The scene Larkin describes in "Faith Healing" seems something from an old clip of Oral Roberts: "Slowly the women file to where he stands / Upright in rimless glasses, silver hair, / Dark suit, white collar." And as they draw close the "deep American voice" asks them, "*Now, dear child, / What's wrong* . . . And, scarcely pausing, goes into a prayer / Directing God about this eye, that knee."

The petitioners in "Faith Healing" are ushered, healed, and dismissed. Some "go in silence," while others "stay stiff, twitching and loud," revealing, as Larkin puts it, "a kind of dumb / And idiot child within them still" ready "To re-awake at kindness." There is pathos in all this, but Larkin doesn't linger there. "What's wrong!" the American asks, as "Moustached [women] in flowered frocks" stand before him then "shake." Larkin himself says, "By now, all's wrong." Then the syntactical complexity of what follows makes an overlay of "life lived" and "love" remaining incomplete. Front stage there is psychological manipulation; back of that, a complex syntax dramatizing need and the unanswerable limits imposed by need. Larkin's method is to develop the situation then delay resolution in order to increase the reader's engagement: "To some it [love] means the difference they could make / By loving others, but across most it sweeps / As all they might have done had they been loved." Larkin adds, "That nothing cures." Instead there is "An immense slackening ache" like a "thawing . . . landscape [that] weeps, / Spreads slowly through them"—with "the voice above / Saying *Dear child*, and all time has disproved." Compassion is not rationed so much as freely given, if in fact Larkin believed it to be compassion.

Larkin wrote Maeve Brennan in March of 1964 that he thought the end of "Faith Healing" was "one of the best things in the book," that book being *The Whitsun Weddings*. By "best" Larkin meant one of his most complete realizations of complicated emotion. In *Further Requirements* Larkin says poetry is emotion. Larkin could have added that doubt and disappointment magnify emotion. The dissonance of Larkin's rhyming "loved" with "disproved" is just one small touch reminding us of this.

Larkin was our hard-boiled poet. But not so in the beginning. His early poems "The Explosion," "Cut Grass," "Forget What Did," "At the chiming of light upon sleep," and the title poem of his first book, "The North Ship," displayed an open sensitivity he later learned to dampen. "The North Ship" opens:

> I saw three ships go sailing by,
> Over the sea, the lifting sea,
> And the wind rose in the morning sky,
> And one was rigged for a long journey.

The poem ends by repeating that the ship, the poet, was "rigged for a long journey." As so young Larkin proved to be. Years later he wrote "The Old Fools," asking of the aged, "Can they never tell / What is dragging them back, and how it will end?" What the "North Ship" and "The Old Fools" share between them is longing—that of the first poem expectantly, that of the second reflectively. In his poem entitled "Larkin," Howard Nemerov says Larkin wrote to be "among the undeceived" and should be praised for his "contempt," which was "sympathy / Of a sort." Wilbur demonstrated sympathy as well, but Larkin used disguises that made him a figure both humorous and dark at once.

Initially characterized as narrow and Hardyesque, Larkin was considered part of the diminished landscape of England following World War II and the breakup of the British Empire. Since that beginning he has been considered a metonymic realist, a modern, a postmodern, a symbolist, dialogical in practice, given to heteroglossia, a sly mystic, a historical materialist, and a postimperial pastoralist. What these characterizations tell us collectively is that Larkin is a multivoiced and emotionally complex poet whose work accounts for a broad range of experience. Larkin affirmed matters, as we are reminded by the lines "this bodying-forth by wind / Of joy my actions turn on" spoken by a farmer's bride in "Wedding Wind." And there are Larkin's affirming poems, "The Whitsun Weddings" and "To the Sea." All three focus on a dearness found in ordinary working-class lives. Larkin memorably describes the limitations of such people, but then he ends magnifying them. His poems range from shy interest to vague contempt to sympathy, then compassion, then full valuation.

And Richard Wilbur? Wilbur has his reservations too. As a young man he experienced the Great Depression, and during the Second World War he fought in Europe. But early and late his best poems stand clear-eyed and patient. Wilbur's poem "Lying" describes the "chuckling ice" and "Toxic zest" of a "dead party" during which someone tells a lie to enliven things. In another study, Wilbur's cowboy described in "Tywater" is an American type whose violence embodies twentieth-century wars as much as any part of the storied past of the American West. The riddles in human behavior that cause doubt in Larkin are just as active in Wilbur's cowboy, whose "whistling silver throwing knife" could "punch the life / Out of a swallow in the air." Even Wilbur's much-affirming and much-anthologized poem "The Beautiful Changes" contains the miniature danger of the praying mantis that Wilbur describes, "arranged / On a green leaf," there waiting for food. Yet at the same time it is the mantis that "makes the leaf leafier," adds to life, even as, again, it tilts up waiting to use its raptorial front legs to catch what it will eat. Here in the guise of one small figure Wilbur includes predacity, camouflage for protection and beauty in the increased green of ongoing life. There is shadow in the wit of this light touch. Other times, as in "Mayflies," Wilbur openly studies a "somber" scene, and, as Larkin finesses so often, captures the angle leaning between things dark, things light.

In "Church Going" Philip Larkin lets "the door thud shut" after he is sure no one is there. In "Mayflies" Richard Wilbur celebrates "How fair the fiats of the caller are." There is Larkin waking early to the dark in "Aubade" and Wilbur in his poem "Love Calls Us to the Things of This World" waking to light and to "a cry of pulleys," comically echoing George Herbert as the urban morning's laundry is pulled out on a line. Larkin's and Wilbur's first two poems reflect different levels of comfort with their worlds. Their second two poems offer views of love. All four were only art, but as far as that goes Larkin doubted while Wilbur affirmed. With both, it seems, there was compassion of a sort, and rationing to last.

CONTRIBUTORS

RICHARD BAUSCH has written twelve novels, including *Peace* and *Before, During, After*, and eight collections of short fiction, among them *Wives & Lovers: 3 Short Novels* and *Living in the Weather of the World*. He has won the PEN/Malamud Award for Excellence in the Short Story, the Rea Award in the Short Story, and the Dayton Literary Peace Prize, among other awards. Two feature-length films have recently been made from his work: *Espèces menacées*, by French filmmaker Gilles Bourdos, from six Bausch stories, and *Recon*, just released, Robert Port's adaptation of *Peace*.

ADRIANNE HARUN is the author of two short-story collections, *The King of Limbo* and *Catch, Release*, winner of the Eric Hoffer Award, as well as a novel, *A Man Came Out of a Door in the Mountain*, which won the 2015 Pinckley Prize for Debut Crime Fiction. Her stories have received "notable" listings in *Best American Short Stories* and *Best American Mystery Stories*, and her books have been short-listed for the Washington State Book Award, Pacific Northwest Booksellers Association Award, and International Dublin Literary Award, among others.

ANDREW HUDGINS is the author of numerous collections of poetry and essays, many of which have received high critical praise, such as *The Never-Ending: New Poems*, a finalist for the National Book Award; *After the Lost War: A Narrative*, which received the Poets' Prize; and *Saints and Strangers*, a finalist for the Pulitzer Prize. Hudgins is an elected member of the Fellowship of Southern Writers, and was the Humanities Distinguished Professor of English at Ohio State University.

NAOMI IIZUKA'S plays include *36 Views*, *Polaroid Stories*, *Anon(ymous)*, *Good Kids*, and *Language of Angels*. Her plays have been produced at Berkeley Rep, the Goodman, the Guthrie, Actors Theatre of Louisville, and the Public Theatre, among others. She is an alumna of New Dramatists and the recipient of a PEN/ Laura Pels Award, an Alpert Award, and a Whiting Award. Iizuka heads the MFA playwriting program at the University of California, San Diego.

RANDALL KENAN was the author of a novel, *A Visitation of Spirits,* and a collection of stories, *Let the Dead Bury Their Dead,* which was a finalist for the National Book Critics Circle Award, a nominee for a *Los Angeles Times* Book Prize for fiction, and a *New York Times* Notable Book. His most recent collection, *If I Had Two Wings,* was long-listed for the National Book Award. He taught creative writing at the University of North Carolina at Chapel Hill.

MARGOT LIVESEY is the author of a collection of stories, eight novels, and a book of essays about writing, *The Hidden Machinery.* Her ninth novel, *The Boy in the Field,* came out in 2020. She is the recipient of fellowships from the Guggenheim Foundation, the National Endowment for the Arts, the Radcliffe Institute, and the Canada Council for the Arts. She grew up on the edge of the Scottish Highlands and teaches at the Iowa Writers' Workshop.

WILLIAM LOGAN'S books of poetry include *Rift of Light, Madame X,* and *Strange Flesh.* His numerous books of criticism include *Our Savage Art: Poetry and the Civil Tongue* and *Guilty Knowledge, Guilty Pleasure: The Dirty Art of Poetry.* A new book of criticism, *Broken Ground: Poetry and the Demon of History,* will be published this spring. He is a regular critic for the *New York Times Book Review* and the *New Criterion* and is Alumni/ae Professor of English at the University of Florida.

MAURICE MANNING has published seven books of poetry, most recently *Railsplitter.* His fourth book, *The Common Man,* was a finalist for the Pulitzer Prize. A former Guggenheim Fellow, Manning teaches at Transylvania University in Lexington and in the MFA Program for Writers at Warren Wilson College. He lives with his family on a small farm in Kentucky.

CHARLES MARTIN is the author of seven books of poetry, most recently *Future Perfect.* His verse translation of Ovid's *Metamorphoses* received the 2004 Harold Morton Landon Award from the Academy of American Poets. In 2005 he received an Academy Award in Literature from the American Academy of

Arts and Letters. Martin has also been the recipient of a Bess Hokin Award from *Poetry* magazine, a Pushcart Prize, and fellowships from the Ingram Merrill Foundation and the National Endowment for the Arts.

JILL MCCORKLE is the author of seven novels, most recently *Hieroglyphics*, and four story collections. Her work has appeared in numerous periodicals, and four of her short stories have been selected for *Best American Short Stories*. She currently teaches in the Bennington College Writing Seminars and at North Carolina State University.

ALICE MCDERMOTT is the author of eight novels, most recently *The Ninth Hour*. Her novel *Charming Billy* won the National Book Award for Fiction in 1998. Three of her novels were finalists for the Pulitzer Prize.

DAN O'BRIEN'S plays include *The Body of an American, The House in Scarsdale: A Memoir for the Stage, The Cherry Sisters Revisited, The Voyage of the Carcass, The Dear Boy*, and many others. His awards include a Guggenheim Fellowship in Drama and Performance Art, the Horton Foote Prize for Outstanding New American Play, the inaugural Edward M. Kennedy Prize for Drama, two PEN America Awards for Drama, and the L. Arnold Weissberger Award. He is also a librettist and an award-winning poet.

WYATT PRUNTY is the Carlton Professor of English at the University of the South and the founding director of the Sewanee Writers' Conference. He is the author of nine collections of poetry—including *Unarmed and Dangerous: New and Selected Poems; The Lover's Guide to Trapping;* and *Couldn't Prove, Had to Promise*—and the critical work *"Fallen from the Symboled World": Precedents for the New Formalism*. He is the general editor of the Johns Hopkins: Poetry and Fiction Series.

MARY JO SALTER is the author of eight books of poems, most recently *The Surveyors*. She is also a lyricist, whose work has been performed by Fred Hersch and Renee Fleming. Salter has coedited the fourth, fifth, and sixth editions of *The Norton Anthology of Poetry*. She is Krieger-Eisenhower Professor in the Writing Seminars at Johns Hopkins University.

CHRISTINE SCHUTT is the author of two short-story collections, *Nightwork* and *A Day, a Night, Another Day, Summer,* and three novels: *Florida,* a National Book Award finalist; *All Souls,* a Pulitzer Prize finalist; and *Prosperous Friends.* Among other honors, Schutt has twice been selected for inclusion in *The O. Henry Prize Stories,* and her work has appeared in the *New American Stories* anthology from Vintage. She is the recipient of New York Foundation for the Arts and Guggenheim fellowships, and she lives and teaches in New York.

A poet and translator, **SIDNEY WADE** is professor emerita of creative writing at the University of Florida. She is the author of eight collections of poetry, including *Bird Book* and *Deep Gossip: New and Selected Poems.* She has also served as president of the Association of Writers and Writing Programs and as secretary/treasurer of the American Literary Translators Association.

ALLEN WIER is the author of two books of stories, including *Late Night, Early Morning,* and four novels, most recently *Tehano.* He has edited a book on style in contemporary fiction and an anthology of stories. The recipient of a National Endowment for the Arts grant, a Guggenheim fellowship, the Paisano Fellowship, the John Dos Passos Prize for Literature, and the Fellowship of Southern Writers' Robert Penn Warren Award, Wier is professor emeritus at the University of Tennessee, Knoxville, where he held the Hodges Chair for Distinguished Teaching.

STEVE YARBROUGH is the author of eleven books, most recently the novel *The Unmade World,* winner of the Massachusetts Book Award for Fiction. Additional prizes for his work include the Mississippi Institute of Arts and Letters Award for Fiction, the California Book Award, the Richard Wright Award, and the Robert Penn Warren Award. A native of Mississippi, he lives in the Boston area and teaches at Emerson College.

INDEX

Aarne-Thompson Classification System, 202
About Fiction (Morris), 204
Abrams, M. H., 65–68
abstractions, 191–92, 214
adjectives, 201
adultery, 184–85
advice, 54, 66, 113, 118–19, 128–29, 171, 199, 204, 208–10, 214, 231
Aeneid (Virgil), 59
aesthetics of ambivalence, 84–97
Albers, Josef, 104
alchemy, 55, 79–80, 83, 211
allegory, 164
All the King's Men (Warren), 50–52
alterations affecting a poem, 193–203
"Always" (Strand), 99
ambivalence, 88–97
American literature, 159–60
American poetry, 154–55
The American Scene (James), 92–93
"American Scenes (1904–1905)" (Justice), 91–93, 96
anagrams, 111–12
"Animals in Heaven," 11–24
animation, 32, 35, 43
"A&P" (Updike), 228–29
architecture and narrative: and the Bunny Lane House, 38–40; and childhood memories, 25–27; form and function, 29–32; and Herrera's *Signs Preceding the End of the World*, 35–38; and libraries, 32–35; and shaping stories, 27–30, 35–38; and Tokarczuk's *House of Day, House of Night*, 40–44
Arduini, Franca, 63
"Aren't You Happy for Me?" (Bausch), 208
Aristotle, 16, 23, 57–58, 63
Ars Poetica (Horace), 58
artifice, 88, 108
The Art of Fiction (Gardner), 47
"An Arundel Tomb" (Larkin), 241–42
The Atlantic (magazine), 117
"Aubade" (Larkin), 69, 237, 241–42, 245
Auden, W. H., 90
Audubon: A Vision (Warren), 160–69
Audubon, John James, 155, 161–69
Austen, Jane, 116
authenticity, 68
autobiographical poets, 98
"Automat" (Hopper), 107

backstory, 36, 47
Baldwin, James, 116, 117, 119–22, 124
The Ballad of the Sad Café (McCullers), 172
Barnstone, Willis, 217
Barthes, Roland, 195
"The Bath" (Carver), 116
Bausch, Richard, 208
"The Beautiful Changes" (Wilbur), 240–41, 244
beginning of a story: in as few words as possible, 228–29; and magic, 16–20; and opening pages of novels, 127–36; and the process of writing, 211–12; and revision, 123–24. *See also* opening paragraphs

INDEX

Bell, Madison Smartt, 27
Bellow, Saul, 209
Beloved (Morrison), 55
Bennington College, 179–81
Bernard Shaw (Holroyd), 54
Bernay, Anne, 121
Berryman, John, 100–101, 106
Bible, 184, 188–89, 205, 224
Birds of America (Audubon), 161
Bishop, Elizabeth, 116, 121, 126, 177, 221
Blaise, Clark, 211
"The Blank Page" (Dinesen), 22
blank verse, 199–200
Bogdanovich, Peter, 135
"Book of Isaiah" (Carson), 224–26
Bowen, Elizabeth, 213
"Boy Wandering in Simms' Valley" (Warren), 157–59
Brennan, Maeve, 243
Brooks, Cleanth, 203
Brown, Bill, 78
Brown, Denise Scott, 29–30
Browning, Robert, 65–67
"Buffalo Bill's / defunct" (Cummings), 236
Bunny Lane House, 38–40, 43–44
Butler building, 38

Campbell, Joseph, 35–37
capitalism, 160
Capote, Truman, 49, 213
Carson, Anne, 224–26
Carver, Raymond, 116, 133
Casey, John, 16
catalog sentences, 230
Catholic Church, 183–85
Catullus, 62–63
The Changing Light at Sandover (Merrill), 112
Chapman University, 190
characters: and backstory, 47; and failure to capture, 45–46; and the human condition, 80–81; and interiority, 59; minor, 125; as mythological, 50; and New Journalism, 49; non-point-of-view characters, 121; and personality, 47–48; and physicality, 46–47; and plot, 67; and revision, 125; and secrets, 76–77; and storytelling, 52–53; and voices, 146; and writing about real people, 49–54; and writing outside the story, 121
chiasmus, 61–64
childhood memories, 25–27, 94
choreography, 79
"Church Going" (Larkin), 239, 244
"Churchill's Black Dog" (Storr), 47
class disparities, 229, 244
cleverness, 21–23
Cloud Atlas (Mitchell), 64
Cobb, Ty, 236
codex, 64
Coleridge, Samuel Taylor, 154–55, 205–6
collage, 104
Collected Poems (Strand), 108–9
Collected Poems (Thomas), 64
combinatory play, 218–19
"Come Back to the Raft Ag'in, Huck Honey" (Fiedler), 56
comedy, 143–44
comfort, 177–79
common metaphors, 217
communication, 190
compassion, 234–45
concealment, 93–94
confessional mode of poetry, 93, 100–101, 106, 109
conflict, 125, 145
conflicting advice, 118–19
Conrad, Joseph, 20–21, 115–16
constructive criticism, 118–19
conventional monologues, 144
conversation, 140–41
"Cottage Street, 1953" (Wilbur), 241
The Country Girls (O'Brien), 136–38
craft, 48, 102, 105–6, 138, 140, 156, 204–7, 208, 227

INDEX

Culler, Jonathan, 194–95, 197
Cummings, E. E., 236

Dale, Peter, 235–36
darkness, 100, 231–32
"The Dead" (Joyce), 175
death, 82–83, 90–91, 159, 231–32
"The Decorated Shed," 29–30
Defoe, Daniel, 53
de Maupassant, Guy, 124
democracy, 160
Democracy and Poetry (Warren), 159–60, 168–69
Departures (Justice), 87
detective stories, 65–67
dialogue, 51–52, 140, 142–45, 208–9
Dickens, Charles, 19
Dickinson, Emily, 111–12, 171, 182, 209, 219
Dillman, Lisa, 38
diminished self, 159–60
Dinesen, Isak, 22
direct address, 144–45
directing sentences, 227–33
Donne, John, 68
doubt, 128, 237, 241–45
Dracula (Stoker), 174
drama and plot, 61
dramatic monologues, 65–68
Dramatic Monologues (Maio), 67
dreams, 40, 172
Dreiser, Theodore, 214
"Drinking Coffee Elsewhere" (Packer), 123–24
"The Duck," 29–30
Du Maurier, Daphne, 174

Earley, Tony, 17–18
East of Eden (Steinbeck), 174–75
editing, 114–26
Ehn, Erik, 73–74
Einstein, Albert, 218–19
Eisenhower, Dwight David, 188
An Elemental Thing (Weinberger), 216–17
Eliot, T. S., 94
Elkin, Stanley, 229–31
Embers (Marai), 129–30
Emerson, Claudia, 171
emotion(s), 93–94, 149, 181, 196–97, 211, 243
endings of novels and stories, 21–23, 124, 136–38
England, 154–55, 244
English poetry, 111
epic poetry, 57–64
epyllion, 62–63
Eva Moves the Furniture (Livesey), 122
everyday language, 90
everyday objects, 78
exercises, 209
exposition, 50, 208

fabrication, 204–5
failure, 45–46
fairy tales, 37–38, 172, 202
"Faith Healing" (Larkin), 242–43
familiarity of form, 30–33
A Farewell to Arms (Hemingway), 138
Faulkner, William, 172
Felicia's Journey (Trevor), 130–33
feminine rhymes, 96
"A Few Don'ts by an Imagiste" (Pound), 84
fiction writing: and advice, 118–19, 129, 171, 208–10; and animation, 43; and dialogue, 51, 208–9; and the directing sentence in short stories, 227–33; and exposition, 50; and failure to capture characters, 45–46; and familiarity of form, 30–33; houses and hauntings, 171–81; and imagination, 205–6; and linear design of novels, 35–38; and narrative movement, 40–41; and New Journalism, 48–49; and nonfiction, 48–50, 53–54; opening pages of novels, 128–36; and ordinary life, 212–13; and personality, 47–48; and process of writing, 211–12; and revision, 114–26; shaping

fiction writing, *(continued)*
stories using architectural dicta, 27–30, 35–38; technique and the imagination, 204–15; and time and space, 210–11; and truth, 54–55; and words, 212–15; and writing rules, 207–8. *See also* structure
Fiedler, Leslie, 56
"Filling Station" (Bishop), 177
Fish, Stanley, 56
Fitzgerald, F. Scott, 23, 48, 116
flashbacks, 122, 125
Flaubert, Gustave, 88, 207
"Flowering Judas" (Porter), 214
forbidden, 172
forgetfulness, 99
form: and American poetry, 155; and familiarity, 30–33; and intimacy, 164; and Justice's "On the Porch," 87; and loyalty to, 94–96; and movement, 154, 157; and Tokarczuk's *House of Day, House of Night*, 40–43; and Warren's *Audubon*, 164, 169
Forster, E. M., 206
framed stories, 40
Frazer, James, 27
free verse, 91, 94, 143
French theater, 82
Freytag's Pyramid, 28, 58, 63
Frost, Robert, 157–59, 164, 193–203
Further Requirements (Larkin), 243

García Márquez, Gabriel, 18, 122
Gardner, John, 47
Garner, Margaret, 55
Gass, William, 213
Geary, James, 218
generosity, 84–85
genre, 28, 65, 102
"Geraniums" (O'Connor), 116
"Gilbert in Arcadia" (Livesey), 117, 121, 125
Gioia, Dana, 91
A Glossary of Literary Terms (Abrams), 65–66
The Golden Bough (Frazer), 27
"A Good Man Is Hard to Find" (O'Connor), 227–28
Gordon, Caroline, 206–7
gospel, 63
Graves, Robert, 219
Great Expectations (Dickens), 19
The Great Gatsby (Fitzgerald), 23, 116
Greek drama, 63
grief, 157

Hadley, Tessa, 115
hallways, 41–42
Hammer, Langdon, 109–10, 112
"Hansel and Gretel," 202
Hartley, L. P., 136
The Haunting of Hill House (Jackson), 179
hauntings, 157, 171–81
Heaney, Seamus, 221–22
Heart of Darkness (Conrad), 20–21
Herbert, George, 111, 245
The Hero's Journey (Campbell), 35–37
Herrera, Yuri, 35–38
Higginson, Thomas, 171
"High Windows" (Larkin), 234–35
Historical Fictions (Kenner), 68
histories of characters, 47
Hitchcock, Alfred, 108
Holroyd, Michael, 54
Homer, 57–59, 190–91
hope, 138, 157, 160, 192, 198, 234, 238–40
Hopkins, Gerard Manley, 189
Hopper, Edward, 103–8, 113, 177, 178
Hopper (Strand), 107
Horace, 58
Hougen, John B., 236
House by the Railroad (Hopper), 178
House of Day, House of Night (Tokarczuk), 40–44
houses, 43–44, 171–81
Housman, A. E., 213
Howard, Richard, 85

Howard's End (Forster), 206
Howl Round (journal), 82
Huey Long (Williams), 52
human behavior, 244
human condition, 80–81
human subjectivity, 102

iamb, 219
"The Idea of Order at Key West" (Stevens), 156
identity, 37, 105, 168
idiosyncrasy, 102
I Is an Other (Geary), 218
Iliad (Homer), 58–59, 190–91
illusory endings, 197–98
imagination, 55, 188–89, 204, 205–6
impersonality, 94
inspiration, 205
integrity of the individual, 160
interiority, 58–59, 61
intimacy, 164
irony, 90–91, 164–65, 197–98
It's a Wonderful Life (film), 178
Izenour, Steven, 29–30

Jackson, Shirley, 179
Jacob's Room (Woolf), 18–19
James, Henry, 91–93
Jaynes, Julian, 58–59
Jefferson Lecture in the Humanities, 159–60, 168–69
Jennings Hall, 179–81
Job, 189
Joe Gould's Secret (Mitchell), 50–52
Journal of Education, 199–200
Joyce, James, 175
"Judgement Day" (O'Connor), 116
Jung, Carl, 172
Justice, Donald, 84–97

Kabuki, 82
Kafka, Franz, 67
Kalkin, Adam, 38–40, 43–44
Keats, George and Georgiana, 154–55
Keats, John, 154–55, 238
Kenner, Hugh, 68, 70
knowledge, 32–33, 159, 167–68, 222
Koolhaas, Rem, 33–34

landscape and the mind, 155–56
"Landscape and the Poetry of Self" (Strand), 100
language; and architectural narrative, 38; and craft, 204–5; of the everyday, 90; and form, 87; and playwriting, 78–79; and style, 91; and technique, 206
Larkin, Philip, 69–70, 234–35, 237–45
"Larkin" (Nemerov), 235, 243–44
"The Last Day in the Field" (Gordon), 206–7
The Last Picture Show (McMurtry), 133–36
Lattimore, Richmond, 190–91
"Lawns" (Simpson), 227
Learning from Las Vegas (Venturi, Brown, and Izenour), 29–30
Le Corbusier, 29
Le Diable boiteux (Lesage), 198
Leonard, Elmore, 209
The Letters of Percy Bysshe Shelley (Browning), 67
Levertov, Denise, 222–23
libraries, 32–35
Library of Congress, 32
The Life and Surprising Adventures of Robinson Crusoe (Defoe), 53
Life Studies (Lowell), 85
linear design, 30–31, 35–38
linearity, 158
listening, 140, 144–45
literacy, 57–61, 64–65
literary borrowing, 91–93
literary critics, 205
literary fiction, 206
literary metaphors, 217

literature: and abstractions, 191–92; and inspiration, 205; and intimacy, 164; and metaphor, 156, 216; and the other, 189; and salvation, 182–92; and the writing profession, 231
live theater, 79–80
longhand, 103–5
Long Room, Trinity College, 32–33
Loos, Adolf, 29
"Lost in Translation" (Merrill), 109–10
love, 159, 166–67, 169, 241–43, 245
"Love Calls Us to the Things of This World" (Wilbur), 235–36, 245
Lowell, Robert, 85, 100–101, 106
loyalty, 23
loyalty to form, 94–96
Luv'd Ones (band), 185–88
"Lycidas" (Milton), 202–3
"Lying" (Wilbur), 240, 244
lyrical poetry, 56–57, 68–69, 106, 197
lyricism, 138, 157–58, 197

MacLaverty, Bernard, 128
MacLeod, Alistair, 129–30
magic, 17–20, 27, 140, 205
Maio, Samuel, 67
Mann, Thomas, 207
A Man of 1794 (Justice), 89–91
Mantel, Hillary, 43
mapping stories, 122
Marai, Sandor, 129
Matthew (evangelist), 63
Maxwell, William, 26
"Mayflies" (Wilbur), 237–38, 244–45
McComiskey, Billy, 14
McCullers, Carson, 172
McLuhan, Marshall, 58
McMurtry, Larry, 133–36
McPhee, John, 55
Mee, Chuck, 82, 146
Melville, Herman, 53
memory, 125, 211
Mercury (Livesey), 122–23
Merrill, James, 64, 109–10, 112
Metamorphoses (Ovid), 59–61
"Metamorphosis" (Kafka), 67
metaphor: and Audubon's *Birds of America*, 161; and the blending of patterns, 222; in Carson's "Book of Isaiah," 224–26; in Heaney's "Squarings," 221–22; in Levertov, 222–23; literary, 217; and motion, 156; in Murray's "Shoal," 221; and physical sensation, 219–21; in Plath's "A Winter Ship," 220–21; Richards on, 216; and synesthesia, 217–19; and the unspeakable, 151; in Violi's "On an Acura Integra," 223–24; in Weinberger's *An Elemental Thing*, 216–17
meter, 156
Michaels, Leonard, 231–32
middle of a story, 20–21
middle style, 88
"Military Industrial Complex" speech, 188
Milton, John, 202–3
mind, 155–56
minor characters, 125
Missouri (ship), 169–70
Mitchell, David, 64
Mitchell, Joseph, 49–53, 55
Mizener, Arthur, 138
Moby-Dick; or The Whale (Melville), 53
monologues, 144–45
Montgomery, Alabama, 185–88
"Moon" (Strand), 110–11
moral vision, 22–23
Morris, Wright, 204
Morrison, Toni, 55
mortality, 191, 207, 237–38
motion, 154–69
mot juste, 88, 91
movement, 41, 156–57, 179–81
Mrs. Dalloway (Woolf), 172
"Mrs. Snow" (Justice), 95–96
"Murderers" (Michael), 231–32

"Murders in the Rue Morgue" (Poe), 65, 67
Murray, Les, 221
"Musée des Beaux Arts" (Auden), 90
music, 133, 158–59
Mutiny on the Bounty, 53
"My Last Duchess" (Browning), 65–67
"My South: On the Porch" (Justice), 85–87, 93–95
mystery, 211, 215
mystery genre, 65–67
mythmaking, 49–50
myths, 216–17

Nabokov, Vladimir, 55
narration and design of stories, 35–38
narration and revision, 124–25
narrative: design and architecture of stories, 34–35, 44; and flashbacks, 125; and framed stories, 40; and Frost's "'Out, Out—,'" 195–97; and lyricism, 157–58; movement, 40–41; and narrative stance when writing, 174–75; and technique, 206; voice in Tokarczuk's *House of Day, House of Night,* 42; and Warren's *Audubon,* 161. *See also* structure
Narrative Design (Bell), 27
nature, 101, 156, 171, 197–98
"The Necklace" (de Maupassant), 124
need, 236–37, 243
"The Need of Being Versed in Country Things" (Frost), 157–59
Nemerov, Howard, 235, 243–44
New and Selected Poems (Justice), 97
New Journalism, 48–49, 55
New Yorker (magazine), 43
New York Review of Books (magazine), 103
'Night, Mother (Norman), 175
nonfiction, 48–50, 54–55
nonperformance, 57
nonpersonal narration, 159
non–point-of-view characters, 121
"No Place for You, My Love" (Welty), 214–15
Norman, Marsha, 175
"The North Ship" (Larkin), 243
nostalgia, 94, 96, 107
"Notes on the Craft of Poetry" (Strand), 102
"Notes Toward a Supreme Fiction" (Stevens), 212
nothingness, 98–99
Novakovich, Josip, 213
novels: and endings, 136–38; and inspiration, 205; and linear design, 35–38; and narrative stance, 174–75; and opening pages, 128–36; and plot, 65; and the process of writing, 211; and structure, 40–43, 179; and time, 210; and words, 213–14; and writing rules, 210

oblivion, 234–35
O'Brien, Edna, 136–38
observation, 173–75
occult, 149–50
O'Connor, Flannery, 116, 209, 227–28
O'Connor, Frank, 136
"Ode to a Dressmaker's Dummy" (Justice), 93
"Ode to a Nightingale" (Keats), 155
Odyssey (Homer), 59
O'Hara, John, 128
"The Old Fools" (Larkin), 243
Old Library at Trinity College, 32–33
Old Testament, 183
Oliver, Mary, 208
OMA architects, 33–34
"On an Acura Integra" (Violi), 223–24
"On Becoming a Poet" (Strand), 102
"One Art" (Bishop), 116, 121, 126
100 Essays I Don't Have Time to Write . . . (Ruhl), 83
One Hundred Years of Solitude (García Márquez), 18
Ong, Walter J., 57–59, 64–65, 68, 70
"On Nothing" (Strand), 98–99
On Writing (Welty), 204
opening pages, 123–24, 127–36

opening paragraphs: "Animals in Heaven," 13–14; Elkin's "A Poetics for Bullies," 230; and magic, 18; Michaels's "Murderers," 231–32; O'Connor's "A Good Man Is Hard to Find," 227–28; pronouncements made in, 227; Updike's "A&P," 228–29. *See also* beginning of a story
The Opposite House (Emerson), 171
orality, 57–58, 61
Orality and Literacy (Ong), 57–59
ordinary life, 212–13
Orem, Faith, 186
"Orientation" (Orozco), 123
ornamentation, 29–30, 32
Orozco, Daniel, 123
"'Out, Out—'" (Frost), 193–203
Ovid, 59–61
"Ozymandias" (Shelley), 95

Packer, ZZ, 123–24
Painter, Pamela, 121
"Pantisocracy" scheme, 154–55
papyrus rolls, 63–64
paragraphs, 158
Paris Review (magazine), 103, 108–9, 113, 137–38, 195
Parks, Suzan-Lori, 71
passion, 164–70, 206
patterns, 61, 143, 219, 222
"Pearl" (Merrill), 64
"People in the Sun" (Hopper), 107
performance, 195, 203
Perfume (Süskind), 213
personality, 47–48
persona poems, 67–69
perspective, 159, 223
Persuasion (Austen), 116
physicality, 46–47, 75, 219–21
Picasso, Pablo, 208
pithy sentences, 230
Pizan, Christine de, 68
Plath, Sylvia, 220–21, 241
playwriting: and alchemy, 79–80; and the human condition, 80–81; and language, 78–79; and physicality, 75; and props, 77–78; and secrets, 75–77; and stage pictures, 79; and structure, 81–83; and the unspeakable, 139–52; and violence, 81
plot, 56–70, 140, 195, 198, 211
Poe, Edgar Allan, 65–67
poetic foot, 156, 219
poetics, 229–30
Poetics (Aristotle), 16, 57
"A Poetics for Bullies" (Elkin), 229–31
The Poetics of Translation (Barnstone), 217
poetry: and advice, 113; and aesthetics of ambivalence, 84–97; alterations to Frost's "'Out, Out—,'" 193–203; and chiasmus, 61–64; confessional mode of, 100–101, 106, 109; dramatic monologues, 65–68; and emotion, 93–94, 196–97, 243; epics, 57–64; and houses and hauntings, 157; and idiosyncrasy, 102; and literary borrowing, 91–93; in longhand, 103–5; and loyalty to form, 94–95; lyrical, 56–57, 68–69, 106, 197; and metaphor, 219–26; in motion, 154–69; and movement, 155–59; persona poems, 67–69; philosophical, 164; as physical art, 219–21; and plot, 56–70; poetic composition, 156–57; poetic foot, 156, 219; poetic form, 155, 157, 164; the poetic line, 157; rationed compassion in Larkin and Wilbur, 234–45; and Sappho, 68–69; and Strand, 98–113; visionary-subjective mode of, 100, 106
"A Poet's Alphabet" (Strand), 99–100, 112
point of view, 121, 129, 172–73, 175, 205, 228–29
Poochigian, Aaron, 68–69
Pope, Alexander, 200
Porter, Katherine Anne, 214
"Potato" (Wilbur), 236–37
Pound, Ezra, 84, 214
"Praise in Summer" (Wilbur), 240

process of writing, 211–12
pronouncements, 227
pronouns, 144
props, 77–78
prosody, 156–57
psychic distance, 125–26
psychological manipulations, 243
public and private spaces, 42
pure cinema, 108

quatrain, 157

racism, 185–88
Railroad Crossing (Hopper), 178
"The Rape of the Lock" (Pope), 200
rationed compassion, 234–45
readers: and critical analysis, 208; and endings, 124; and familiarity of form, 30–31; and metaphor, 224; and opening pages, 123; and rationed compassion, 243; and writing rules, 208
reality, 49, 54
Rebecca (Du Maurier), 174
recognizable form, 30–33
redaction, 141
remembering, 158–59
restrictive settings, 228–29
retrospective writing, 227–29
revision/rewriting, 43, 114–26
rhymes, 95–96, 158
rhythm, 125, 142, 156, 209, 219
Rich, Charlie, 174
Richards, I. A., 216
Rohe, Mies van der, 29
"A Rose for Emily" (Faulkner), 172
Ruhl, Sarah, 83

The Saint Plays (Ehn), 73–74
salvation, 182–92
Sandburg, Carl, 204
San Diego, California, 73–74
Sappho, 68–70
scarcity, 237
scenes, 28, 124–25
Schlegel, Margaret, 206
scripts, 142–44
secrets, 75–77, 152
secret sympathy, 27
Seeing Things (Heaney), 222
self, 105, 116, 159–60, 165, 168
Selkirk, Alexander, 53
A Sense of Things (Brown), 78
sentences, 79, 116–17, 230–33
Shakespeare, William, 205–6
The Shape of the Book From Roll to Codex (Arduini), 63
shaping a story, 27–30, 35–38
Shawn, Wallace, 113
Shelley, Percy Bysshe, 95
Shepard, Sam, 72–83
Shklovsky, Viktor, 195, 197–98
"Shoal" (Murray), 221
Shorer, Mark, 207
short stories, 227–33
Signs Preceding the End of the World (Herrera), 35–38
Simpson, Mona, 227
Sledgehammer Theatre, 73–74
"A Small, Good Thing" (Carver), 116
"The Snow Man" (Stevens), 234
soliloquy, 65, 144
"Soliloquy of the Spanish Cloister" (Browning), 65
So Long, See You Tomorrow (Maxwell), 26
"Sonny's Blues" (Baldwin), 119–22
the South, 93
Southey, Robert, 154
speech on stage, 139–45
Spiegelman, Willard, 108–9
"Squarings" (Heaney), 221–22
stage pictures, 79
stanzas, 157–58
Steinbeck, John, 174–75
Stevens, Wallace, 88, 108, 156, 212, 234

Stoker, Bram, 174
stories: "Animals in Heaven," 11–24; and the directing sentence in short stories, 227–33; and grace, 189–90; mapping, 122; not working at the highest level, 117–18; in poetry, 157–58; and questions, 119–21; and revision, 114–26; and salvation, 188–92; shaping of, 27–30, 35–38; and time, 211
Storr, Anthony, 47
storytelling: fiction v. nonfiction, 48–50, 53–54; and truth, 54–55; writing about real people, 49–54. *See also* stories
Strand, Mark, 98–113, 178
Structuralist Poetics (Culler), 194–95, 197
structure: and houses, 179; and illusory endings, 198; and linear design, 30–31, 35–38; and narrative movement, 40–41; of plays, 81–83; and revision, 126; and strategy, 28–29; and techniques of fiction, 205; and Warren's *Audubon*, 161, 164
stuff, 200–201
style, 88, 91, 204, 214
submergence, 100–101
Sullivan, Louis, 29
The Sunset Maker (Justice), 97
surface of the page, 142–44
Süskind, Patrick, 213
Suspicion (Hitchcock), 108
symbolism, 214
sympathy, 243–44
synesthesia, 217–19
syntax, 158, 198, 243
systematic discrimination, 185–88

talent, 207
technique and process of writing, 211
technique and the imagination, 204–15
"Technique as Discovery" (Shorer), 207
Tehano (Wier), 210
Ten Commandments, 183–85
Tennyson, Hallam, 199–200
"Tennyson's Geese," 199–200
"Ten Rules for Good Writing" (Leonard), 209
Terminal Hip (Wellman), 73
theater, 71–83
"Things About to Disappear" (Wier), 210
Thomas, Dylan, 64
Thompson, Hunter S., 49
time and space, 40, 71, 210–11
"Toads" (Larkin), 234
"Toads Revisited" (Larkin), 234
"To Autumn" (Keats), 238
Tokarczuk, Olga, 40–44
tone: and the directing sentence, 231; fluidity of, in novels, 133; and Larkin's "Aubade," 242; and writing exercises, 209
"To the Sea" (Larkin), 239–40, 244
"Tradition and an Individual Talent" (Gioia), 91
tragedy, 57
transcendence, 100–101, 111
transitions, 124, 240–41
translation, 38, 68
Trevor, William, 130–33
Trinity College, 32–33
True West (Shepard), 72–83
truth(s), 23, 54–55, 151, 165, 182, 189–90, 192
Twain, Mark, 209
"Tywater" (Wilbur), 236, 244

"The Undead" (Wilbur), 236
Understanding Poetry (Warren and Brooks), 203
universality, 102, 106
the unspeakable, 139–52
Updike, John, 228–29
urban age, 106–7
urbanization, 101

Van Doren, Mark, 191
Vendler, Helen, 231
Venturi, Robert, 29–30
"Vers de Société" (Larkin), 239
verse, 143, 156, 165–66

Vinnedge, Char, 185–87
violence, 81, 160, 164, 189, 244
Violi, Paul, 223–24
Virgil, 59
visionary-subjective mode of poetry, 100, 106
visual art, 102–8, 178, 213
vivid verbs, 199–200
voice(s): and authority, 205; and characterization, 51; in Frost's "'Out, Out—,'" 196–97; and playwriting, 145–50; and the unspeakable, 151–52

Ward, Edna, 241
Warren, Robert Penn, 50–53, 157–69, 203
Washburn, Anne, 80–81
The Waste Land (Eliot), 94
Watson, Paul, 148–49, 151–52
The Weather of Words (Strand), 99–100
"Wedding Wind" (Larkin), 239, 244
Weinberger, Eliot, 216–17
Wellman, Mac, 73
Welty, Eudora, 128, 204, 214–15
What If? (Painter and Bernay), 121
"The Whitsun Weddings" (Larkin), 238–39, 244
The Whitsun Weddings (Larkin), 243
"Why Don't You Dance?" (Carver), 133
Wilbur, Richard, 235–45
Williams, T. Harry, 52
Williams, William Carlos, 88
"A Winter's Ship" (Plath), 220–21
Woods, James, 43
Woolf, Virginia, 18–19, 172, 175
wordplay, 112
words: and abstractions, 192; and ambivalence, 88–91; and dialogue, 209; in Frost's "'Out, Out—,'" 199–202; and metaphor, 217; and ordinary life, 212–13; and playwriting, 139–45; search for in poetry, 110–11; and sensory perception of, 213–14; writers on, 213–14
words first poets, 111–12
Wordsworth, William, 100–102, 104, 106
workshops, 118–19
"The Writer" (Wilbur), 241–42
writing outside the story, 121
writing rules, 116–17, 207–8, 214
writing tasks, 121–22

"Year's End" (Wilbur), 240–41
Yeats, William Butler, 14–15
Young, Arthur, 153–54

CPSIA information can be obtained
at www.ICGtesting.com
Printed in the USA
LVHW111303210521
688131LV00003B/101

9 780807 175064